Peter of Damascus
Byzantine Monk and Spiritual Theologian

There are countless under-studied or ignored authors from the Byzantine Empire awaiting scholarly attention. In the area of Byzantine spirituality the twelfth century as a whole has received little consideration, primarily owing to the perceived lack of any significant or noteworthy author. While the tenth-century mystic Symeon the New Theologian and the fourteenth-century hesychast Gregory Palamas have been the focus of much academic industry, little serious attention is paid to figures from the intervening centuries. Recognizing that literature on monasticism and empire in the twelfth century is extensive, this book hopes to fill the void that appears to have marked the study of spirituality of the same period by taking as its subject the twelfth-century monk and spiritual theologian Peter of Damascus. Although he is the second most voluminous writer included in the Philokalia, Peter is one of the least studied of the philokalic authors. The main study devoted to him, now seventy years old, by Jean Gouillard was incomplete and, on some points, erroneous. As well, Gouillard's reading of the Petrine philokalic texts through an Evagrian or Maximian lens gives the reader an inadequate and inaccurate picture of Peter's spiritual theology. *Peter of Damascus: Byzantine Monk and Spiritual Theologian* seeks to renew interest in a figure who was an important contributor to the larger field of Byzantine monasticism and spirituality. Using unedited manuscripts, prosopographical evidence, and published sources, this study attempts not only to recover the shape of Peter's life and work but also to elucidate his spirituality through a detailed examination of both *The Admonition to His Own Soul* and *The Spiritual Alphabet*, demonstrating the ways in which that spirituality remained accessible to both monastics and non-monastics.

STUDIES AND TEXTS 175

Peter of Damascus

Byzantine Monk and Spiritual Theologian

GREG PETERS

PONTIFICAL INSTITUTE OF MEDIAEVAL STUDIES

Acknowledgments

This book has been published with the help of grants from Biola University's Torrey Honors Institute, School of Arts and Sciences and Institute for Spiritual Formation.

Library and Archives Canada Cataloguing in Publication

Peters, Greg, 1971–
 Peter of Damascus : Byzantine monk and spiritual theologian / Greg Peters.

(Studies and texts, ISSN 00825328 ; 175)
Includes bibliographical references and index.
ISBN 978-0-88844-175-1

 1. Peter, of Damascus, Saint, fl. 12th cent.   2. Monks – Byzantine Empire – Biography.   3. Christian saints – Byzantine Empire – Biography. 4. Spirituality – Orthodox Eastern Church – History of doctrines – Middle Ages, 600–1500.   I. Pontifical Institute of Mediaeval Studies   II. Title. III. Series: Studies and texts (Pontifical Institute of Mediaeval Studies) ; 175

BX395.P445P48 2011   281.9092   C2011-904923-6

© 2011
Pontifical Institute of Mediaeval Studies
59 Queen's Park Crescent East
Toronto, Ontario, Canada M5S 2C4
www.pims.ca

To my wife, Christina,
for unconditional love and support

Contents

Abbreviations

BMFD   *Byzantine Monastic Foundation Documents: A Complete Translation of the Surviving Founders' Typika and Testaments*, ed. John Thomas and Angela Constantinides Hero, 5 vols. (Washington: Dumbarton Oaks Research Library and Collection, 2000).

ODB   *The Oxford Dictionary of Byzantium*, ed. A.P. Kazhdan, Alice-Marie Talbot, Anthony Cutler, Timothy E. Gregory and Nancy P. Ševčenko, 3 vols. (Crestwood, NY: Oxford University Press, 1991).

PG   Patrologiae cursus completus: Series Graeca, ed. J.-P. Migne, 161 vols. (Paris: Migne, 1857–1866).

Phil.   *The Philokalia: The Complete Text Compiled by St. Nicodemus of the Holy Mountain and St. Makarios of Corinth*, ed. and trans. G.E.H. Palmer, Philip Sherrard and Kallistos Ware (London: Faber and Faber, 1981, 1984), vols. 2 and 3.

PL   Patrologiae cursus completus: Series Latina, ed. J.-P. Migne, 221 vols. (Paris: Migne, 1844–1864).

Acknowledgments

To research and write on an obscure figure like Peter of Damascus has proved both rewarding and challenging. The rewards came with uncovering new and previously undiscovered connections between Peter and twelfth-century Byzantium, identifying new texts and pieces of information related to him, as well as with the joy of spending so much time concentrating exclusively on his spiritual theology. The challenges came in trying to stay connected with the larger discipline of Byzantine studies, when a lack of peers with whom I could share my discoveries made it difficult for me to keep the forest in view for the trees. However, I have enjoyed the work, and if my efforts serve to stimulate interest in Peter among Byzantinists as well as scholars and students of Christian spirituality, then it will have been time well spent. For understanding both the opportunities and the challenges presented by the project, I wish to thank especially T. Allan Smith, csb, of the Pontifical Institute of Mediaeval Studies, both for overseeing my first foray into the thought of Peter of Damascus and for his support over the past eight years while I have continued researching and writing on this neglected Byzantine spiritual theologian.

As all authors acknowledge, the writing of a book is impossible without the support of many people. I would like to thank my sons, Brendan and Nathanael, for bringing so much joy to the end of each day of researching and writing. Knowing that they would be at home each evening waiting for me helped to get me through many days when I would rather have forsaken the project. I would also like to thank Flo Ebeling and the entire Biola University Interlibrary Loan staff for the constant and diligent procuring of books. Thanks are also due to Professor Robert Sinkewicz at the University of Toronto for help with citing and locating Greek manuscripts, and to Professor Amy Obrist at Biola for assistance in translating Russian texts. The larger part of this study was written while on research leave from Biola University. For this I thank the administration of Biola University for funding this leave and for my colleagues and students in the Torrey Honors Institute, who make teaching and working at Biola University such a joy. Appreciation is also extended to my research assistant Stephanie Greer for her help in many areas of the project, and to Monica Hopson for her work on the index. Finally, my greatest supporter over the past eighteen years has been my wife, Christina. Without her there never would have been a doctoral thesis on Peter of Damascus, much less a book. I dedicate this book to her in loving affection.

Recovering a Lost Spiritual Theologian

With the publication of the *Philokalia* at Venice in 1782, the text's editors, Nicodemus of the Holy Mountain and Macarius of Corinth,[1] not only helped to rejuvenate the reading and study of spiritual texts in eighteenth-century Greece, they also re-introduced to Orthodox Christianity a number of forgotten or neglected spiritual authors.[2] Among these authors were John of Carpathos, Philotheus of Sinai, Theophan the Monk, Theoleptos of Philadelphia, and most important for this study, Peter of Damascus, a Byzantine monk and spiritual theologian.[3]

1   The *Philokalia*'s full Greek title is Φιλοκαλία τῶν ἱερῶν νηπτικῶν. On the *Philokalia* generally, see *Dictionnaire de spiritualité: Spiritualité ascétique et mystique: Doctrine et histoire*, ed. Marcel Viller, F. Cavallera and A. Solinac (Paris, 1984), s.v. "Philocalie" by Kallistos Ware, 12: cols. 1336–1352; and Vassa Conticello and Elia Citterio, "La Philocalie et ses versions," in *La théologie byzantine et sa tradition II*, ed. Carmelo Giuseppe Conticello and Vassa Conticello (Turnhout, 2002), 999–1021. On Nicodemus of the Holy Mountain, see Elia Citterio, "Nicodemo Agiorita," in *La théologie byzantine et sa tradition II*, 905–997; and Elia Citterio and Antonio Rigo, eds., *Nicodemo l'Aghiorita e la Filocalia: Atti dell'VIII Convegno Ecumenico internazionale: Di Spiritualità Ortodossa: Bose, 16–19 settembre 2000* (Magnano, 2001). A critical introduction and study of Macarius of Corinth is lacking. A more popular treatment is available from Constantine Cavarnos, *St. Macarios of Corinth* (Belmont, MA, 1972). For both Nicodemus and Macarius, see Gerhard Podskalsky, *Griechische Theologie in der Zeit der Türkenherrschaft (1453–1821)* (Munich, 1988).

2   The appearance of the *Philokalia* was part of the larger renaissance of spirituality occurring in Greek Orthodox countries during the late eighteenth and early nineteenth centuries, which was connected to the *Kollyvades* movement. On this movement, see George S. Bebis, "Introduction," in *Nicodemus of the Holy Mountain: A Handbook of Spiritual Counsel*, by Nicodemus the Hagiorite (New York, 1989), 11–13. As well, Bebis cites the pertinent studies published in Greek.

3   The *Philokalia* was published originally as a folio volume of 1207 pages in double columns, containing the (spurious and authentic) texts of thirty-six authors who lived from the fourth to the fifteenth century. All are Greek authors with the exception of John Cassian. Of the lesser known authors in the collection, only Theoleptus of Philadelphia and Peter of Damascus have received scholarly attention. On

It takes a reader much longer to read through Peter's philokalic works than it does the published secondary literature on this neglected theologian. This despite Peter's two works in the *Philokalia* being second in length only to those of Maximus the Confessor. That Nicodemus of the Holy Mountain and Macarius of Corinth included all of the then-known Petrine texts in the *Philokalia* suggests that Peter's texts were regarded as important, and that fact alone calls for a serious study of his writings. Their popularity in the early modern era is evidenced by Paisius Velichkovsky's response when seeing a monk reading the texts on Mt Athos in Greece. Paisius writes:

> While I was walking alone with two brothers from the holy and great Lavra of St. Athanasius toward the great Skete of the Lavra, St. Anne's, we came straight to the very high hill of the Holy Prophet Elias, which is in height one-third of the great peak of holy Athos. Under this hill, on a very high place on the side toward the sea, there is the Skete of St. Basil the Great, which was established in recent times by monks who came from Caesarea of Cappadocia ... And so we came to this Skete and sat down near the holy church, and a monk of reverent appearance saw us, and after we had venerated the holy icons in the church and gone out, he invited us with love into his cell and went out to prepare some food for us in order to refresh us from the labor of walking. Looking at a little table which was near the window, I saw an opened book lying on it, from which he was making a copy, for by craft he was a calligrapher, and looking closely at this book I saw that it was the book of St. Peter Damascene, and seeing it I cannot express with what unutterable spiritual joy I was filled; for I thought that I had been enabled to see a heavenly treasure upon earth ... When the brother returned to the cell, I began to ask him with great joy and unutterable astonishment, how it was that such a book, beyond all my hopes, was to be found in this holy place. He told me that there was even another book of this same Saint, having 24 Homilies in alphabetical order ... Having heard this and rejoiced greatly with unutterable joy at obtaining such

---

Theoleptus, see, *Theoleptos of Philadelphia, The Monastic Discourses: A Critical Edition, Translation and Study*, ed. and trans. Robert E. Sinkewicz (Toronto, 1992); and Angela Constantinides Hero, *The Life and Letters of Theoleptos of Philadelphia* (Brookline, MA, 1994). For an earlier study of Peter of Damascus, see Greg Peters, "Recovering a Lost Spiritual Theologian: Peter of Damascus and the *Philokalia*," *St. Vladimir's Theological Quarterly* 49 (2005): 437–459.

a heavenly treasure upon earth, I began to entreat him fervently, for the love of God, to copy such books for me also.[4]

Though Peter flourished in the mid-twelfth century and was known on Mt Athos as recently as the eighteenth century, no serious examination of his life or literary output appeared in print until 1939,[5] and this in spite of the fact that there are over 100 extant manuscripts of Peter's texts.[6] His works were also known in Russia as early as 1500[7] – where we know they were used by Archpriest Avvakum to defend the form of the sign of the cross used by the Old Believers[8] – and were translated into both Slavonic and Russian in the nineteenth century.[9] Peter also received scant attention in Russian encyclopedic literature around the turn of the twentieth century,[10] but not until this author's own recent work has he received any sustained scholarly attention.[11]

4 Schema-monk Metrophanes, *Blessed Paisius Velichkovsky: The Man Behind the Philokalia: The Life and Ascetic Labors of Our Father, Elder Paisius, Archimandrite of the Holy Moldavian Monasteries of Niamets and Sekoul*, trans. Seraphim Rose (Platina, CA, 1976), 82, 85. It appears that the monk was copying the *Admonition of His Own Soul* since he mentions the *Spiritual Alphabet* as "another book." See also Peters, "Recovering a Lost Spiritual Theologian," 456–458.

5 Jean Gouillard, "Un auteur spirituel byzantin du XIIe siècle, Pierre Damascène," *Échos d'Orient* 38 (1939): 257–278; reprinted in Jean Gouillard, *La vie religieuse à Byzance* (London: Variorum, 1981).

6 See "Petrus Damascenus" in Robert E. Sinkewicz, *Manuscript Listings for the Authors of the Patristic and Byzantine Periods* (Toronto, 1992).

7 It is known with certainty that Iosif of Volokolamsk copied extracts of Peter's works around this time. See Peters, "Recovering a Lost Spiritual Theologian," 453–455.

8 Petrovich Protopope Avvakum, *The Life of Archpriest Avvakum, by Himself*, trans. Jane Ellen Harrison and Hope Mirrlees (London, 1924), 121: "our first shepherds made the sign of the cross and blessed men as of old with two fingers, according to the tradition of our Holy Fathers, Meletina of Antioch, Theodoret, the blessed Bishop of Cyrene, Peter of Damascus, and Maxim the Greek."

9 For the Slavonic translation, see *Dobrotoliubie*, in *Dobrotoliubie: La Philocalie slavonne de Païssy Velitchkovsky: Reproduction anastatique intégrale de l'édition princeps, Moscou, 1793* trans. Paisius Velichkovsky (Bucharest, 1990).

10 This literature is noted by Gouillard, "Un auteur spirituel byzantin," 257–258.

11 In addition to Peters, "Recovering a Lost Spiritual Theologian," see also Greg Peters, "Peter of Damascus and Early Christian Spiritual Theology," *Patristica et Medievalia* 26 (2005): 89–109. There is a brief discussion of Peter's description of making the sign of the cross in Andreas Andreopoulos, *The Sign of the Cross: The Gesture, the*

I have argued elsewhere that this inattention, at least in the past century, is likely the result of the negative assessment that Peter received from Jean Gouillard.[12] Gouillard concludes, "[i]n summary, entirely concentrated on putting into clear formulas the teachings of the greatest contemplatives of the east, the Damascene does not invent, nor does he prepare anything. Whence the dull effect that his work leaves that edified so many generations of monks."[13] Yet, it is doubtful that Gouillard knew his topic well. For example, Gouillard, in reconciling the conflicting dates provided for Peter's writing in Paris, Bibliothèque Nationale, Ancien gr. 1134 and Vatican City, Bibliotheca Apostolica Vaticana, Palat. gr. 210, explains that a haplography accounts for the radically different dating of the Vatican manuscript. However, upon examination of the actual manuscript, it is impossible that such a scribal error explains the discrepancy. It would appear, therefore, that Gouillard, though he talks extensively about a number of the manuscripts of Peter's works, must have been working primarily (at least for the non-Parisian manuscripts) from printed catalogs and not from the manuscripts themselves. As well, Gouillard goes to great pains to conform Peter's teachings to the ever-growing, popular designation of "hesychast," demanding that Peter must be perceived as a continuator of the Evagrian/Maximian spiritual tradition. Why? There is a general tendency in Byzantine historiography to see most authors as being Evagrian and/or Maximian: that is, espousing the same theology of the spiritual life as that promoted by the fourth-century monk Evagrius of Pontus and/or that of the seventh-century monk Maximus the Confessor. Such a historiography claims that the teaching of these two icons of Eastern Orthodox spiritual theology set the tone and agenda for all that followed. This Evagrian/Maximian theology, it is claimed, was then bequeathed to the late Byzantine church and fully codified by Gregory Palamas. Thus such a theology can then adopt a number of labels in the literature: Evagrian, Maximian, hesychastic or Palamite. In truth, such a convenient historiography is more the creation of twentieth-century scholars than a true repre-

---

Mystery, the History (Brewster, MA, 2006), 24–26 and a short discussion in Augustine Casiday, "Church Fathers and the shaping of Orthodox theology," in *The Cambridge Companion to Orthodox Christian Theology*, ed. Mary B. Cunningham and Elizabeth Theokritoff (Cambridge, 2008), 180–182. It should be noted that although Casiday is aware of my publications he still misdates Peter.

12   See Peters, "Recovering a Lost Spiritual Theologian," 437–438.

13   Gouillard, "Un auteur spirituel byzantin," 278. The translation is my own.

sentation of Byzantine spiritual history.[14] For these reasons, Gouillard's work is of a limited value.

Believing that Gouillard's assessment was in error, this book seeks to properly situate Peter of Damascus in the Byzantine spiritual tradition. Chapter 1 will locate Peter geographically, since where he spent his life as a monk has hitherto been uncertain. Using a reference to "the monk Peter" that appears in the *Typikon* of Leo, bishop of Nauplia, for the Monastery of the Mother of God at Areia, it will be argued that Peter was Leo's brother and a monk in this monastery – providing both a location and firmer dates for Peter's life.

Chapter 2 will take up the question of Peter's name. As will be explained in this chapter, it is highly doubtful that Peter had any connection to the city of Damascus.[15] It will be shown here that Peter's surname, Mansur, caused confusion between Peter and the better-known theologian, John of Damascus (whose surname was also Mansur). This, in turn, led to Peter's mis-appellation as "of Damascus." This will lead to establishing finally that Peter of Damascus and Peter Mansur are the same person. Being the same person, those works that have come down to us under the name of Mansur will need re-attribution to Peter of Damascus.

Counter to Gouillard's assessment that Peter's spiritual theology is unsystematic and more a thesaurus than a coherent system,[16] chapters 3 and 4 will explicate the spiritual theology of Peter of Damascus as found in his two philokalic texts: the *Admonition to His Own Soul* (ὑπόμνησις πρὸς τὴν ἑαυτοῦ ψυχήν) and the *Spiritual Alphabet* (Λόγοι κατ᾽ ἀλφαβῆτον).[17] In these chap-

---

14   On Byzantine spiritual historiography in general, see Greg Peters, "Towards a Definition of 'Spiritual Theology': A Historiography of Recent Writings on Byzantine Spirituality," *Studia Monastica* 46 (2004): 25–41. One example of such a historiographical reading is John Meyendorff, *A Study of Gregory Palamas*, trans. George Lawrence (New York, 1964), 134–156.

15   Cf. Peters, "Recovering a Lost Spiritual Theologian," 439–440.

16   Interestingly, like Gouillard, Nicodemus of the Holy Mountain himself viewed Peter's works as thesaurus, calling it a "treasury of divine knowledge and wisdom": τῆς θείας γνώσεως καὶ σοφίας τὸ ταμεῖον. See Φιλοκαλία τῶν ἱερῶν νηπτικῶν, Τόμος Γ, ed. Nicodemus of the Holy Mountain and Macarius of Corinth (Athens, 1991), 4.

17   The naming of Peter's two Philokalic works is quite diverse. I am adopting the titles *Admonition to His Own Soul* and *Spiritual Alphabet* from the best extant manuscripts of Peter's texts. The translators and/or editors of the English translation of the

ters, I will assume that Peter employed a literary technique that is now known as intertextuality.[18] This technique, as defined by Julia Kristeva, is the theory that "every text builds itself as a mosaic of quotations, every text is absorption and transformation of another text."[19] As Graham Allen explains,

> [L]iterary texts possess meaning; readers extract that meaning from them. We call the process of extracting meaning from texts reading or interpretation ... Works of literature, after all, are built from systems, codes and traditions established by previous works of literature. The systems, codes and traditions of other art forms and of culture in general are also crucial to the meaning of a work of literature. Texts ... are viewed by modern theorists as lacking in any kind of independent meaning. They are what theorists now call intertextual. The act of reading ... plunges us into a network of textual relations. To interpret a text, to discover its meaning, or meanings, is to trace those relations. Reading thus becomes a process of moving between texts. Meaning becomes something which exists between a text and all the other texts to which it refers and relates, moving out from the independent text into a network of textual relations. The text becomes the intertext.[20]

Elizabeth Clark, when discussing early Christian texts, expands on this by writing, "Intertextuality thus stands *against* the notion of a book or poem's autho-

---

Philokalia give Peter's *Admonition* the title of "Book I: A Treasury of Divine Knowledge." This phrase is that applied by Nicodemus of the Holy Mountain to the Petrine corpus (see above, n. 16). They refer to the *Spiritual Alphabet* as "Book II: Twenty-four Discourses." Gouillard refers to the two works simply as A and B. On the naming of these texts, see Peters, "Recovering a Lost Spiritual Theologian," 445–446; and Gouillard, "Un auteur spirituel byzantin," 258–264.

18 By using the word "intertextuality" I realize that I am at risk of being misunderstood since "Intertextuality is one of the most commonly used and misused terms in contemporary critical vocabulary ... Such a term is in danger of meaning nothing more than whatever each particular critic wishes it to mean." Graham Allen, *Intertextuality* (London, 2000), 2.

19 Translated by and quoted in Jeanine Parisier Plottel, "Introduction," in *Intertextuality: New Perspectives in Criticism*, ed. Jeanine Parisier Plottel and Hanna Charney (New York, 1978), xiv. See also Elizabeth A. Clark, *History, Theory, Text: Historians and the Linguistic Turn* (Cambridge, 2005), 74.

20 Allen, *Intertextuality*, 1.

rial 'originality'[21] and *for* that of a text's productivity. Texts are here seen as synchronous: whether as allusions or as explicit citations, intertexts stand on the same temporal plane as the passage-at-hand."[22] In short, the theory of intertextuality says that all written texts contain either explicit allusions to or echoes of earlier texts and other cultural "codes" and "traditions." According to Michael Worton and Judith Still, the "theory of intertextuality insists that a text ... cannot exist as hermetic or self-sufficient whole, and so does not function as a closed system."[23] Worton and Still state that this is for two reasons: (1) "the writer is a reader of texts (in the broadest sense) before s/he is a creator of texts, and therefore the work of art is inevitably shot through with references, quotations and influences of every kind;"[24] and (2) "a text is available only through some process of reading" so that what is "produced" when reading is the result of the influence of all the texts (broadly defined) informing both author and reader.[25] All readers and users of written texts employ them in specific ways, especially when they are engaged in a constructive project. Peter is no exception. For Peter, then, his reading of earlier Christian texts is informed by his own cultural conditioning, and the original texts themselves are laden with "codes" and accretions from the "traditions." Thus in quoting from these texts and finding as well as giving them meaning in the moment of his reading, Peter is not merely a copious collector and arranger of texts but is employing them to some end that is original.

Chapter 5 will examine how Peter understood that his spiritual "program" is open to both monks and laity. Such a contention is shared in middle Byzantine spirituality with Symeon the New Theologian and Theodore the Stoudite and should be viewed by scholars as a radically different from the spiritual theologies of Peter's successors, especially Gregory Palamas. Given that Peter was writing during the height of Byzantine monastic renewal, it is significant that he understands his spirituality not to be uniquely monastic (though he himself was a monk) but available to all.

---

21 Clark is quoting from Plottel, "Introduction."

22 Elizabeth A. Clark, *Reading Renunciation: Asceticism and Scripture in Early Christianity* (Princeton, 1999), 123. Italics in the original.

23 Michael Worton and Judith Still, "Introduction," in their *Intertextuality: Theories and Practice* (Manchester, 1990), 1–44, at 1.

24 Ibid., 1.

25 Ibid., 1–2.

Chapter 6 will offer the following conclusions: 1) Peter's spiritual theology is original and it does not strictly follow the so-called Evagrian/Maximian paradigm; and 2) Peter employs the literary technique of intertextuality, accounting for how he uses past authors innovatively and originally. Three appendices provide a comparison of the contents of the *Admonition* and the *Spiritual Alphabet*, a translation of the verse epigrams that begin each of the *logoi* of Peter's *Spiritual Alphabet*, and a textual emendation and translation found in Paris, Bibliothèque Nationale, Ancien gr. 1135.

❧ ❧

Though mostly ignored and rarely studied, Peter of Damascus has much to contribute to the scholarly renaissance of Byzantine spiritual theology.[26] It seems especially peculiar that an author as prolific as Peter – whose works were apparently quite popular in both the regions of the former Byzantine empire and in Orthodox settings outside of the empire (especially in Russia)[27] – would go virtually unnoticed for so many centuries. Furthermore, that his philokalic works have been easily available to monks, nuns, students and scholars for well over two hundred years but have, until recently, only resulted in one academic essay, is lamentable, especially given Peter's accessible spiritual theology and his unique emphasis on its applicability to both monastics and laity. So, this book is as much about rehabilitating an unfamiliar theologian as it is with distilling the author's spiritual theology.[28] Most importantly, this book seeks to move its readers beyond these pages to the very texts of Peter

26 For examples of this renaissance, see Hilarion Alfeyev, *St. Symeon the New Theologian and Orthodox Tradition* (Oxford, 2000); and Catia Galatariotou, *The Making of a Saint: The Life, Times and Sanctification of Neophytos the Recluse* (Cambridge, 1991).

27 For example, a Slavonic translation of the Philokalic works of Peter appear in a manuscript from 1779 in the St Panteleimon Monastery on Mt Athos, while four manuscripts of Peter's works dating from the fourteenth to the eighteenth centuries are extant in the Cyrillic manuscripts of the Chilander Monastery, also on Mt Athos. For Peter's works in Russian, see above. See also Peters, "Recovering a Lost Spiritual Theologian," 458.

28 The phrase "spiritual theology" was given prominence in 1926 by the Jesuit theologian Joseph de Guibert in his *Theologia spiritualis, ascetica et mystica: Quaestiones selectae in praelectionum usum* (Rome, 1926). The first use of the phrase, however, .

himself where the knowledge and wisdom of this neglected spiritual theologian is most evident.

On Reading Byzantine Spiritual Texts

How one should go about reading a "Byzantine text" is a complicated question, as Jakov Ljubarskij recently resolved.[29] In fact, Ljubarskij wonders if the task of answering such a question is even possible or if the task should be undertaken at all. He concludes "that the traditional methods of classical philology (by which I mean the correct interpretation and emendation of a text and the extraction of historical information from it) can and must be used by Byzantinists." There are two perspectives regarding texts, he says, among Byzantinists. First, there are the scholars of Byzantine texts who believe that Byzantine writers were more concerned with exercising their rhetorical skills and imitating earlier authors than they were with "describing historical reality; therefore the historical information to be extracted from their texts is scarce, worthless, and cannot be taken at face value."[30] Scholars of this kind, Ljubarskij states, spend their time making statements about how well Byzantine authors were educated or how well they practiced rhetoric, but the scholar "fails to learn what [the original author] really felt and thought." Second, since Byzantine authors believed "that the surrounding world was ... full of signs and symbols," then "the main task of the modern scholar is to penetrate beneath the surface and try to understand and explain what was in reality meant by the author." Scholars adopting this perspective believe that real life in Byzantium "was nothing more than the means of

---

likely comes from the seventeenth century work of F. Simplex, *Theologia spiritualis fundamentalis* (Oliva, 1687). On this, see Joseph de Guibert, *Leçons de théologie spirituelle* (Toulouse, 1946), 18, n. 31. Since Christian scholarship often functions with different subdivisions within the theological disciplines, I have chosen to designate Peter as a "spiritual theologian" though Peter would have never used this phrase in reference to himself. In twelfth-century Byzantine terminology Peter is simply a Θεολόγος, "one who speaks of God." For a longer discussion of the use of "spiritual theology," see Peters, "Towards a Definition of 'Spiritual Theology,'" 25–41.

29   Jakov Ljubarskij, "How should a Byzantine text be read?," in *Rhetoric in Byzantium*, ed. Elizabeth Jeffreys (Burlington, VT, 2003), 117–125.

30   Ibid., 117.

revealing or, on the contrary, concealing these signs and symbols."[31] Latent in this view of Byzantine texts is the suspicion that the texts are hiding something and the modern scholar must unlock this meaning. Yet, all of Ljubarskij's examples concern non-spiritual texts: that is, they come from histories. Both ways suggested by Ljubarskij for reading Byzantine texts fail to account for the straightforward way in which spiritual texts should be read. That does not mean, of course, that spiritual authors did not make use of rhetorical or literary techniques. Rather, I am suggesting that a hermeneutic of suspicion should not be applied to a spiritual text unless good reason is found to do so.[32] Spiritual texts begin with a religious experience that the author then concretizes into written form. The spiritual text then enters the broader community of spiritual readers whose "later generations enter into conversation with these texts ... both to understand them and to find nourishment in them."[33] Summarizing Walter Principe, Lawrence Cunningham writes that the "salient point is that texts derive from experience so that a correct approach to the text demands that we try to uncover the experience that motivates the text."[34] This being the case, the most appropriate way to read a spiritual text is to allow the original author to guide the reading: that is, by taking seriously the author's personal revelations about his/her life, motives, and circumstances for writing.

In this book I do not read the spiritual texts of Peter of Damascus as an analytic philosopher, or as a French structuralist or *Annaliste*, or even as a Marxist or someone engaged in what is now called the "new literary turn." Rather, I read the texts of Peter of Damascus like a Victorine. That is, according to the principles laid out by Hugh of St Victor in his *Didascalicon* wherein he writes, "The method of expounding a text consists in analysis. Every analysis begins from things which are finite, or defined, and proceeds in the direction of things

---

31 Ibid., 118.

32 Such a hermeneutic is most appropriate to overt hagiographical texts and visionary literature, where the author is claiming direct communication from God.

33 Lawrence S. Cunningham, "Theological Table Talk: On Reading Spiritual Texts," *Theology Today* 56, no. 1 (1999), 98–104, at 101. Cunningham is summarizing Walter H. Principe, "Towards Defining Spirituality," *Studies in Religion/Sciences Religieuses* 12 (1983): 127–141.

34 Cunningham, "On Reading Spiritual Texts," 101.

which are infinite, or undefined."[35] Elsewhere he expands on this textual analysis by saying that "[a]nalysis takes place through separating into parts or through examination. We analyze through separation into parts when we distinguish from one another things which are mingled together. We analyze by examination when we open up things which are hidden."[36] For Hugh, the goal of reading and analyzing a text is to find the meaning that lies hidden within the text itself. The reader does not read meaning into a text, for the text's meaning is already there. Rather, the reader's task is to find that meaning, using appropriate methods of analysis. First, the reader analyzes the text grammatically, syntactically and semantically. Second, the reader analytically studies the central topic of the text and the order of thought therein. Next, the reader orders and compiles textual extracts that illustrate this analytical work. Finally, the reader "engages in deeper analytical thought about the implications of the work read."[37] I hope that this book is a good example of Victorine reading.

I also hope that my reading of Peter of Damascus' spiritual texts is true to Peter's own manner of reading texts. Peter took the texts that he read seriously, trying to let the texts speak for themselves and not impose his own interpretation upon them.[38] For Peter, "[t]he purpose of spiritual reading is to keep the intellect from distraction and restlessness" (155; 69.9–10)[39] and a text, especially

---

35   Hugh of Saint Victor, *Didascalicon* 3.9; in *The* Didascalicon *of Hugh of St. Victor: A Medieval Guide to the Arts*, trans. Jerome Taylor (New York, 1961), 92. Original Latin text in *Hugonis de Sancto Victore Didascalicon de studio legendi: A Critical Text*, ed. Charles Buttimer (Washington, 1939).

36   Hugh of St Victor, *Didascalicon* 6.12; *The* Didascalicon *of Hugh of St. Victor*, 150.

37   Paul J. Griffiths, "Reading as a Spiritual Discipline," in *The Scope of Our Art: The Vocation of the Theological Reader*, ed. L. Gregory Jones and Stephanie Paulsell (Grand Rapids, 2002), 44. In this article, Griffiths summarizes three processes of reading, which he calls academic reading, Proustian reading and Victorine reading. The quotation comes from his analysis of Hugh of St Victor's *Didascalicon*.

38   This is not to say that texts do not have multivalent meanings but that the meaning of a text is not exclusively the domain of the reader. On the readings of texts and their multiple meanings, see Peter J. Leithart, *Deep Exegesis: The Mystery of Reading Scripture* (Waco, TX, 2009).

39   Throughout the book, references to Peter's works include the page number in the English translation followed by page and line number of the Greek *Philokalia* edition. All quotations from Peter's *Admonition to His Own Soul* and *Spiritual Alphabet* are taken from the English translation of Peter in *Phil*.

the Scriptures, "presents one aspect to most people, even if they think that they understand its meaning [κᾶν δοκοῦσι γινώσκειν], and another to the person who has dedicated himself to continual prayer, that is, who keeps the thought of God always within him, as if it were his breathing" (154; 68.16–19). In short, Peter sees real meaning in texts, claiming, in fact, that the deepest meaning of a text is most evident to the one who is spiritual. Thus this book will take for granted that the most natural reading of the Petrine corpus is the one that takes Peter at his word, as opposed to assuming that Peter is merely engaged in rhetorical or hagiographical convention. Thus when Peter says he is a monk, then it can be assumed that Peter is a monk. I will not make an assumption that Peter is employing some hagiographical *topos*, as opposed to simply revealing the truth about his life (which is of great enough interest already to merit further study).

CHAPTER ONE

Locating and Dating Peter of Damascus

At the time of Jean Gouillard's article in 1939, where Peter was born, lived and died was unknown. Though Peter carries the geographical designation τοῦ Δαμασκηνοῦ, it is unlikely that he had any connection with the city.[1] Elsewhere I have summed up what, until now, has been known about when Peter lived:

We know little of Peter's personal history. Since he refers to Symeon Metaphrastes, who died in the last quarter of the tenth century, he lived at least after Symeon (103; 28.17). Gouillard, using two manuscript notations, argues convincingly that Peter flourished around 1156–1157. Both Paris, Bibliothèque Nationale, Ancien gr. 1135 (14th century) [*sic*][2] and Vatican City, Bibliotheca Apostolica Vaticana, Palat. gr. 210 (13th century) contain chronological indications, though they do not agree with one another. The Paris manuscript gives the date of the world in figures as the fifth indiction of the 6665th year, that is 1156–1157. The Vatican manuscript gives the date in letters: "(testatur Petrus se id scripisse) ἰνδικτιῶνος πεμπτῆς ἔτους ἑξακισχιλιοστοῦ ἑξακοσιοστοῦ ε΄," 1096–1097. Gouillard follows the Paris manuscript dating .... Three Greek codices further confirm this date, says Gouillard, citing a Russian article that bases its decision to date Peter to the twelfth century (favoring the date of 1156–1157) on these codices.[3]

---

1   This will be discussed in detail in chapter 2.
2   Unfortunately, I wrongly referenced Paris, Bibliothèque Nationale, Ancien gr. 1135 when I should have referred to Paris, Bibliothèque Nationale, Ancien gr. 1134, as Gouillard correctly cites. See Jean Gouillard, "Un auteur spirituel byzantin du XIIe siècle, Pierre Damascène," *Échos d'Orient* 38 (1939): 257-278, at 265.
3   Greg Peters, "Recovering a Lost Spiritual Theologian: Peter of Damascus and the *Philokalia*," *St. Vladimir's Theological Quarterly* 49 (2005): 438–439.

Any further, definitive dating for Peter's life depends in great part on knowing where Peter lived. An additional aid in determining Peter's dates would be to identify other Petrine works still in manuscript form that might contain chronological markers or whose composition and transmission history would shed light on this topic. Of course, identifying additional works would be significantly facilitated by knowing firm dates for Peter's life, so there is an obvious tension between knowing when Peter lived to help give attribution to unknown works while at the same time seeking the assistance of this very same manuscript evidence for establishing these dates. This tension will need to be held in check. Therefore, this chapter will take up the question of where and when Peter lived while the next will take up the question of Peter's name, which is more closely connected with the question of identifying additional works as coming from the hand of Peter.

Peter's own writings reveal that Peter is, first and foremost, a monk. He refers to himself as a monk on four occasions (5.32; 99.6–7; 38.7 and 64.27) and says that he lives in a cell (for example, 64.16). Because of Peter's self-description, the task of locating Peter within the vast geographical area of twelfth-century Byzantium is limited, at least, to the monasteries. Yet, this does not give too great a solace considering there were at least 345 monasteries in and around Constantinople alone during the Byzantine era, with many more in other major monastic and urban centers such as Mts Athos and Olympus.[4] Though Peter describes his monastic manner of life as the "royal way" (βασιλικὴν ὁδὸν) – that is, "living in stillness with one or two others, neither alone in the desert nor in great company" (197; 101.17–20) – this is not necessarily a true indication of how Peter himself lived as a monk.[5] He could merely

---

4   See R. Janin, *La géographie ecclésiastique de l'Empire Byzantin, Première partie, La siège de Constantinople et la Patriarcat œcuménique*, vol. 3: *Les églises et les monastères* (Paris, 1969), xiii–xiv; and R. Janin, *Les églises et les monastères des grands centres byzantins Bithynie, Hellespont, Latros, Galèsios, Trébizonde, Athènes, Thessalonique* (Paris, 1975). H.-G. Beck estimates that there were about 100 monasteries on the Asian side of the Bosphorus alone with thousands of monks. See Hans-Georg Beck, *Kirche und Theologische Litteratur in Byzantinischen Reich* (Munich, 1959), 208–209.

5   The phrase "royal way" is taken from Numbers 29:17 and is used in more than one sense in early Christian monastic literature. For example, Abba Poemon referred to a modest daily meal for a monk as opposed to extreme fasting as the "royal way." Benedicta Ward, trans., *The Sayings of the Desert Fathers: The Alphabetical Collection* (Kalamazoo, 1975), 171; and Greek text in PG 65: 330. In the letters of Barsanuphius and John, Abba Paul wrote that remaining faithful to the Nicene faith is the "royal

be reflecting what he sees as the ideal form of monastic life, as portrayed by John Climacus in one of the most popular texts of the Byzantine period, the *Ladder of Divine Ascent*,[6] or merely reflecting the twelfth century realities of Byzantine monasticism.

By the early twelfth century, Byzantine monasticism was experiencing a period of intense fervor. During the eleventh century, noteworthy monasteries were founded by a number of monastic reformers, including Christodoulus of Patmos, Nikon of the Black Mountain, Lazarus of Mt Galesion and, most notably, Timothy of the Theotokos Evergetis. This practice of founding new, reformed monasteries continued well into the twelfth century.[7] Based upon surviving sources, the stimulus for this new period of monastic reformation and expansion is largely attributable to the inspiration of the Evergetis monastery in Constantinople, which exercised great influence upon new twelfth-century monastic foundations.[8] As Robert Jordan writes, the "history of the foundation in the late eleventh and early twelfth centuries during the height of the monastic reform is unfortunately obscure, but its impact, traceable in the adoption of its founder's *typikon* in the foundation documents of other patrons, is indisputable."[9] Of the surviving monastic *typika* of the twelfth cen-

---

way" while Barsanuphius says that applying oneself to one's labour is also the "royal way." *Barsanuphius and John: Letters*, trans. John Chryssavgis (Washington, 2006), 1: 73, 231. Finally, in the mid-eleventh century, Nikon of the Black Mountain says that Chariton of Jerusalem's practice of giving only bread, salt and water to his monks "is the royal road." See the Κανονάριον of Nikon of the Black Mountain 45, in *BMFD*, 398.

6   John Climacus, *Ladder of Divine Ascent*, Step 1; trans. Colm Luibheid and Norman Russell (New York, 1982), 79.

7   See Rosemary Morris, "The Resurgence of the Monastic Life," in her *Monks and Laymen in Byzantium, 843–1118* (Cambridge, 1995), 9–30; and Michael Angold, "Monasteries and Society," in his *Church and Society in Byzantium under the Comneni, 1081–1261* (Cambridge, 1995), 263–382. See also section II in C. Bakirtzis, "Byzantine Monasteries in Eastern Macedonia and Thrace (Synaxis, Mt. Papikion, St. John Prodromos Monastery)," in *Mount Athos and Byzantine Monasticism*, ed. Anthony Bryer and Mary B. Cunningham (Brookfield, VT, 1996), 47–54.

8   On the Theotokos Evergetis monastery, see *BMFD*, 454–506; and Margaret Mullett and Anthony Kirby, eds., *The Theotokos Evergetis and Eleventh-Century Monasticism* (Belfast, 1994).

9   *BMFD*, 455. It must be understood that the founder's *typikon* of the Theotokos Evergetis was not a new invention. Rather, it stands in a long tradition of such doc-

tury, of which there are nine, five are textually dependent on the Evergetis *typikon* and a sixth is "sympathetic to Evergetian concerns."[10] Of these nine extant *typika*, five are from imperial or royal monasteries – monasteries where members of the imperial or royal family established and/or wrote the founder's *typikon*.[11] Private individuals founding constitutionally independent houses composed the remaining four *typika*.[12] Since so little is known biographically about Peter of Damascus, it is impossible with this paucity of information to easily establish whether he was at either an imperial or royal monastery, or an independent house. Monasteries of the twelfth century, despite their dependency on the Evergetis *typika*, at times either followed closely the Evergetis regulations or modified them to suit their unique circumstances and desires. This illustrates well Rosemary Morris's conclusion that "Byzantine monasticism never possessed 'rules' that were common to families of houses (such as those of the Benedictines or Cistercians in the West)."[13] In short, there is no unified monastic observance in the Byzantine church in the twelfth century since "each monastic founder organised such matters in his own way and each monastery carefully preserved its own customs, for Byzantine monasticism was highly indi-

---

uments but it exercised a degree of influence far greater than both earlier and contemporary *typika*. On *typika* and the types of Byzantine *typika* in general, see Abraham-Andreas Thiermeyer, "Das Typikon-Ktetorikon und sein literarhistorischer Kontext," *Orientalia Christiana Periodica* 58 (1992): 475–513.

10 *BMFD*, 859.

11 These five *typika* are: (1) the Testaments of Gregory for the Monastery of St Philip of Fragala in Sicily; (2) the *Typikon* of Luke for the Monastery of Christ Savior (San Salvatore) in Messina; (3) the *Typikon* of Empress Irene Ducaena Comnene for the Convent of the Mother of God Full of Grace in Constantinople; (4) the *Typikon* of Emperor John II Comnenos for the Monastery of Christ Pantocrator in Constantinople; and (5) the *Typikon* of the Sebastocrator Isaac Comnenos for the Monastery of the Mother of God Savior of the World near Bera. See *BMFD*, 621–858.

12 These are: (1) the *Rule of John* for the Monastery of St. John the Forerunner of Phoberus; (2) the *Memorandum* and *Typikon* of Leo, bishop of Nauplia, for the Monastery of the Mother of God in Areia; (3) the *Typikon* of Athanasius Philanthropenus for the Monastery of St Mamas in Constantinople; and (4) the *Typikon* of Nikephoros Mysticus for the Monastery of the Mother of God of the Altars of the Son or Elegmon. See *BMFD*, 872–1092.

13 Morris, *Monks and Laymen in Byzantium*, 17.

vidualistic."[14] Also of importance is the lack "of clearly defined forms" of monastic life in Byzantium.[15] Morris writes,

> an institution long considered by modern scholars to have developed over time from lavriote to the coenobitic style, had always, in fact, demonstrated an ability to adjust and adapt itself to changing circumstances. The different traditions amalgamated in a variety of ways: hermits could live in a loose, but recognisable relationship with communities; the more experienced members and even the *hegoumenoi* of houses which were clearly *koinobia* often lived a solitary life some little distance away from them. It is these very cross-fertilisations which have led to the impossibility of providing any precise semantic definitions for the various words used in contemporary sources to describe monastic houses in this period. Efforts to point fine distinctions between the terms *koinobion, mone, monasterion, phrontisterion* and, indeed, *lavra* are doomed to failure simply because many houses contained elements of both the eremitic and the communal life.[16]

Though writing about the ninth century, Alexander Kazhdan demonstrates that Morris's comments are true for the twelfth century as well: "In the twelfth century, the paramount contrast was not that of the *koinobion* and atomized eremitic cell."[17] In light of this cross-fertilization, Morris uses the term "'hybrid' monasticism" for "the combination of elements drawn from the coenobitic and lavriote traditions."[18] Keeping this "hybrid" monasticism in mind, it is possible

---

14 Ibid., 2.
15 Ibid., 33.
16 Ibid., 33–34.
17 A.P. Kazhdan, "Hermitic, Cenobitic and Secular Ideals in Byzantine Hagiography of the Ninth Centuries," *The Greek Orthodox Theological Review* 30 (1985): 473–487, at 482.
18 Morris, *Monks and Laymen in Byzantium*, 2. Consider also Peters' description of a *lavra* in *The Encyclopedia of Christian Civilization*, vol. 3: *M–R*, ed. George Thomas Kurian (Malden, WA; Oxford, 2011), s.v. "Monasteries," by Greg Peters, 1556: "The Greek word *laura* means 'lane' or 'alley' and originally referred to the paths that connected individual monastic cells to a main, centralized church. In time, the term came to designate the whole monastic complex. In lavriotic monasteries, the monks spend the week praying, working and eating in their individual cells, coming

that Peter, when describing the royal way of monasticism, was merely stating what he thought to be true: that is, that living a form of monasticism – like the one he describes as the royal way – was a more superior form of monastic lifestyle, though he himself may have not been living in such a manner. In fact, the earliest monastic reference to the royal way, that of (Pseudo-)Basil in his *Constitutiones asceticae*, refers to the cenobitic monastic life as the "royal way."[19] For another example of a monk who viewed one form of monastic life as ideal while living another manner of life, one does not need to look any further than Peter's own exemplar of the royal way – John Climacus.

Though Climacus lived for about forty years as a hermit at St. Catherine's in Sinai, the monastery itself was not organized along the lines laid out by Climacus in his *Ladder of Divine Ascent*, at least not at the time of his arrival. A description of the monastery provided by the pilgrim Egeria around 381–384, describes "some monastic cells [*monasteria quaedam*]" scattered throughout the area.[20] However, between 548–565 emperor Justinian I constructed the still-extant monastery, moving the eremitical monks inside the monastery walls and establishing a cenobitic manner of life. According to Kallistos Ware, by the time John Climacus came to Sinai in about 600 "he would have found a monastic center already well established, containing in close proximity all the three forms of the monastic life that he describes in Step 1 of *The Ladder*": the cenobitic,

---

together on Saturday and Sunday for a common liturgy. When returning to his cell, a monk would take the next week's provision of food and supplies to complete his assigned manual labor. Lavriotic monasticism had three primary characteristics: (1) it was a life of both eremiticism and coenobitism; (2) monks spent time in private and communal prayer and meals each week; and (3) lavriotic monks performed manual labor that benefited the whole lavra."

19   (Pseudo-)Basil, *Constitutiones asceticae* 4.2; PG 31: 1349B. The editors of the *Byzantine Monastic Foundation Documents* believe that this text was not written by Basil, whereas Rosemary Morris appears to believe that it was. Compare *BMFD*, 30, with Morris, *Monks and Laymen in Byzantium, 843–1118*, 16.

20   Egeria, *Diary of a Pilgrimage*, trans. George E. Gingras (New York; Ramsey, NJ, 1970), 51. According to a footnote by Gingras, "monastic cells" is the preferable translation of *monasteria* since *monasteria* is the same as καλύβας, the designation of the huts of Sinaitic hermits. This connection between *monasteria* and καλύβας is found in Pseudo-Nilus's *Narrationes* 3.4 and explained by Augustinus Bludau, *Die Pilgerreise der Aetheria* (Paderborn, 1927), 263. For Pseudo-Nilus, see Nilus of Ancyra, *Narratio*, ed. Fabrizio Conca (Leipzig, 1983). Compare with John Chrysostom, *Ad populum Antiochenum* 1.2 (PG 49: 18).

the eremitical and the "royal way."[21] Climacus writes in Step 1 that "[a]ll monastic life may be said to take one of three forms. There is the road of withdrawal and solitude for the spiritual athlete; there is the life of stillness shared with one or two others; there is the practice of living patiently in community."[22] According to Climacus' biographer, Daniel of Raithu, Climacus arrived in Sinai at the age of sixteen, placing himself under the elder Martyrius and thus following the "life of stillness" or "the royal way."[23] At thirty-five years old, writes Daniel, Climacus became a hermit at Tholas, where he remained for the next forty years until he was elected (against his will) the hegumenos of the larger, cenobitic community. In this way, we may also assume that though Peter of Damascus preferred the royal way, this does not signify with any certainty that he actually lived his entire monastic life in this manner. Like Climacus, Peter could have begun his life as one living under the tutelage of a spiritual master and in time retired to either a hermitage, a cenobitic foundation, or both (especially since all of these forms of monastic life were available in twelfth-century Byzantium, as discussed above).

Returning to Peter, it may be possible to discern that Peter is *not* living as a hermit in the royal way since he refers twice to "us monks" (75; 5.32 [ἡμῖν τοῖς Μοναχοῖς] and 194; 99.6–7 [ἡμῶν τῶν Μοναχῶν]). In another place, he reminds his fellow monks that they are not to leave their cell (149; 64.19–20). Of course, these references to other monks could simply be directed toward his monastic readers and not necessarily toward other monks at his own monastery. Yet, given that Peter is writing for both monastics and non-monastics, it is reasonable to propose that these allusions to other monks are referring to his immediate monastic brothers, suggesting that Peter is living either the royal way manner of monastic life or is living in a cenobitic monastery, though the history of twelfth-century Byzantine monasticism would suggest that Peter was likely leading a cenobitic way of life. This is further confirmed by other extant monastic texts of the eleventh and twelfth centuries. The life of St Lazarus of Mt

---

21 Kallistos Ware, "Introduction," in *The Ladder of Divine Ascent*, by John Climacus, trans. Colm Luibheid and Norman Russell (New York, 1982), 1–70, at 3.

22 John Climacus, *The Ladder of Divine Ascent*, 79.

23 For Climacus' life by Daniel, see Βίος ἐν ἐπιτομῇ τοῦ ἀββᾶ Ἰωάννου in PG 88: 596–608; and for an English translation, see John Climacus, *The Ladder of Divine Ascent*, trans. Archimandrite Lazarus Moore (Boston, 1979), xxxiv–xxxviii. See also John Chryssavgis, *John Climacus: From the Egyptian Desert to the Sinaite Mountain* (Aldershot, UK, 2004), 15–20, 42–44.

Galesion from the mid-eleventh century also refers to cenobitic monasticism as the royal way:

> If [a brother], seeing [the father's] mode of life, was in a hurry to emulate it and imitate it to the best of his ability, or troubled by the affections of the flesh, wished to cope by a rather harsher regimen than that of the monastery [κοινόβιου], and went to the father to beg permission, he would put him on his guard, and say: 'Take a good look, brother, at what you are undertaking; perhaps you will be unable to carry it through. For many have started off and, unable to complete that which they had begun, gone backwards [instead of forwards], losing [the benefit of] their self-willed and premature achievement twice over, because they were not content with what the monastery [κοινόβιου] offered them. But those who proceed by the rule of the monastery, treading untroubled the 'royal road' [βασιλικὴν ὁδόν] the fathers prescribed, advancing with discretion and not singularity, do not stumble, for they have not stirred up against themselves the ingenious and multiform malice of the demons, because they proceed in simplicity.'[24]

In like manner, John, the author of the Ὑποτύπωσις for the monastery of St John the Forerunner of Phoberos, states that "because I travel this main 'royal road' that I outline this rule and pattern for the monastery [μονῆς] which is brief and appropriate for the weaknesses of the brotherhood [ἀδελφότητος]. One thing alone I affirm, that what I say comes not from me but from what the divine fathers rightly prescribed for us."[25]

In an important article on tenth- and eleventh-century monasticism, Rosemary Morris writes that there was around the year 1000 "an important turning-point in the history of Byzantine monasticism: the move away from the following of individual askēsis in solitude towards the incorporation of personal spiritual development into the context of the communal monastic life."[26] Also,

---

24   *Testament* of Lazarus of Mt Galesion 196 in *BMFD*, 162. Greek text in Hippolyte Delehaye, ed., *Acta sanctorum novembris* (Brussels, 1910), 3: 508–588. See also *Testament* of Lazarus of Mt Galesion 197.

25   Ὑποτύπωσις of John 4 in *BMFD*, 889. Greek text in Athanasios Papadopoulos-Kerameus, *Noctes Petropolitanae: Sbornik vizantiĭskikh tekstov XII–XIII viekov* (1913; repr. Leipzig, 1976), 1–87.

26   Rosemary Morris, "Monasteries and their Patrons in the Tenth and Eleventh Centuries," *Byzantinische Forschungen* 10 (1985), 185.

the editors of *Byzantine Monastic Foundation Documents* write that "though historically Byzantium had been home to several coexisting forms of monasticism, the reformers [show] ... a strong bias towards cenobitic monasticism."[27] Morris's understanding of such communal monastic life as a combination of different forms of lifestyle (her "hybrid" monasticism) was noted above and, most importantly, this form of monasticism, incorporating primarily cenobitic and lavriotic elements, was the most common form during the twelfth century. For example, four early twelfth-century foundations (Phoberos, Helious Bomon, Areia and Mamas) are each textually connected to the aforementioned Theotokos Evergetis monastery, employing the Evergetis *typikon* "either directly or indirectly."[28] Most importantly in this context is that "these four authors also shared the Evergetian view of the centrality of cenobitism in the monastic life."[29] It is most likely, then, that Peter lived in some form of a cenobitic monastery that would have included aspects of both cenobitic and lavriotic monasticism – Morris's "hybrid" monasticism. This being the case, it is now necessary to ask: Where was Peter living as a monk? Using the preferred dating of 1156–1157 for when Peter flourished, one can begin to search extant sources for references to mid-twelfth-century persons named Peter.

There are 108 items in the database of the Prosopography of the Byzantine World that reference someone named Peter.[30] Of these references, only seventeen are dated to the twelfth century, when Peter of Damascus was active. Several are easily dismissed as referring to someone other than Peter of Damascus. The first (Petros 61)[31] is the well-known Frenchman called Peter the Hermit, leader of the disastrous "Peasants' Crusade" of 1096.[32] Two (Petros 4006 and

---

27 *BMFD*, 444.

28 *BMFD*, 859.

29 *BMFD*, 863.

30 According to the website, "The *Prosopography of the Byzantine World* aims to record all surviving information about every individual mentioned in Byzantine textual sources, together with as many as possible of the individuals recorded in seal sources, in the period 642–1261." British Academy and Berlin-Brandenburg Academy of Sciences and Humanities, "The Propography of the Byzantine World, http://www.pbw.kcl.ac.uk/content/aboutpbw/projectdef.html (accessed on 8 October 2008).

31 Parenthetical references are to the enumeration of the database of the Prosopography of the Byzantine World, s.v. "Petros," http://www.pbw.kcl.ac.uk/pbw/apps/ (accessed 8 October 2008).

32 See Heinrich Hagenmeyer, *Peter der Eremite: Ein kritischer Beitrag zer Geschichte des erstan Kreuzzuges* (Leipzig, 1879).

4007) are Latin monks referred to by William of Tyre in his *History of the Deeds Done Beyond the Sea*.[33] A third (Petros 15002) is one of three Latin soldiers mentioned by Anna Comnena in her *Alexiad*.[34] A fourth individual (Petros 20105) is known through a thirteenth-century seal that refers to Peter, the Latin archbishop of Caesarea.[35] A number of the individuals in the database contain biographical details establishing that they too are not Peter of Damascus. Four of the Peters (Petros 118, 121, 122 and 123) are married and/or have children. Though it is possible that Peter of Damascus was married prior to his entrance to the monastic life, one statement in his *Philokalia* writings suggest otherwise. Peter claims to have never owned any books; rather, all of his physical needs have been met by friends (74; 5.14–15). In fact, he claims emphatically that this has always been and continues to be the case: ἀλλὰ ξένος καὶ πένης ὑπάρχων ἀεὶ καὶ ταῦτα ἐν πάσῃ (98.33).[36] If so, it would seem illogical that any of the four married Peters mentioned in the prosopographical database would be Peter of Damascus since this would necessitate that these close friends would have been caring for Peter *and* his entire family. Though possible, it seems unlikely. Finally, the acts of the Athonite monastery of Iveron mention one Peter, father of Nedanos (Petros 127).[37] Like those named Peter that are married, that this Peter has a son implies that he also was likely (though not necessarily) married at some time[38] – thus he too is not Peter of Damascus.

33 *Historia rerum in partibus transmarinis gestarum* 13.27: Petrus Latinator, monachus Sancti Pauli; and 15.15: legatus quidam Ecclesiae Romanae, Petrus nomine, natione Burgundio. Latin text in William of Tyre, *Chronicon*, ed. R.B.C. Huygens (Turnhout, 1986).

34 *Alexiadis* 4.6: τῶν Λατίνων τρεῖς ... ὁ δὲ ἕτερος Πέτρος ὁ τοῦ Ἀλίφα. Greek text in Anna Comnena, *Alexiadis*, ed. and trans. Ludovicus Schopenus (Bonn, 1839), 212. Cf. *Alexiadis* 5.5; 11.6; and 13.12.

35 Jean-Claude Cheynet, Cécile Morrisson and Werner Seibt, *Les sceaux byzantins de la collection Henri Seyrig* (Paris, 1991), no. 385.

36 "I ... am always a stranger and poor" (193).

37 Jacques Lefort, Nicolas Oikonomidès and Denise Papachryssanthou, eds., *Actes d'Iviron*, vol. 2: *Du milieu du XIe siècle à 1204*, pt. 1: *Texte* (Paris, 1990), 266: Νεδάνου τοῦ Πέτρου.

38 It is less likely that Nedanos was Peter's illegitimate son. On illegitimate children in the Byzantine era, see Hélène Antoniadis-Bibicou, "Quelques notes sur l'enfant de la moyenne époque byzantine," *Annales de Démographie Historique* (1973): 77–84.

Having eliminated ten of the seventeen twelfth-century persons named Peter found in the database of the Prosopography of the Byzantine World, the remaining seven individuals need to be investigated. The prosopographical information for several of the remaining individuals named Peter is quite scant. However, the main reason for not equating these persons named Peter with Peter of Damascus is the lack of an explicit reference to them as monks. One Peter (Petros 119), from the acts of Iveron, is simply known as Peter, son of Nikolaos.[39] Lacking any further designation, especially that of τοῦ μοναχοῦ, it seems reasonable to not identify this Peter with Peter of Damascus. The same is true for a Peter (Petros 125) who owns properties at Radolibos, also recorded in the Iveron *acta*.[40] Another Athonite monastery, Xeropotamou, records the name, in 1142, of ἀρχιερέα Peter.[41] That Peter of Damascus never suggests that he is a bishop would seem sufficient proof that, once again, this Peter is not Peter of Damascus. Finally, a seal dated to 1125 records one Πέτρῳ πρωτοσπαθαρίῳ (Petros 20138).[42] The πρωτοσπαθάριος was "a dignity of the imperial hierarchy ... [that] usually conferred membership in the SENATE ... Up to the 10th C. *protospatharios* was a high title granted mostly to commanders of THEMES; in the 11th C. it lost this significance."[43] Given the secular nature of the term it would appear that Peter of Damascus, as a monk, would not have held such a title. As well, he himself never alludes to having held any form of high office. Further, given that the office of πρωτοσπαθάριος was paid 72 nomismata a year seems to be in direct conflict, again, with Peter's assertion that he never owned anything and that others cared for him.

In summary, though listing seventeen individuals named Peter from the twelfth century, it appears that the database of Prosopography of the Byzantine World lends no assistance to identifying Peter of Damascus with greater certainty. Of course, the database is certainly incomplete and so it is possible to

---

39 *Actes d'Iviron*, 2: 207; cf. ibid., 2: 245.

40 Ibid., 254, 262, 265. It is possible that this is the same Peter as Πέτρου τοῦ Μανόηλα (Petros 126) mentioned in another act from Iveron. See ibid., 254–255.

41 Jacques Bompaire, *Actes de Xéropotamou* (Paris, 1964), 75. Though there are examples from earlier Christian literature where the word ἀρχιερεύς can also be in reference to a priest, I would suggest that Leo's use is clearly to a bishop.

42 *Spink Auction 135: Byzantine Seals from the collection of George Zacos, Part III with Ancient and Islamic Coins* (London, 1999), 300.

43 *ODB*, s.v. "Protospatharios," by Alexander P. Kazhdan and Anthony Cutler, 1748. Rodolphe Guilland, *Recherches sur les institutions byzantines* (Berlin, 1967), 2: 99–131.

imagine that at a later date it would yield different results. However, the database does allow us to see that though Peter was a somewhat common name, it was not a uniquely monastic or a uniquely non-monastic name. That is to say, that any additional persons named Peter that will come to light later from either textual or sigillographical sources will likely be a mix of both monastic and non-monastic individuals, suggesting that locating Peter of Damascus from these sources will remain elusive. That said, there is one textual reference of special note to a "monk Peter" (τοῦ μοναχοῦ Πέτρου) that has escaped the notice of the compilers of the database.

Sometime prior to October 1143, Leo Antzades, bishop of Nauplia and Argos in the Peloponnese, built "a monastery in the name of our exceedingly pure Lady, the Mother of God, at Areia," intending to have thirty-six nuns live there.[44] However, due to pirates (λῃστῶν), Leo moved the monastery inland to Bouze, fearing for both the loss of the monastic property (φθορὰ τῶν μοναζουσῶν) and that the nuns might be the victims of rape (ἀφαιρέσεσι τῶν ἐνόντων τῇ μονῇ).[45] In its place he established another monastery, this time of monks: "As for the previous convent [at Areia], after transforming it into a male monastery, I assembled sufficient monks, and installed them there."[46] Sometime after this, likely around 1149, he composed a *typikon* for the men's monastery.[47] This *typikon* is what is of greatest concern vis-à-vis Peter of Damascus. In this document Leo makes mention of his biological family members: "... the monk Nikodemos and nun Catherine, and for my brothers and sisters in the flesh."[48] Leo proceeds to name his brothers and sister: Joseph,

---

44 *Memorandum* of Leo, BMFD, 960–964, at 960. Original Greek text in George A. Choras, Ἡ "ἁγία μονὴ" Ἀρείας ἐν τῇ ἐκκλησιαστικῇ καὶ πολιτικῇ ἱστορίᾳ τοῦ Ναυπλίου καὶ Ἄργους (Athens, 1975), 239–244. For biographical details concerning Leo and historical details on the monastery at Areia, see Choras, Ἡ "ἁγία μονὴ" Ἀρείας; BMFD, 954–960; and Michael Lamprinidou, Ἡ Ναυπλία ἀπὸ τῶν ἀρχαιοτάτων χρόνων μέχρι τῶν καθ᾽ ἡμᾶς, Ἔκδοσισ B v (Athens, 1950), 20–28.

45 *Memorandum* of Leo 3 in BMFD, 961.

46 *Memorandum* of Leo 4 in BMFD, 961. See also *Memorandum* of Leo 5: "Therefore for the above reasons the nuns were transferred from their original convent to another, which I have just constructed from the foundations, and I changed the former nunnery into a male monastery." BMFD, 961.

47 English translation by Alice-Mary Talbot in BMFD, 964–970. Greek text in Choras, Ἡ "ἁγία μονὴ" Ἀρείας, 244–252.

48 *Typikon* of Leo 12 in BMFD, 968; and Choras, Ἡ "ἁγία μονὴ" Ἀρείας, 251: τοῦ` τε

Nikon, Symeon and Peter, all monks; Helen; and John, also a bishop.[49] He continues by mentioning two "uncles who raised me, lord Constantine Antzas and the monk lord Iakobos."[50] What is of greatest interest here is the reference "τοῦ μοναχοῦ Πέτρου." That this reference could possibly be to Peter of Damascus is based primarily on several considerations: (1) this Peter is clearly a monk, as is Peter of Damascus;[51] (2) according to manuscript and (supposed) codicological evidence, Peter flourished in 1156–1157, a date that corresponds closely to Leo's foundation of the male monastery at Areia; and (3) the monks at Areia were forbidden "to have any private possession in his cell."[52]

I have already discussed above that Peter refers to himself as a monk in his philokalic writings,[53] and it is most likely that he was living in a cenobitic monastery. As a monk, Peter states that he lives in a κελλίον.[54] The word κελλίον, however, is not indicative of a particular form of monasticism.[55] It

---

Νικοδήμου μοναχοῦ καὶ Αἰκατερίνης μοναχῆς, καὶ τῶν καθ᾽ αἷμα αὐταδέλφων μου.

49 *Typikon* of Leo 12 in *BMFD*, 968; and Choras, Ἡ "ἁγία μονὴ" Ἀρείας, 251: τοῦ τε μοναχηοῦ Ἰωσήφ, τοῦ μοναχοῦ Νίκωνος, τοῦ μοναχηοῦ Συμεών, τοῦ μοναχοῦ Πέτρου καὶ τῆς Ἑλένης καὶ Ἰωάννου ἐπισκόπου. The English translationin *BMFD* inexplicably omits the names of Joseph, Nikon and Symeon.

50 *Typikon* of Leo 12 in *BMFD* ,968; and Choras, Ἡ "ἁγία μονὴ" Ἀρείας, 251: τῶν ἀναθρεψαμένων με καὶ θείων μου, κυροῦ Κωνσταντίνου τοῦ Ἀντζᾶ καὶ τοῦ μοναχοῦ κυροῦ Ἰακώβου.

51 Johann Albert Fabricius, Gottlieb Harles and Christopher Heumann, *Bibliotheca graeca sive notitia scriptorum verterum graecorum*, new ed. (1804; repr. Hildensheim, 1966), 9: 718: "qui vero simplex monachus erat."

52 *Typikon* of Leo 3in *BMFD*, 965; and Choras, Ἡ "ἁγία μονὴ" Ἀρείας, 246: ἀλλ᾽ οὐδέ τι ἔχειν ἰδιόκτητον ἐν τῷ κελλίῳ αὐτοῦ. Recall that Peter never owned private property.

53 Twice he writes about "us monks" (75; 5.32 [ἡμῖν τοῖς Μοναχοῖς] and 194; 99.6–7 [ἡμῶν τῶν Μοναχῶν]); once he makes reference to his monastic habit (114; 38.7 [τοῦ μοναχικοῦ σχήματος]); and once he refers to himself as a "fully-tested monk" (149; 64.27 [δόκιμος γέγονε Μοναχός]).

54 He talks of entering his cell (262; 154.34: καὶ εἰς τὸ κελλίον εἰσελθών), being outside a cell (90; 18.2–3: ἔξωθεν τῆς κέλλης διάγων ποτέ; and 91; 19.2: ἔξω τῆς κέλλης ὤν), being in his cell (149; 64.16: ἐν τῷ κελλίῳ; and 150; 65.16: ἐν τῷ κελλίῳ) and of standing outside a cell (262; 154.36–37: καὶ ἔξω τῆς κέλλης ἱστάμενος). He also reminds his fellow monks that they are not to leave their cell (149; 64.19–20: ἂν μὴ ἐξέλθη τῆς κέλλης)

55 *ODB*, s.v. "Kellion," by Alice-Mary Talbot, 1120.

can refer to a cell in a cenobitic monastery,[56] a cell at a lavra,[57] the cell of a hermit or even to small Athonite monasteries.[58] Again, it is highly likely that Peter lived in a cenobitic monastery, like that at Areia.

According to Gouillard, in addition to Paris, Bibliothèque Nationale, Ancien gr. 1134, there are three Greek codices confirming that Peter flourished in the mid-twelfth century.[59] However, an examination of the article cited by Gouillard in support of the dating of the three Greek codices yields no references to either Peter *or* any Greek codices.[60] Unfortunately, then, apart from Vatican City, Bibliotheca Apostolica Vaticana, Palat. gr. 210, which misdates Peter, there are no other textual indicators of when Peter lived. The maturity and detail of Peter's own philokalic works would suggest someone a number of years into the monastic life. For example, Peter writes, "I went through all these [books] slowly and diligently, trying to discover the root of man's destruction and salvation, and which of his actions or practices does or does not bring him to salvation" (74; 5.25–26). Peter's list of the books that he used and investigated is quite impressive, including the Holy Scriptures and "all the writings of

---

56 *Typikon* of Timothy for the Monastery of the Mother of God *Evergetis*, 24: "it is very good that there should be two of you in your cells" in *BMFD*, 490. Greek text in Gautier, "Le typikon de la Théotokos Évergetis," 67: εἶναι δὲ οὖν δύο ἐν τοῖς κελλίοις.

57 "[A] monk who lived in a lavra (in contrast to a *koinobion*) was frequently called a *kelliotes.*" *ODB*, s.v. "Kellion," by Alice-Mary Talbot, 1120. See also G.W.H. Lampe, ed., *A Patristic Greek Lexicon* (Oxford: Clarendon Press, 1961), 741: "κελλιώτης, ὁ, monk who has left the cenobitic life for greater solitude in a laura"; and Theodore the Stoudite, *Epistle* 1.11: ἡγουμένων ἐπίσκεψις, κελλιωτῶν ἐπίκρισις, πρεσβυτέρων καὶ διακόνων χειροτόνησις, καὶ βίου τούτων πάντων ἐπιτήρησις, χηρῶν προστασία, ὀρφανῶν ἐπικουρία, καταπονουμένων ἐκδίκησις, ἀδικουμένων ὑπερμάχησις, καὶ μέντοι καὶ ὑπεροχῆς διατήρησις (PG 99: 948AB).

58 Denise Papachryssanthou, *Actes de Prôtaton* (Paris, 1975), 86 n. 245; and cited in *ODB*, s.v. "Kellion," by Alice-Mary Talbot, 1120.

59 Gouillard, "Un auteur spirituel byzantin," 266.

60 Gouillard's citation is "*Bratskoe slovo*, 1876, fasc. 3, 196." The article is entitled "Letopis' proiskhodiashchikh" v" raskole sobytyi [Chronicle of events taking place during the schism]" and runs from pages 196–234. The periodical itself was published by the Russian Holy Synod in its attempt to combat the "schismatic" Old Believers who used Peter's teaching on how to make the sign of the cross as proof that their method was correct. It is possible, of course, that Gouillard is correct about the existence of these codices but mistaken in his reference. I have been unable, however, to locate another reference to these codices.

the great fathers and teachers – Dionysios, Athanasios, Basil, Gregory the Theologian, John Chrysostom, Gregory of Nyssa, Antony, Arsenios, Makarios, Nei-
los,[61] Ephrem, Isaac, Mark, John of Damaskos, John Klimakos, Maximos,
Dorotheos, Philimon, as well as the lives and sayings of all the saints" (74; 5.20–
25). Peter's philokalic works reveals that he did, in fact, go through these authors
carefully, borrowing much from them. Such an exercise would not only take a
rich library, or perhaps even multiple libraries, but quite an understanding of
spiritual theology and experience in the spiritual/monastic life to identify with
it and arrange it appropriately.

The latest source used by Peter is Symeon Metaphrastes "the Logothete," a
high Constantinopolitan official who died ca. 1000.[62] Symeon was the author
of many saint's lives, organized according to the liturgical year. Peter makes reference to Symeon once in the *Admonition*: "Symeon Metaphrastis the Logothete said with reference to John Chrysostom that it would be wrong not to use
the saint's words and to substitute his own" (103; 28.17–19). This is likely a reference to Symeon's *vita* of Chrysostom written as part of his *Menologion*.[63] In
this *vita*, Symeon praises Chrysostom's use of words, reinforcing the judgment
that Chrysostom is, in fact, the golden-mouthed saint.[64] There is a slight varia-
tion between scholars regarding when Symeon's *Menologion* was compiled into

61 That is, Evagrius of Pontus.

62 ὁ Λογοθέτης Συμεὼν ὁ Μεταφραστὴς (28.17). It would appear that Peter has
conflated two different persons named Symeon: "Although [Symeon Metaphrastes]
is usually identified with SYMEON LOGOTHETE, the hagiographer apparently
belonged to the next generation and worked in a different genre." *ODB*, s.v. "Symeon
Metaphrastes," by A.P. Kazhdan and Nancy P. Ševčenko, 1983. Most glaringly absent
as a direct textual source for Peter is Symeon the New Theologian, a contemporary
of Symeon Metaphrastes and a highly influential spiritual writer. This, perhaps, is
best accounted for by Peter's apparent lack of exposure to the writings of Symeon
as opposed to some sort of rejection of the thought of the New Theologian since,
as will be discussed in chapter 5, Peter and Symeon both shared a common ideal
regarding holiness and the monastic life.

63 See Nancy P. Ševčenko, *Illustrated Manuscripts of the Metaphrastian Menologion*
(Chicago, 1990). The Greek text of Symeon's *vita* of Chrysostom is in PG 114: 1045–
1210. On *Menologia* in general, see Jacques Noret, "Ménologes, Synaxaires, Menées:
Essai de clarification d'une terminologie," *Analecta Bollandiana* 86 (1968): 21–24.

64 For example, Symeon claims that those who heard the words of Chrysostom were
convinced that his soul was an exact copy of the apostle Paul's soul (PG 114: 1093)
and that the church was watered by the life-giving words of Chrysostom (PG 114:
1173).

a unified text and begun to be circulated, especially to monasteries, which is where Peter would have likely encountered Symeon's comments on John Chrysostom. Kazhdan and Ševčenko state that the *Menologion* "became standard reading in monastic circles from the 11th C. onward."[65] Elsewhere, Ševčenko argues that surviving manuscripts for the illustrated versions of the *Menologion* are dated at the earliest to around 1055–1063.[66] Christian Høgel believes that the individual lives circulated during Symeon's lifetime but that they were only later published as whole during the reign of Constantine VIII (1025–1028).[67] Given the time needed for copies of the assembled *Menologion* to be made and circulated, it would appear that both Ševčenko and Høgel would affirm that, at the earliest, Peter would have had access to Metaphrastian texts about the year 1050. Thus Peter's reference to Symeon Metaphrastes establishes a *terminus post quem* for his life of about 1050.

Establishing an *terminus ante quem* relies on manuscript evidence. According to the Greek Index Project,[68] there is one manuscript dating to the twelfth century that contains Petrine texts: Athos, M. Koutloumousion, Ms gr. 14.[69] According to Lampros, this twelfth-century manuscript contains 521 pages (σελίδας), with selections from many of the church fathers. On page 468 begins a work described as Ἐκ τοῦ βιβλίου τοῦ ἁγίου Πέτρου τοῦ Δαμασκηνοῦ, followed on page 479 by Τοῦ αὐτοῦ Λόγος πενθικὸς τῷ πενθεῖν βουλομένῳ.[70] The first work, according to Lampros, begins with "Πᾶσα γνῶσις ἀρετή τε καὶ ἰσχὺς χάρις Θεοῦ εἰσιν" and ends with "ἥτις ἐστὶ γνῶσις θείων καὶ ἀνθρωπίνων πραγμάτων." This beginning line is from Peter's introduction of the *Admonition to His Own Soul*: "Πᾶσα δὲ γνῶσις, ἀρετή τε καὶ ἰσχυς, χάρις Θεοῦ εἰσιν, ὥσπερ τἆλλα πάντα"

---

65 *ODB*, s.v. "Symeon Metaphrastes," 1983.

66 Ševčenko, *Illustrated Manuscripts of the Metaphrastian Menologion*, 197–200.

67 Christian Høgel, *Symeon Metaphrastes: Rewriting and Canonization* (Copenhagen, 2002), 127–134.

68 A database containing approximately 300,000 records listing manuscripts for Greek authors who lived before 1600 C.E.

69 Robert E. Sinkewicz, *Manuscript Listings for the Authors of the Patristic and Byzantine Periods* (Toronto, 1992), J14.

70 Spyrindon P. Lampros, *Greek Manuscripts on Mount Athos* (Cambridge, 1895), 1: 274. Cf. Marcel Richard, *Répertoire des bibliothèques et des catalogues de manuscrits grecs*, 2nd ed. (Paris, 1958), 41.

(17.13–14),[71] whereas the concluding line occurs nine pages later in the printed *Philokalia* edition in a section entitled "Concerning the Second Commandment That Fear Generates Mourning": "καὶ νοῦν ἔχειν διὰ Χριστὸν νοοῦντα τῇ τοῦ πενύματοσ καὶ σοφίᾳ, ἥτις ἐστι γνῶσις θείων καὶ ἀνθρωπίνων πραγμάτων" (26.17–19). The latter text mentioned by Lampros, Τοῦ αὐτοῦ Λόγος πενθικὸς τῷ πενθεῖν βουλομένῳ, is not found in the printed *Philokalia* text.[72] Of great interest, however, is the fact that this manuscript, dated to the twelfth century by Lampros, contains a portion of Gregory of Sinai's *Chapters on Prayer*. Gregory was not born until sometime around 1275,[73] making it impossible that this Koutloumousion manuscript is truly from the twelfth century. Yet, it is possible that the pages containing Gregory's *Chapters on Prayer* are a later addition, especially since they are located at the end of the manuscript. Apart from examining the manuscript anew, it is not possible to suggest other alternatives at this time.[74] Proceeding, then, with Lampros's dating provides the *terminus ante quem* of Peter's life as sometime during the twelfth century. This corresponds appropriately with the dating indication in Paris, Bibliothèque Nationale, Ancien gr. 1134 whose text is cited by Johann Albert Fabricius:

> Fuit alter Petrus Damascenus, cuius ascetica opera in bibliothecis adseruantur nondum edita: qui vero simplex monachus erat, et inter Graecos Byzantinos morabatur. Viuebat anno mundi 6695. Seu Christi 1157. ut ipse testatur in fine libri tertii his verbis, quae excerpsi ex regio cod. MMCMXCIV. fol. 122. ὁ γὰρ νικήσας χάριτι Χριστοῦ τὰ ὀκτὼ πάθη ταῦτα φησιν, ἐνίκησε καὶ τὰ λοιπὰ πάντα ἅ τινα προεγράφησαν ἐν τῷ πρώτῳ βιβλίῳ ὑπὸ τοῦ συγγράψαντος

71 A similar theme is found later in the *Admonition*: "Ἐπειδὴ τί ὠφελεῖται ἄνθρωπος, ἐὰν πᾶσαν γνῶσιν ἔχων, μᾶλλον δὲ λαβὼν ἀπὸ Θεοῦ κατὰ χάριν." (27.19–20).

72 Similar themes, however, are discussed in the *Admonition*. See especially the section "Περὶ τῆς τρίτης θεωρίας" (37.24–43.41).

73 On Gregory, see Antonio Rigo, "Gregorio il Sinaita," in *La théologie byzantine et sa tradition*, ed. Carmelo Giuseppe Conticello and Vassa Conticello (Turnhout, 2002), 2: 35–122.

74 I have not been able to consult the manuscript.

αὐτὸν Πέτρου ταπεινοῦ μοναχοῦ τοῦ Δαμασκήνοῦ κατ᾽ αὐτὸ σξέ ἔτος, ινδ. ἑ.[75]

More modern corroboration is provided by the *Entsiklopedicheskii Slovar*, which dates Peter to the second half of the twelfth century.[76] Karl Krumbacher gives Peter's date as around 1158, basing this on Munich, Bayerische Staatsbibliothek, Ms gr. 318, fols. 288–291, along with Paris, Bibliothèque Nationale, Ancien gr. 1134–1137.[77] Munich, Bayerische Staatsbibliothek, Ms gr. 318, f. 288r begins Πέτρου τοῦ ὁσιωτάτου καὶ τρισμάκαρος τοῦ Δαμασκηνοῦ.[78] The remainder of the folios are a catalog of the supposed works with summaries of Peter's thought. Gouillard was aware of this manuscript, using it to show that there were some compilers and authors who thought that Peter had written a num-

---

75 Johann Albert Fabricius, Gottlieb Harles and Christopher Heumann, *Bibliotheca graeca sive notitia scriptorum veterum graecorum*, new ed. (1804; repr. Hildersheim, 1966), 9: 718. Reprinted as part of the introduction to the works of John of Damascus in PG 94: 39–40. In the PG reprint, the codex is given as MMCMXIV, a misprint of Fabricius. Facricius' "ex regio cod. MMCMXCIV" is the older way of citing manuscripts in the French Royal Library, now the Bibliothèque Nationale. See Henri Omont, *Inventaire sommaire des manuscrits grecs de la Bibliothèque Nationale*, vol. 1: *Ancien fonds grec, Théologie* (Paris, 1886), 226. As Gouillard points out, Omont does not mention the text ὁ γὰρ νικήσας χάριτι Χριστοῦ τὰ ὀκτὼ πάθη ταῦτα as does Fabricius (Gouillard, "Un auteur spirituel byzantin," 263). Elsewhere in the same volume of Fabricius, Peter is described as "monachus, qui circa a. 1158. vixit, variorum asceticorum scriptor, quae in bibliothecis adhuc inedita delitescunt" (page 336). See also William Cave, *Scriptorum ecclesiasticorum historia literaria* (Oxford, 1743), 2: Dissertatio Prima, 15: "Vixit an. 1157."

76 *Entsiklopedicheskii Slovar*, ed. I.E. Andreevskii, F.F. Petrushevskii, V.T. Sheviakov and K.K. Arsenev (St Petersburg, 1893), s.v. "Damaskin (Petr)," 10: 62: "zhivshii vo 2-i polovine XII v." However, the brief entry still mislabels Peter as a martyr-monk ("sviashchennomuchenik") who lived in Damascus.

77 Karl Krumbacher, A. Ehrhard and Heinrich Gelzer, *Geschichte der byzantinischen Literatur von Justinian bis zum Ende des Oströmischen Reiches (527–1453)*, 2nd ed. (Munich, 1897), 157: "Mehrere asketische Schriften des Petros von Damaskos, auch Petros Mansur genannt, der um 1158 gelebt haben soll, sind vorhanden z. B. in den codd. Monac. 318 saec. 13 fol. 288–291, Paris. 1134–37."

78 See Ignaz Hardt, *Catalogus codicum manuscriptorum Graecorum Bibliothecae Regiae Bavaricae* (Munich, 1806), 3: 292. For the Greek manuscripts in Munich in general, see Kerstin Hajdú, *Die Sammlung griechischer Handschriften in der Münchener Hofbibliothek bis zum Jahr 1803: Eine Bestandsgeschichte der Codices graeci Monacenses 1–323 mit Signaturenkonkordanzen und Beschreibung des Stephanus-Katalogs (Cbm Cat. 48)* (Wiesbaden, 2002). Hajdú makes no direct reference to Ms gr. 318.

ber of additional texts, such as the opuscules περὶ τῶν τρίων δυνάμεων τῆς ψυχῆς ἐν ἐπιτόμῳ and περὶ τῶν ὀκτὼ λογισμῶν, as listed in the Munich manuscript.[79] It would appear, however, that these "works" are actually just listings of sections of the *Admonition*,[80] suggesting that as early as the thirteenth century portions of Peter's philokalic works were already being circulated and copied. More important is Peter's description as "holy" and "thrice-blessed." To ascribe these titles to Peter demonstrates that within about a hundred years of his death, Peter's works were at least somewhat well-known and that he was viewed as a saint and a gifted teacher and spiritual writer whose works were worthy of being copied.

Peter of Damascus states that he never owned any books or "other possession" (74; 5.14 and 193; 98.32–33).[81] Granted that Peter's admission to such absolute poverty could be looked upon with suspicion, that is, as a merely literary or hagiographic convention, the most natural reading of the text would be to accept Peter's words as an honest admission. Touched upon above is the strong influence of the Theotokos Evergetis *typikon* on many twelfth-century monasteries, which disallows monks from owning private property. Also mentioned previously is that Leo's monastery at Areia is textually connected to the Theotokos Evergetis monastery. Furthermore, it must be noted that the liturgical and dietary regime of the monks at Areia were dependant not on the Evergetis *typikon* but the lost *typikon* of Meletius the Younger.[82] Alice-Mary Talbot suggests that Meletius' *typikon* "was probably structurally like" the *Stoudios* or *Athonite typika*: that is, "a document closer to a liturgical than a founder's *typikon* like *Evergetis*."[83] However, "since the author [Leo] does not incontrovertibly reveal his dependence on *Evergetis* by using literal transcriptions ... we

---

79 Gouillard, "Un auteur spirituel byzantin," 262. Hardt lists the contents as follows: περὶ τῶν ὀκτὼ διαλογισμῶν καὶ τοῦ τριαμέρου τῆς ψυχῆς καὶ περὶ τοῦ ἐλευθερῶσαι τὸ πάθος, ἔι τι ποιήσει ἄνθρωπος. Α. χρὴ γινώσκειν πάντα ἄνθρωπον. Τ. οὕτω καταξιούμεθα.

80 Hence Hardt's judgment that the manuscript lists a number of "Opusc. ignotum."

81 ἐπειδὴ οὐδ᾽ ὅλως βίβλων ἰδίαν κέκτημαι, ἢ ἐκτησάμην ποτέ, ἀλλ᾽ ἐκ τῶν φιλοχρίστων ἐλάμβανον, ὥσπερ καὶ τὰς σωματικὰς χρείας ἁπάσας (5.14–16); and μηδ᾽ ὅλως ἰδίαν ἔχων βίβλον ἢ ἄλλο τι τὸ παράπαν (98.32–33).

82 See *Memorandum* of Leo 8 in *BMFD*, 962. On Meletius, see François Halkin, *Bibliotheca hagiographica graeca*, 3rd ed. (Brussels, 1957), nos. 1247 and 1248; and Chrysostomos Papadopoulos, Συμβολαί εἰς τὴν ἱστορίαν τοῦ μοναχικοῦ βίου ἐν Ἑλλάδι. Ὁ ὅσιος Μελέτιος ὁ Νέος (1035–1105) (Athens, 1968).

83 *BMFD*, 955.

must leave open the possibility that he was drawing upon an earlier or parallel reform tradition with which the Evergetian *typikon* shared much of its content."[84] Yet, there are certainly Evergetian themes in the Areia *typikon*: for example, the superior is the monk's confessor and he determines how frequently a monk receives the Eucharist;[85] monks are not to visit one another's cell;[86] both monasteries were to be free from episcopal control;[87] and admission criteria were comparable in the two monasteries.[88] Similar to both the Stoudite tradition and Evergetis, monks at Areia were forbidden to have private property.

> You shall not possess anything of this world nor store up anything for yourself as your own, not even one piece of silver. (Testament of Theodore the Studite, "Rules for the Superior" 2);[89]

> Those who acquire some possessions contrary to the rule of the monastery, even so much as an obol or a piece of fruit, without the knowledge of the superior, will be liable to punishment. Similar to them is the person who eats and drinks in secret … and the person who receives messages from friends and relatives, and replies to them. (Evergetis *Typikon* 22);[90]

> No monk is to have permission to eat by himself in his own cell, unless he is confined to bed by illness, or this is permitted by the superior as a dispensation. Nor is he to have any private possession in his cell. (*Typikon* of Leo 3)[91]

---

84   *BMFD*, 955. This earlier tradition would be the Stoudite *synaxarion*: "I ordain that on each occasion every doxology be celebrated zealously and without any omission and with the fitting attention and sobriety in accordance with the Studite *synaxarion* of the ecclesiastical office" (Leo, *Typikon* 1). For a translation and discussion of the Stoudite *typikon*, see the prefatory analysis to "*Stoudios: Rule* of the Monastery of St. John Stoudios in Constantinople," in *BMFD*, 84–119.

85   Compare *Typikon* of Leo 2 (*BMFD*, 965) and *Evergetis* 5 (*BMFD*, 474).

86   Compare *Typikon* of Leo 9 (*BMFD*, 967) and *Evergetis* 21 (*BMFD*, 489).

87   Compare *Typikon* of Leo 12 (*BMFD*, 968) and *Evergetis* 12 (*BMFD*, 482).

88   Compare *Typikon* of Leo 6 (*BMFD*, 966) and *Evergetis* 37 (*BMFD*, 494).

89   *BMFD*, 77. Greek text in PG 99: 1817.

90   Ibid., 490. Greek text in Paul Gautier, "Le typikon de la Théotokos Évergétis," *Revue des études byzantines* 40 (1982): 15–95, at 66–67.

91   *BMFD*, 965.

Areia placed a strong emphasis on poverty, yet this was not always one of the distinctive features of Byzantine monasteries, even in the twelfth century.[92] For as the editors of the *Byzantine Monastic Foundation Documents* write, "Although Byzantine monasteries remained in principle opposed to private property, personal poverty was not a rule, and exceptions were regularly made, especially for monks and nuns who came from powerful and wealthy families and who, by the standards of the time, could not be expected to live a common life with other members of a community."[93] This is corroborated by Kazhdan and Constable who write that the "individualistic features of monastic organization became more prominent in the later Middle Ages, when the so-called idiorhythmic type of monastic community developed. The monks in these communities formed small quasi-familial groups holding their property in common. Even private ownership was allowed."[94] Emperor John Tsimiskes' *typikon* for Mount Athos from 971–972 allows, and thereby presupposes, that monastic superiors will own private property: "If one of the superiors should choose to sell, donate, or otherwise transmit his *own* plot of land to any person he wishes ... we consent that he be permitted to exercise his own ownership and authority with full freedom."[95] Michael Attaleiates' Διάταξις for the monastery of Christ Πανοικτίρμονος from March 1077 speaks of the monk's personal servants,[96] as does Christodoulus of Patmos in March 1093.[97] Both

---

92 See Emil Herman, "Die Regelung der Armut in den byzantinischen Klöstern," *Orientalia Christiana Periodica* 7 (1941): 406–460.

93 Giles Constable, "Preface," in BMFD, xxxiii.

94 A.P. Kazhdan and Giles Constable, *People and Power in Byzantium: An Introduction to Modern Byzantine Studies* (Washington, 1982), 91. On idiorhythmic monasticism, see *ODB*, s.v. "Idiorrhythmic Monasticism," by Alice-Mary Talbot, 981–982: "The term *idiorrhythmia* (ἰδιορρυθμία), meaning 'following one's own devices,' is found as early as the 5th C ... but this type of MONASTICISM did not become at all common until the Palaiologan era and has a negative connotation throughout the Byz. Period ... Idiorrhythmic monks are permitted to acquire personal property ..."

95 *Typikon* of Emperor John Tzimiskes 6 in *BMFD*, 237. Greek text in Papachryssanthou, *Actes du Prôtaton*, 209–215. See also *Typikon* of Emperor John Tzimiskes 7. The following examples are summarized in *BMFD*, xxxiii–xxxiv.

96 Διάταξις of Michael Attaleiates 42 in *BMFD*, 353. Greek text in Paul Gautier, "La diataxis de Michel Attaliate," *Revue des études byzantines* 39 (1981): 17–130.

97 *Codicil* of Christodoulos of Patmos 4 in *BMFD*, 599: "The servants working for the monastery ..." Greek text in Franz Miklosich and Joseph Müller, *Acta et diplomata graeca medii aevi sacra et profana* (Vienna, 1890), 6: 85–90.

the *typikon* of Gregory Pakourianos for the monastery of the Θεοτόκου τῆς
Πετριτζιωτίσσης in Bačkovo, dated to December 1083, and the *typikon* of
Emperor John II Comnenos for the monastery of Christ Pantokrator in Constantinople, dated to October 1136, allow certain comforts for monks accustomed to "luxurious living" [ἀβροδιατίτης]. Pakourianos writes that there will
be one common dining table where only one type of bread and wine is allowed,
since one monk should not eat better bread or drink better wine than another
monk. He forbids the monks from making any private decisions or personal
arrangements and hiding anything edible in his cell. As well, "a vessel for heat-
ing water" or preparing "cooked food privately" is also forbidden. However, he
then writes that "if someone truly desires these things perhaps through weakness of body or very advanced old age this should be considered a necessity and
be provided for this reason, and more so if it happens to be one of the very
exalted or someone used to luxurious living (ἐξ ὑψωτάτων τις τέτευχεν εἶναι
ἢ ἀβροδιαίτης).[98] Similarly, John II Comnenos writes, "But if someone is necessary for the monastery, since the requirements of its activities demand people
who are able to contribute as they can, or if a person for certain reasons needs
some concession, either because he happens to be from a pre-eminent family
[συγκαταβάσεως] or he has been brought up in a rather luxurious way of life
[ἀβροτέρα], it will rest with the superior after consideration to devise measures
for the care of that person in accordance with the benefit to the monastery as
he perceives it."[99] In other monasteries the monks or nuns were given cash
allowances with which to purchase private possessions. For example, Michael
Attaleiates writes that the "allowance of the monks and the other pious dona-
tions [ῥόγα τῶν μοναχῶν καὶ τὰ λοιπὰ ψυχικὰ]" should be "paid out without my heir keeping back or removing anything."[100] As well, the *typikon* of
Athanasius Philanthropenos for the monastery of St Mamas in Constantinople, founded with certainty in November 1158 – during Peter of Damascus's
lifetime – says,

---

98 *Typikon* of Gregory Pakourianos 4 in *BMFD*, 528. Greek text in Paul Gautier, "Le
   typikon du sébaste Grégoire Pakourianos," *Revue des études byzantines* 42 (1984):
   19–133, at 48.
99 *Typikon* of John II Komnenos 17 in *BMFD*, 748. Greek text in Paul Gautier, "Le
   typikon du Christ Sauveur Pantocrator," *Revue des études byzantines* 32 (1974): 27–
   131.
100 Διάταξις of Michael Attaleiates 33 in *BMFD*, 349.

Concerning, indeed, clothes and footwear and various other bodily coverings of the monks it is our wish that there be given to each of them anything he needs in accordance with the cenobitic pursuit and regimen which has been traditional from long ago. Inasmuch, however, as contention accompanies, as it often does, the distributions of this sort, and it is one of the most troublesome things to satisfy the pleasure and wish of each, we considered it better that the items of clothing be supplied to each of the brothers through the use of money, putting an end to contentions and grumblings even in this matter.[101]

From this survey, it appears that Areia's emphasis on personal poverty is somewhat unique for its time and therefore seems to suggest that it would be the kind of monastery where Peter, who forfeited all earthly possessions, would feel most at home. Monastic poverty had come, throughout much of monastic history, to be a *sine qua non* of "true monasticism."[102] Theodore the Stoudite, in the ninth century, went so far as to state that it is poverty (and celibacy) that distinguishes a monk from a non-monastic person. He wrote in a letter to the Spatharios Marian,

Poverty of spirit, tears of compunction, gentleness, peace, mercy, the mind's contemplation of God, contempt of money, hatred towards the world, frugality, temperance over each power of the faculties; and simply to love the Lord more than wife, children, parents, brothers and all persons ... and similar things are of the true Christian. Do not think my Lord, that what I have said only concerns the monk. Although it affects the monk more

101 *Typikon* of Athanasios Philanthropenos 38 in *BMFD*, 1013–1014. Greek text in Sophronios Eustratiades, "Τυπικὸν τῆς μονῆς τοῦ ἁγίου μεγαλομάρτυρος Μάμαντος," *Hellenica* 1 (1928): 256–311. See also V. Laurent, "Remarques critiques sur le texte du typikon du monastère de Saint-Mamas," *Echos d'Orient* 30 (1931): 233–242. That Athanasios Philanthropenos would allow for such distribution of cash is even more revealing when one considers its significant textual dependence on the *typikon* for the Theotokos Evergetis monastery, which legislated for individual poverty.

102 See Adalbert de Vogüé, "Monastic Poverty in the West," *Monastic Studies* 13 (1982): 99–112; and Verna E.F. Harrison, "Poverty in the Orthodox Tradition," *St. Vladimir's Theological Quarterly* 34 (1990): 15–47.

intensely all these things equally affect the lay person, with the exception of celibacy and poverty, for which a secular is not to be condemned.[103]

John IV/V Oxeites, Chalcedonian patriarch of Antioch from ca. 1089–1100, wrote his *Oratio de monasteriis laicis non tradendis* in 1085 or 1092.[104] In this treatise, directed against the *charistike*,[105] John places emphasis on monastic poverty on several occasions. In one instance he claims that poverty among the monks is scarce and that the lack of poverty among the monks in monasteries under the *charistike* is placing them at risk for being withdrawn from communion in the heavenly kingdom.[106] For John, as for Theodore the Stoudite, there were different requirements for monks and non-monastics (κοσμική) vis-à-vis poverty. To have non-monastics in charge of monasteries, thinks John Oxeites, was detrimental to the need of the monks to have no personal property and to live in poverty. Fortunately for monks like Peter of Damascus there were monasteries, like that at Areia, which legislated for monastic poverty, giving the monk who "neither own[s] nor ever ... owned any books" an opportunity to continue to live that form of monastic life.

---

103 *Letter* 464; English translation in Roman Cholij, *Theodore the Stoudite: The Ordering of Holiness* (Oxford: Oxford University Press, 2002), 227, but omitting Cholij's Greek insertions.

104 On John Oxeites in general, see Paul Gautier, "Jean V l'Oxite, patriarche d'Antioche: Notice biographique," *Revue des études byzantines* 22 (1964): 128–157.

105 John Philip Thomas, *Private Religious Foundations in the Byzantine Empire* (Washington, 1987), 157: "The *charistike* was a public program sponsored by the emperor and the ecclesiastical hierarchy for the private management of religious institutions." In short, it was placing a monastery under lay patronage.

106 John IV/V Oxeites, *Oratio de monasteriis laicis non tradendis* 13; *Joannis Oxeitae oratio de monasteriis laicis non tradendis*, ed. Tiziana Creazzo (Spoleto, 2004), 75.444–448: φημὶ δὴ τὸ τῶν μοναχῶν καὶ μοναζουσῶν, οὐ μόνον διὰ τῆς τῶν ἀναγκαίων ἐνδείας πιέζων καὶ στενοχωρῶν ἀλλὰ καὶ διὰ δωρεᾶς ἀνθρώποις καταδουλῶν καί, ὅσον τὸ ἐπ' αὐτόν, ἀφιστάνων αὐτοὺς τοῦ ἐπουρανίου βασιλέως, πῶς δύναται εἶναι ἢ λέγεσθαι χριστιανός. See also John Oxites, *Joannis Oxeitae oratio de monasteriis laicis non tradendis*, ed. Tiziana Creazzo (Spoleto, 2004), 15. When employing John Oxeites it is good to heed the wisdom of Michael Angold: "John of Oxeia's tract against *kharistike* is polemic, but nonetheless instructive for that." In, *Church and Society in Byzantium Under the Comneni, 1081–1261* (Cambridge, 1995), 277.

CHAPTER TWO

Naming Peter of Damascus

In my earlier study of Peter of Damascus I briefly discussed Peter's name and his designation of τοῦ Δαμασκηνοῦ.[1] In summary, according to Jean Gouillard, Peter's appellation is not proof that he came from Damascus: "If, later, the famous preacher of the sixteenth century was able to call himself Damascene, although born in Thessaloniki, if the homonymous scribe of *Hieros. patr. 109*, seventeenth century, was descended from Adrianople, why would Peter have to come from Damascus to justify his surname?"[2] In his introduction to Peter's texts in the *Philokalia*, Nicodemus of the Holy Mountain said that Peter was a monk-bishop who lived in the middle of the eighth century.[3] Some, especially G.E. Steitz, have argued for a connection of Peter of Damascus with Peter Mansur.[4] It is necessary to take up these in turn.

Gouillard's main contention is simply that there are other examples of Eastern Orthodox persons who were supposedly connected to the city of Damascus but were not. This is not sufficient proof, however, that Peter also falls into this category. Rather, it is instructive as a reminder that some epithets are inaccurate.

---

1   Greg Peters, "Recovering a Lost Spiritual Theologian: Peter of Damascus and the *Philokalia*," *St. Vladimir's Theological Quarterly* 49 (2005): 437-459, at 439-440.
2   Jean Gouillard, "Un auteur spirituel byzantin du XIIe siècle, Pierre Damascène," *Échos d'Orient* 38 (1939): 257-278, at 265: "Si, plus tard, le fameux prédicateur du XVIe s. a pu s'appeler Damascène, bien que né à Thessalonique, si le scribe homonyme du *Hieros. patr. 109*, XVIIe s., était issu d'Andrinople, pourquoi Pierre devrait-il venir de Damas pour justifier son surnom?" I am unsure who Gouillard is referring to as the "famous preacher of the sixteenth century." His reference to the scribe of *Hieros. patr. 109* comes from Anastasios Papadopoulos-Kerameus, Ἱεροσολυμιτκὴ Βιβλιοθήκη, Τομος Πρῶτος (En Petroupodei, 1891), 192.
3   Φιλοκαλία τῶν ἱερῶν νηπτικῶν, Τόμος Γ, ed. Nicodemus of the Holy Mountain and Macarius of Corinth (Athens, 1991), 3-4.
4   G.E. Steitz, "Die Abendmahlehre der griechischen Kirche in ihrer geschichtlichen Entwicklung," *Jahrbücher für deutsche Theologie* 13 (1868), 23-31.

Concerning Nicodemus of the Holy Mountain's misappellation, there is, notably, a Peter τοῦ Δαμασκηνου from the eighth century. Theophanes the Confessor, in his *Chronographia*, records the following for the year 741–2: "Oualid ordered that Peter, the most holy metropolitan of Damascus, should have his tongue cut off because he was publicly reproving the impiety of the Arabs and the Manichees, and exiled him to Arabia Felix, where he died a martyr on behalf of Christ after reciting the holy liturgy."[5] Theophanes, immediately after recounting the martyrdom of the eighth-century Peter of Damascus, also records in Damascus the martyrdom of another Peter, one Peter of Maiouma (or Capitolias), who "has been honoured in a laudation by our holy father John [of Damascus]."[6] The former Peter is who Nicodemus has in mind when attributing the philokalic works of Peter τοῦ Δαμασκηνου. Furthermore, John of Damascus states that his work *Contra Jacobitas* was "ἐκ προσώπου Πέτρου τοῦ ἁγιωτάτου ἐπισκόπου Δαμασκοῦ"[7] and John's *Libellus de recta sententia* was sent to "ἐπισκόπου Πέτρῳ μητροπολίτη Δαμασκοῦ."[8] Despite the presence of this eighth-century Peter of Damascus, chronologically it is not possible that he is the author of the philokalic texts.

5 Theophanes the Confessor, *The Chronicle of Theophanes Confessor: Byzantine and Near Easter History AD 284–813*, trans. with introduction and commentary by Cyril Mango and Roger Scott with the assistance of Geoffrey Greatrex (Oxford, 1997), 577. Greek text in Theophanes the Confessor, *Theophanis chronographia*, ed. Carl de Boor (Leipzig, 1883–1885), 1.416.

6 Theophanes the Confessor, *The Chronicle of Theophanes Confessor*, 577–578. This laudation only survives in Georgian and is attributed to John of Damascus. See Paul Peeters, "La passion de S. Pierre de Capitolias (†13 janvier 715)," *Analecta Bollandiana* 57 (1939): 299–333; and 58 (1940): 123–125. The *Martyrologium Romanum Gregorii XIII jussu editum* (Rome, 1583) lists the feast day of both Peters on February 21: "Damasci sancti Petri episcopi et martyris, cui Arabum et Manichaeorum errores arguenti, Saracenorum rex linguan praecidi iussit eumque in Arabiam Felicem relegavit, ubi diro affectus supplicio, martyrium consummavit. Ibidem, sancti Petri Mauimeni, qui cum Arabis ipsum aegrotum visitantibus diceret: 'Omnis qui sanctam fidem Christianam catholicam non amplectitur damnatus est, sicut et Mahumet pseudopropheta veste,' ab illis necatus est. "

7 John of Damascus, *Die Schriften des Johannes von Damaskos*, vol. 4: Liber de haeresibus: Opera polemica, ed. P. Bonifatius Kotter (Berlin; New York, 1981), 109.

8 PG 94: 1421–1422. According to the note in the PG, it is "ex Vaticano cod. n. 1262" which says that the *Libellus de recta sententia* is being sent to Peter, metropolitan of Damascus.

The argument that Peter of Damascus is the same person as Peter Mansur is of great interest. As early as 1712, Michel Lequien argued that two short treatises on the Eucharistic body of Christ attributed to John of Damascus by earlier scholars were not, in fact, authentic.[9] The first text is a letter to Zacharias, bishop of Doaroi.[10] The second work is entitled Περὶ τοῦ ἀχράντου σώματος οὗ μεταλαμβάνομεν, *caput de immaculato corpore, cujus participes sumus*.[11] Lequien then makes reference to a Parisian manuscript that attributes the letter to Zacharias to Peter Mansur.[12] Lequien proceeds to name the three Peters

---

9 John of Damascus, *Opera omnia*, ed. Michel Lequien (Paris, 1712), 1.652–655. Lequien's text was reprinted in Johann Albert Fabricius, Gottlieb Harles and Christopher Heumann, *Bibliotheca graeca sive notitia scriptorum veterum graecorum*, new ed. (1804; repr. Hildesheim, 1966), 9: 718; which was later republished in PG 94: 39–40. These treatises had been attributed to John of Damascus in the earlier editions of his works by Petrus Pantinus (Antwerp, 1601) and Fronto Ducaeus (Paris, 1603 and 1619). The earliest attribution to John of Damascus was by the twelfth-century anti-Comnenian Michael Glykas and the canonist and theologian John Zonaras. See Franz Renz, *Die Geschichte des Messopfer-Begriffs*, vol. 1: *Altertum und Mittelalter* (Freising, 1901), 515; Heinrich Pachali, "Soterichos Panteugenos und Nikolaos von Methone," in *Zeitschrift für wissenschaftliche Theologie* 50 (1907), 347–374 at 373; and Hans-Georg Beck, *Kirche und Theologische Litteratur im Byzantinischen Reich* (Munich, 1959), 644.

10 Given by Lequien as Δοάρων. Fabricius, Harles and Heumann, *Bibliotheca graeca sive notitia scriptorum veterum graecorum*, 9: 717. Steitz is unsure of this designation but suggests it could be a reference to a small town ("Städtchen") near Damascus. See Steitz, "Die Abendmahlehre der griechischen Kirche in ihrer geschichtlichen Entwicklung," *Jahrbücher für deutsche Theologie* 13 (1868): 23–31, at 24, n. 1; and also George Dahl, *The Materials for the History of Dor* (New Haven, 1915), 108. The text in PG 95: 401–403 gives the title as Ἐπιστολὴ τοῦ ἁγιωτάτου Πέτρου τοῦ Μανσοὺρ πρὸς Ζαχαρίαν ἐπίσκοπον Δοάρων.

11 PG 95: 405–412. Lequien gives the title as follows: κεφάλιον περὶ τοῦ ἀχράντου σώματος οὗ μεταλαμβάνομεν, de immaculato corpore, cuius participes reddimur. Fabricius, Harles and Heumann, *Bibliotheca graeca sive notitia scriptorum veterum graecorum*, 9: 717.

12 This is Paris, Bibliothèque Nationale, Coislin gr. 201. The catalog describes the relevant contents as follows: "On lit auparavant, sous le nom de. S. Jean Damascène, deux opuscules: a (f. 1) lettre de Pierre Mansour à Zacharie (M. 95, 401 A6–404 B8); b (ff. 1–2) le petit traité 'de immaculato corpore Christi' (M. 95, 405–412)." Robert Devreesse, *Catalogue des manuscrits grecs*, vol. 2: *Le fonds Coislin* (Paris, 1945), 179. Also, in Paris, Bibliothèque Nationale, Ancien gr. 2315 there is a "S. Joannis Damasceni fragmentum de corpore et sanguine Christi" beginning on f. 346 and in Paris, Bibliothèque Nationale, Ancien gr. 364 a "s. Joannis Damasceni tractatus

to whom this treatise could belong: the two Peters in Theophanes the Confessor's *Chronographia* discussed above, and Peter of Damascus. Lequien rejects its attribution to any of these Peters.[13] Regarding Peter of Damascus as the author, he writes that such a conclusion is not fully established.[14] In his article, G.E. Steitz speaks about these two Pseudo-John of Damascus texts from the twelfth century concerning the Eucharist. He then proceeds to discuss Peter Mansur, with his information taken from Lequien, perhaps directly or from the reprints of Fabricius or the *Patrologia graeca*. Discussions in Byzantium regarding such topics, writes Steitz, did not begin to happen until the mid-twelfth century when Soterichos Panteugenos became involved in discussions on the nature of Christ's sacrifice.[15] In fact, two theological controversies dominated the eleventh- and twelfth-century Byzantine church: the azymes controversy and questions concerning the *filioque* and the natures of the Son of God, including those questions related to the Eucharist's implications of Christ's humanity and divinity.[16] "Azymes" (ἄζυμος) was the term for the unleavened bread used

---

de sacris mysteriis" beginning on f. 34. See, respectively, Henri Omont, *Inventaire sommaire des manuscrits grecs de la Bibliothèque nationale*, vol. 2: *Ancien fonds grec, Droit-Histoire-Sciences* (Paris, 1888), 236; and Henri Omont, *Inventaire sommaire des manuscrits grecs de la Bibliothèque Nationale*, vol. 1: *Ancien fonds grec, Théologie* (Paris, 1886), 37.

13 For an English overview of Lequien's argument, see William Smith, ed., *A Dictionary of Greek and Roman Biography and Mythology by Various Writers*, vol. 3: *Oarses–Zygia* (New York, 1967), 223. See also Joseph Langen, *Johannes von Damaskus: Eine patristische Monographie* (Gotha, 1879), 196.

14 John of Damascus, *Opera omnia*, 1.653; and PG 95: 397–398: "Horum alterum fuisse epistolae et oratiunculae scriptorem non affirmavero."

15 Steitz, "Die Abendmahllehre der griechischen Kirche in ihrer geschichtlichen Entwicklung," 25. Gouillard confirms Steitz's assertion when he writes that "[l]es écrits appartiennent bien à l'époque qui vit paraître" the *Admonition* and *Spiritual Alphabet*. Gouillard, "Un auteur spirituel byzantin du XIIe siècle," 263. Beck also believes that these treatises belong to a later era, in his estimation the eleventh century: "Wenn tatsächlich ein Petros Mansur der Verfasser sein sollte – J. Hoeck konnte noch keine Hs. mit seinem Namen feststellen – so müßte er wohl spätestens dem 11. Jahrhundert zugewiesen werden; der theologischen Problemgeschichte nach, das hat schon Lequien gezeigt, wäre die Abfassung freilich schon Jahrhunderte früher möglich und denkbar." Beck, *Kirche und Theologische Litteratur im Byzantinischen Reich*, 645. Panteugenos will be discussed in greater detail below.

16 The following discussion relies on Beck, *Kirche und Theologische Literatur im Byzantinischen Reich*, 609–662; and A.P. Kazhdan and Simon Franklin, *Studies on Byzantine Literature of the Eleventh and Twelfth Centuries* (Cambridge; New York; Paris, 1984).

by the Armenian and Latin churches in the Eucharist, whereas the Byzantine church used leavened bread. Controversy between the Byzantine church and the Latin church on this subject began in the eleventh century and culminated in 1054 with the excommunication of Patriarch Michael I Cerularius by the Latin Cardinal Humbert. Many Byzantine writers wrote works concerning this topic. For example, John II, metropolitan of Kiev in the late eleventh century, addressed a letter around 1090 to (anti-pope) Clement III with a treatise on the azymes attached to it.[17] The letter was not sent in a spirit of antagonism, given that it was addressed "to our very holy and venerable father in the same service of God, Clement, pope of ancient Rome."[18] John accused the Latins of making innovations, including Saturday fasts, celibate clergy, the *filioque* and azymes.[19] He pleaded with Clement, "I ask you in grace ... prostrate on your knees, I beg you to quit your mistake, especially that which concerns the azymes and the Holy Spirit: because the first compromises the Holy Communion, the second, the orthodoxy of the faith."[20] According to A.S. Pavlov, John may have, at a later date, written a longer treatise dedicated to the question of the azymes, but this is uncertain.[21] A short irenic treatise condemning the use of azymes is attributed to Symeon II (†1098–9), patriarch of Jerusalem,[22] and another three trea-

17 *ODB*, s.v. "John II," by Simon C. Franklin, 1045–1046.

18 Bernard Leib, *Rome, Kiev et Byzance à la fin du XIe siècle: Rapports religieux des Latins et des Gréco-Russes sous le Pontificat d'Urban II (1088–1099)* (1924; repr. New York, 1968), 34. Greek text of the letter in Aleksej Stepanovič Pavlov, ed., *Kritičeskie opyty po istorii drevnejšej greko-russkoj polemiki protiv latinjan* (St Petersburg, 1878), 169–186. Greek text also available in S.K. Oikonomos, ed., Τοῦ ὁσίου πατρὸς ἡμῶν Ἰωάννου μητροπολίτου Ρωσίας ἐπιστολὴ πρὸς Κλήμεντα παπαν Ῥώμης (Athens, 1868). I have been unable to consult either Pavlov or Oikonomos.

19 Leib, *Rome, Kiev et Byzance à la fin du XIe siècle*, 36.

20 Ibid., 37: "Je vous demande en grâce, écrit-il, et, posterné à vos genoux, je vous conjure de quitter vos errement, surtout ceux qui touchent les azymes et le Saint-Esprit: car les premiers compromettent la sainte communion, les seconds, l'orthodoxie de la foi."

21 Ibid., 37, n. 2.

22 Greek text of the treatises in Bernard Leib, "Deux inédits byzantins sur les azymes au début du XIIe siècle," *Orientalia Christiana Periodica* 2 (1924): 177–239; with French translation in Leib, *Rome, Kiev et Byzance à la fin du XIe siècle*, 260–263. That these two treatises are, in fact, from the hand of Symeon, see Anton Michel, *Amalfi und Jerusalem im griechischen Kirchenstreti (1054–1090): Kardinal Humbert, Laycus von Amalfi, Nicetas Stethatos, Symeon II. Von Jerusalem, und Bruno von Segni über die Azymen* (Rome, 1939).

tises on the azymes, entitled Λόγος περὶ ἀζύμων, were written by John VIII, also patriarch of Jerusalem, in 1106–7.[23] Of great importance is the contribution of Leo of Ohrid, an eleventh-century polemicist.[24] Leo was the spokesman of Patriarch Michael I Cerularius between the Byzantine and Latin clergy in southern Italy. Though he addressed many issues, his main argument against the Latin church concerned the use of azymes in the Eucharist. Leo addressed at least three letters to Rome about this issue, the first of which received a sharp answer from Cardinal Humbert, initiating a series of exchanges that ultimately led to the condemnation of Patriarch Michael in 1054.[25] Leo argued that the use of unleavened bread was a Jewish practice, that it contradicts the synoptic Gospels, which claim that Jesus took "bread" (ἄρτον, which implies that the bread was leavened), and that "its symbolic value is that of 'death,' not of 'life,' for yeast in the dough is like the soul in the body."[26] Finally, Theodore of Smyrna, who engaged in discussions with the Latin theologian Peter Grossolano in Constantinople in 1112, also wrote a theological tract on the azymes that remains unpublished.[27]

In addition to the azymes controversy, authors also concerned themselves with the nature of Christ, and with the nature of the Son's relationship to the

23   Joseph Patrich, *The Sabaite Heritage in the Orthodox Church from the Fifth Century to the Present* (Leuven, 2001), 91. The treatise is found in Jerusalem, Greek Orthodox Patriarchate, St Sabas 366. An edition was prepared by Dositheos II of Jerusalem, *Τόμος ἀγάπης, συλλεγεὶς καὶ τυπωθεὶς παρὰ Δοσιθέου, πατριάρχου Ἱεροσολύμων* (Jassy, 1698), 516–527. This was reprinted in PG 151: 693–715. See also Johannes Pahlitzsch, "Die Bedeutung der Azymenfrage für die Beziehungen zwischen griechisch-orthodoxer und lateinischer Kirche in den Kreuzfahrerstaaten," in *Die Folgen der Kreuzzüge für die orientalischen Religionsgemeinschaften*, ed. Walter Beltz (Halle; Wittenberg, 1996), 75–92.

24   See Louis Bréhier, *Le schisme oriental du XIe siècle* (Paris, 1899), 93–102 and 151–153.

25   Greek text of the letters in Pavlov, ed., *Kritičeskie opyty po istorii drevnejšej greko-russkoj polemiki protiv latinjan*, 146–151; and Cornelius Will, ed., *Acta et scripta quae de controversiis ecclesiae graecae et latinae saeculo undecimo composita extant* (1861; repr. Frankfurt am Main, 1963), 56–60.

26   John Meyendorff, *Byzantine Theology: Historical Trends and Doctrinal Themes* (New York, 1979), 95. This was, in essence, the same argument made by Nicetas Stethatos, a disciple and biographer of Symeon the New Theologian. On Stethatos, see Nicetas Stethatos, *Opuscules et Lettres*, ed. Jean Darrouzès (Paris, 1961).

27   V. Laurent, "Légendes sigillographiques et familles byzantines," *Echos d'Orient* 31 (1932), 331–335.

procession of the Holy Spirit. Eustratius of Nicaea, a philosopher and theologian who flourished around 1100, wrote a treatise on the *filioque*, as did the theologian John Phournes, who rejected the *filioque* and emphasized the monarchical principle of the Godhead. As well, he stressed the equality of the Son and the Holy Spirit, referring to them as "the two hands of the same substance and of the same power."[28] Eustratius also held that the Son and the Holy Spirit were the hands of God the Father. Nicholas IV Mouzalon, patriarch of Constantinople who died in 1152, addressed a treatise to Emperor Alexius I on the procession of the Holy Spirit. In this treatise he refuted the concept of the *filioque*.[29] Nicetas "of Maroneia" made one of the most important contributions in this debate. Nicetas wrote six dialogues between a Greek theologian and a Latin theologian on the procession of the Holy Spirit, in which he sided with the Latin position.[30] In these dialogues he defended the Latin point of view though he refused to accept the change to the Nicene-Constantinopolitan creed that had been initiated by the Latin church. This led the fifteenth-century theologian and papal representative, Bessarion, to comment that Nicetas "was fighting the 'donkey's shadow,' since he accepted the idea of FILIOQUE, but refused to make a corresponding addition to the symbol of the creed."[31] Finally, note must be made of Nicholas of Methone, who died between 1160 and 1166. Nicholas was a vocal proponent of the unity of God; therefore, he polemicized against the *filioque*, fearing that it would lead to the denigration of the Son of God. Further, he emphasized the equality of the Holy Spirit with regard to the divine essence.

---

28 *ODB*, s.v. "Phournes, John," by A.P. Kazhdan, 1671.

29 Theodoros N. Zeses, "Ὁ πατριάρχης Νικόλαος IV Μουζάλων," Ἐπιστημονικὴ Ἐπετηρὶς τῆς Θεολογικῆς Σχολῆς τοῦ Πανεπιστημίου Θεσσαλονίκης 23 (1978), 309–329.

30 The Greek text of book 1 of the *Dialogues on the Procession of the Holy Spirit* is in PG 139: 169–202, with excerpts from the other five books in cols. 201–222. A Greek edition of books 2–4 is in Nicholas Festa, "Niceta di Maronea e i suoi dialoghi sulla processione dello Spirito Santo," *Bessarione* 16 (1912): 80–107, 266–286; 17 (1913): 104–113, 295–315; 18 (1914): 55–75, 243–259; 19 (1915): 239–246. There appears to be no Greek edition of books 5–6. See also Corrado Giorgetti, *Nicetas de Maronée et ses dialogues V et VI sur la procession du Saint-Esprit* (Rome, 1965); and Corrado Giorgetti, "Un teologo greco del XII sec. precursore della riunificazione fra Roma e Costantinopoli: Niceta di Maronea, arcivescovo di Tessalonica," *Annuario 1968 della biblioteca civica di Massa* (Lucca, 1969): 129–148.

31 Kazhdan, "Nicetas 'of Maroneia.'" See the Greek text in PG 161: 329A.

Apart from treatises on azymes and the *filioque*, other authors discussed the divine and human natures of Christ. Demetrius of Lampe was a secular theologian who rejected the Latin teaching that Christ was at the same time both inferior to God the Father and equal to him. Demetrius had a disputation with Emperor Manuel I Comnenos who defended this Latin doctrine and emphasized the two natures of Christ. Following this disputation, Demetrius wrote a treatise in which he developed his views, ultimately leading to the Council of Constantinople in 1166.[32] Constantine of Kerkyra was a theologian condemned in 1170 for his heretical interpretation of John 14:28, "for the Father is greater than I." Constantine stressed the hypostatic unity of the Father and the Son, denying that "the Son was inferior on account of the real and concrete humanity which he assumed in the incarnation."[33]

Therefore, given the nature of the theological debates in the eleventh and twelfth centuries, Peter Mansur must have been writing in the mid-twelfth century and not in the eighth century as some scholars believe. Of Lequien's three Peters, only Peter of Damascus is from the twelfth century. Therefore, Peter Mansur and Peter of Damascus are necessarily the same person. Steitz says that because the time frame of their literary output is the same, he considers it highly probable that Peter of Damascus is the author of the two Eucharistic homilies.[34] Furthermore, Steitz on two occasions says that Peter Mansur is a monk: "Mönchs Petrus Mansur" and "Mönch Mansur."[35] He may have said this based on the fact that he knows that Peter of Damascus was a monk, therefore, if Peter of Damascus and Peter Mansur are the same person then Peter Mansur was a monk. If, however, Peter Mansur has been identified elsewhere as a monk, a possibility even if Steitz does not provide external documentation, the connection between the two Peters would be strengthened.

This identification of Peter Mansur with Peter of Damascus was subsequently accepted, or at least not challenged, by Albert Ehrhard who wrote that

---

32 P. Classen, "Das Konzil von Konstantinopel 1166 und die Lateiner," *Byzantinische Zeitschrift* 48 (1955), 339–368.

33 *ODB*, s.v. "Constantine of Kerkyra," by A.P. Kazhdan, 506.

34 Steitz, "Die Abendmahllehre der griechischen Kirche in ihrer geschichtlichen Entwicklung," 25: "Da nun diese chronologische Bestimmung haarscharf mit der Zeit der schriftstellerischen Thätigkeit des Mönchs Petrus Mansur zusammenfallt, so halte ich es für sehr Wohl möglich, daß dieser der Verfasser der Homilie gewesen ist." Elsewhere he refers to these two works as "den angeblichen Schriftstücken" (39) and "in dem angeblichen Briefe des Mansur" (42).

35 Ibid., 25, 45.

"[t]his Peter is also regarded as the author of two treatises on the Eucharist."[36] Hans-Georg Beck, on the other hand, rejected this position since "the respective writings of 'Petros Mansur' never appear under the name Peter Damascene and the genuine works of [Peter] Damascene never [appear] under the name of Mansur."[37] As well, Beck says that there is a manuscript from 1105 with a work attributed to Peter Mansur, though he fails to identify this manuscript. Since Peter's dates are later than this, he writes, it is unlikely that Peter of Damascus is the same person as Peter Mansur.[38] Gouillard also rejects Steitz's theory since he "was not able to take advantage of any serious argument."[39] For Gouillard, as for Beck, who is Gouillard's likely source, "the thesis is defensible with difficulty ... But two important observations are in order: a writing of Peter Damascene never comes with the denominator of Mansur; and nowhere do the chapters on the Eucharist bear the name of Peter Damascene."[40] Another reason Gouillard rejects the identification of the two Peters is that "the title and tone of the first controversial pamphlet are that of a bishop rather than of a monk like the author of" *Admonition* and *Spiritual Alphabet*.[41]

---

36 Karl Krumbacher, A. Ehrhard and Heinrich Gelzer, *Geschichte der byzantinischen Literatur von Justinian bis zum Ende des Oströmischen Reiches (527–1453)*, 2nd ed. (Munich, 1897), 157: "Dieser Petros wird auch als Verfasser von zwei Schriftstücken über das Abendmahl betrachtet."

37 Beck, *Kirche und Theologische Litteratur im Byzantinischen Reich*, 644: "die entsprechenden Schriften des 'Petros Mansur' nie unter dem Namen Petros Damaskenos erscheinen und die echten des Damaskenos nie unter dem Namen eines Mansur."

38 Ibid., 644: "Zu den Gründen Gouillards kommt die Tatsache, daß eine Handschrift ... schon dem Jahre 1105 entstammt."

39 Gouillard, "Un auteur spirituel byzantin du XIIe siècle," 265: "ne peut se prévaloir d'aucun argument sérieux."

40 Ibid., 263–264: "La thèse est difficilement défendable ... Mais double constatation importante: jamais un écrit de Pierre Damascène ne vient ave le terme de Mansur; nulle part, les chapitres mentionnes sur l'eucharistie ne portent le nom de P. Damascène."

41 Ibid., 264: "la titulature et le ton du premier factum sont d'un évêque plutôt que d'un moine comme l'était l'auteur de ..." This tone had also been noted by Lequien when he stated, "Tandem quae epistolae initio voces leguntur ... non satis referunt humilem nostri Joannis modestiam erga viros episcopali dignitate ornatos, innuuntque ab episcopo potius, quam monacho aut presbytero fuisse scriptam". John of Damascus, *Opera omnia*, 1.653; PG 95: 397–398. See also William Smith and Henry Wace, eds., *A Dictionary of Christian Biography, Literature, Sects and Doctrines: Being a Continuation of "The Dictionary of the Bible,"* vol. 3: *Hermogenes–Myensis* (London, 1882), 417.

However, this could be accounted for if Peter is the brother of a bishop, as discussed in chapter 1.

Returning to the observation that only in the mid-twelfth century were there discussions about the nature of the Eucharist, on 26 January 1156 Emperor Manuel Comnenos called into synodical session in Constantinople bishops and theologians from across the Byzantine empire to discuss a text from the liturgy of St John Chrysostom: "You are he who offers and is offered and received."[42] The debate began when Basil, a deacon of Hagia Sophia and teacher of the Gospels at the patriarchal school in Constantinople, explained that God the Son is both the victim and the recipient of the Eucharistic sacrifice.[43] Soterichos Panteugenos, the patriarch-elect of Antioch,[44] then attacked this position in the form of a Platonic dialogue, which was initially published anonymously.[45] A statement issued at the end of the first session in 1156 condemned those who affirmed that the sacrifice of Christ was offered to God the Father alone and not to all three persons of the Holy Trinity.[46] Panteugenos, along

---

42 PG 140: 138B: "Βασιλεύοντος Μανουὴλ, ὃσ προπάτορα μὲν τὸν βασιλέα ἔσχεν Ἀλέξιον, τοκέα δὲ Ἰωάννην τὸν εν ἄναξι περιώνυμον, ἐκινήθη δόγμα περὶ τοῦ, "Σὺ ὁ προσφέρων καὶ προσφερόμενος καὶ προσδεχόμενος?" This text is spoken by the priest while the people are singing the Cherubic Hymn. For a summary of the events surrounding these two councils, see Jean Gouillard, "Le Synodikon de l'Orthodoxie: Édition et commentaire," *Travaux èt mémoires* 2 (1967): 1-316, at 210-215.

43 On the patriarchal school, see Robert Browning, "The Patriarchal School at Constantinople in the Twelfth Century," *Byzantion* 32 (1962): 167-202; 33 (1963): 11-40; and reprinted in Robert Browning, *Studies on Byzantine History, Literature and Education* (London, 1977).

44 *ODB*, s.v. "Constantinople, Councils of: Local Council of 1156-57," by A.P. Kazhdan, 514; and s.v. "Panteugenos, Soterichos," by John Meyendorff, 1574: "A deacon of the Great Church of Hagia Sophia in Constantinople, then patriarch-elect of Antioch, Panteugenos (Παντευγενός) became the major figure in theological debates on the nature of Christ's sacrifice."

45 This dialogue was preserved by the late-twelfth- /early-thirteenth-century Byzantine historian Nicetas Choniates. Greek text in Johannes Dräseke, "Der Dialog des Soterichos Panteugénos," *Zeitschrift für wissenschaftliche Theologie* 29 (1886): 228-237; PG 140: 140-148; and John Sakkelion, Πατμιακὴ βιβλιοθήκη (Athens, 1890), 328-331.

46 *ODB*, s.v. Meyendorff, "Panteugenos, Soterichos," 1574. See also PG 140: 153C: "ὅθεν καὶ διατόρῳ στόματι ἀνακηρύττο τε καὶ ὁμολογῶ πιστεύειν ἀληθῶς μὴ τῷ Πατρὶ μόνῳ, ἀλλὰ δὴ καὶ τῷ Υἱῷ καὶ τῇ παναγια Τριάδι, τὸ ζωοποιὸν αἷμα καὶ σῶμα τοῦ Σωτῆρος Χριστοῦ καὶ πρώτως ἐπὶ τοῦ Δεσποτικοῦ πάθους

with the deacon and teacher of the Pauline epistles, Nikephoros Basilakes, refused to accept the council's decision.[47] This elicited a response in the form of a tract from George Tornikios, teacher of the Psalms and Gospels and, from 1155, metropolitan of Ephesus.[48] From the extant sources, it is possible to conclude that Soterichos "affirmed that the [Eucharistic] sacrifice could not be offered to the Holy Trinity, for this would imply that the one Christ performs two opposing actions, the human action of offering and the divine action of receiving, and would mean a Nestorian separation and personalization of the two natures."[49] Between the two synods, Panteugenos affirmed his authorship of the *Dialogue*, even presenting a profession of faith that conformed to the council of 1156's teaching. However, using the anathemas of the *Synodicon of Orthodoxy*, it would appear that Panteugenos continued to resist full conformity. Thus on 12 May 1157, the bishops and theologians were called again into synod at the Blachernai Palace to explicitly discuss the Christological teachings of Panteugenos, as well as the consequent implications for the Eucharistic sacrifice.[50] This synod, presided over by Emperor Manuel I Comnenos himself, confirmed the doctrinal affirmations of the previous synod. Panteugenos then confessed his error, abandoning his unorthodox position. In the end, the synod put forward five anathemas that are included in the *Synodicon of Orthodoxy*.[51]

The significance of these synods, especially that of May 1157, regarding Peter of Damascus as the likely author of the two Eucharistic treatises rests with those present at the synod. According to the historian Nicetas Choniates, the synod of 1157 was attended by Leo, bishop of Nauplia, who affixed his signa-

---

προσενεχθῆναι, καὶ ἔκτοτε τὰς ὁσημέραι τελουμένας ἐν ταῖς ἱεραῖς τελεταῖς μυστικὰς ἁγιστείας τῇ τρισυποστάτῳ πάντως Θεότητι παρὰ τῶν ταύτας ἱερουργούντων προσάγεσθαι."

47 Antonio Garzya, "Precisazioni sul processo di Niceforo Basilace," *Byzantion* 40 (1970), 309–316.

48 Jean Darrouzès, *Georges et Dèmètrios Tornikès: Lettres et discours* (Paris, 1970); and Browning, "The Patriarchal School at Constantinople in the Twelfth Century," 34–37.

49 Meyendorff, *Byzantine Theology*, 40.

50 For additional summary, see Giovan Domenico Mansi, *Sacrorum Conciliorum nova et amplissima collectio* (Venice, 1776), 21: 837–838.

51 Greek text of these anathemas in Gouillard, "Le Synodikon de l'Orthodoxie," 73–75; and PG 140: 176B–178B. The most sustained treatise against Panteugenos was

ture to the five anathemas: του Ἀργους Λέοντος.⁵² This is confirmed by Codex Parisinus, supplément grec 1090, which says, "ὀνόματα τὰ εὑρεθέντα ἐν τῷ συνοδικῷ γεγραμμένα τῶν ἀοιδίμων καὶ μακαρίων ἀρχιερέων καὶ ἐπισκόπων ἡμῶν Ναυπλοίου [sic] καὶ Ἀργους εἰσὶ ταῦτα ... "⁵³ It would appear, then, that Leo was involved in the Christological and Eucharistic debates of 1156–1157. If Peter is his biological brother, as discussed in chapter 1, it is reasonable to conclude that Leo asked Peter to write the Eucharistic treatise Περὶ τοῦ ἀχράντου σώματος οὑ μεταλαμβάνομεν as well as the letter to bishop Zacharias on his behalf. Therefore, though the treatises are written in an episcopal tone on behalf of Leo, their true author is Peter, Leo's brother, and a monk at his monastery at Areia.⁵⁴

---

by Nicholas of Methone in his Λόγοι δύο where he "rejected the innovations of Soterichos PANTEUGENOS. Stressing the unity of Christ in the act of the Eucharist, Nicholas reproached Soterichos for raising the dispute at a time of danger from barbarians." *ODB*, s.v. "Nicholas of Methone," by A.P. Kazhdan, 1469.

52 PG 140: 180C. Cf. Mansi, *Sacrorum Conciliorum nova et amplissima collectio*, 838.

53 Quoted in Choras, Ἡ "ἁγία μονὴ" Ἀρείας ἐν τῇ ἐκκλησιαστικῇ καὶ πολιτικῇ ἱστορίᾳ τοῦ Ναυπλίου καὶ Ἀργους, 60. See also John Sakkelion, "Ἀργους καὶ Ναυπλίου παλαιοὶ Ἱεράρχαι," Δελτίον τῆς Ἱστορικῆς καὶ Ἐθνολογικῆς Ἑταιρείας τῆς Ἑλλάδος (1885), 2: 37–38; and *BMFD*, 954.

54 Given that Peter says little in the *Admonition* and *Spiritual Alphabet* concerning the Eucharist; it is difficult to compare these texts with the Eucharistic treatises for a common theology. However, Peter does discuss the Eucharist in two places in the *Admonition* that appear to reveal a mature theology of Holy Communion. The first: "We pray as well for the whole world, as we have been taught to do by the Church, and that though sinful we may be found worthy to partake of holy communion as we should, and that by praying before taking it we may find him ready to help us when the moment for communion comes. We pray that we may remember the holy Passion of our Saviour and may cleave with love to this remembrance. We pray that through the sacrament we may enter into communion with the Holy Spirit; for in this world and in the next the Paraclete Himself solaces those who are filled with godlike grief, and who with all their soul and with many tears call upon Him for help and say, 'O heavenly King, Paraclete, the Spirit of truth...' We pray that our participation in the undefiled mysteries may be a pledge of eternal life in Christ, through the intercessions of His Mother and of all the saints" (200–201; 104.8–19). The second: "[A]nd how these awesome mysteries – I refer to holy baptism and holy communion – cannot take place without the priesthood, as St John Chrysostom says. Here, too, we see the significance of the power given to St Peter, chief of the apostles; for if the gates of the kingdom of heaven are not opened by priestly actions, no one can enter. As the Lord says: 'Unless a man is born of water and the Spirit...'; and again: 'Unless you eat the flesh of the Son of man and drink His blood, you have no life in you'" (208–209; 110.10–17).

Accepting Steitz and Ehrhard's conclusion that Peter of Damascus and Peter Mansur are the same person, it is necessary to explain how one Peter is known by both names. The name "Mansur"[55] entered the Byzantine era primarily through Mansur ibn Sarjun, the man in charge of the fiscal administration of Damascus in the early seventh century.[56] Mansur was succeeded in this position by his son, Sarjun ibn Mansur, mentioned by Theophanes the Confessor in the year 690–691 as a "most Christian man."[57] Sarjun's son also worked in the administration of Damascus and, like his grandfather, was named Mansur ibn Sarjun, though he is known in history as John of Damascus. For as Louth writes, "[A]t some stage, perhaps in the second decade of the eighth century, John resigned from his post in the administration at Damascus, and became a monk in Palestine, taking as his monastic name John, the name by which he has been known ever since."[58] It would appear then that the name Mansur became closely connected to eighth-century Damascus. Thus it is only a short step for the name Peter Mansur to be distorted into Peter of Damascus, especially since there was already a somewhat well-known Peter of Damascus martyred in the eighth century as discussed above. On occasion, Peter is said to be the brother or, at least, a kinsmen of John of Damascus.[59] This identification as brothers/kinsmen is also the result of John of Damascus' family name of Mansur. This helps to explain why as late as the eighteenth century, when Nicodemus of the Holy Mountain was writing his introduction to Peter's works for the *Philokalia*, that he too thought that the philokalic Peter had lived and died in the mid-eighth century.

55 On the etymology of the word "Mansur," see Stephen Gero, *Byzantine Iconoclasm during the Reign of Leo III* (Louvain, 1973), 62, where Gero says that the name is of Hebrew origin meaning "bastard." See also Theophanes the Confessor, *The Chronicle of Theophanes Confessor*, 579: "Mansūr = 'victorious', or 'aided [by God]'..." According to the fifth- or sixth-century lexicographer Hesychius of Alexandria μανσούρ is equivalent to κύων, meaning "bitch." See Kurt Latte, *Hesychii Alexandrini lexicon* (Copenhagen, 1953–1966), μ232.

56 Discussion of the name Mansur comes from Andrew Louth, *St. John Damascene: Tradition and Originality in Byzantine Theology* (Oxford, 2002), 5–6; and *ODB*, s.v. "Mansūr, Ibn Sarjūn," by Walter Emil Kaegi and A.P. Kazhdan, 1288.

57 Cited in Louth, *St. John Damascene*, 5. See also Theophanes the Confessor, *Theophanis chronographia*, 1.365: τις ἀνὴρ χριστιανικώτατος.

58 Louth, *St. John Damascene*, 6.

59 See Henry Riley Gummey, *The Consecration of the Eucharist: A Study of the Prayer of Consecration in the Communion Office* (Philadelphia; London, 1908), 85; and E.G. Cuthbert F. Atchley, *On the Epiclesis of the Eucharistic Liturgy and in the Consecration of the Font* (Oxford, 1935), 132.

CHAPTER THREE

The Spiritual Theology of Peter of Damascus I: *The Admonition to His Own Soul* (ὑπόμνησις πρὸς τὴν ἑαυτοῦ ψυχήν)

This chapter will systematize Peter's teachings from the philokalic work *Admonition to His Own Soul* topically instead of sequentially; in other words, the discussion will not follow the order of Peter's arrangement.[1] This approach will help to counter the misjudgment that "Peter's work is not systematic."[2] It is true that it may not be sequentially systematic but, as will be shown, it is topically systematic; that is to say, the *Admonition* is not an eclectic collection of random thoughts. Rather, it appears that Peter's organization was purposeful and that he chose his material carefully. As discussed below, the dialectic of destruction versus salvation is the hinge upon which the *Admonition* turns. For Peter and for Christian theology in general, each person will ultimately either experience salvation or damnation (i.e., destruction). In Peter's thought, that which leads one toward salvation and away from destruction is a proper spiritual life. Hence, Peter's purpose in the *Admonition* is to explicate a spiritual theology that leads a believer to live a proper spiritual life.[3] Peter does not accomplish this by laying out the stages of the spiritual life in a sequential order, beginning with the fall of humankind and ending with the deification or theosis of each believer. Instead Peter lays out his systematic understanding of the spiritual life in the introduction to the *Admonition* and then meanders topically throughout the remainder of the book to touch upon those areas dis-

---

1 The *Admonition to His Own Soul* is a lengthy text. It occupies 106 pages in the reprinted Greek edition and 136 pages in the English translation of the *Philokalia*.

2 *Phil.*, 3: 72.

3 On "spiritual theology" in this context, see Greg Peters, "Towards a Definition of 'Spiritual Theology': A Historiography of Recent Writings on Byzantine Spirituality," *Studia Monastica* 46 (2004): 25–41.

cussed in his introduction.[4] He uses the bulk of the *Admonition* to paint the full picture of the spiritual life that is only sketched out in the introduction. Using quotations from earlier Christian writers and his own original thoughts, Peter explicates fully, though not sequentially, his unique spiritual theology.[5] Yet, by using the introduction to the *Admonition* as the skeleton of Peter's thought, one is able to use the remainder of the *Admonition* to flesh out those topics discussed in the introduction.

It is a common judgment that Peter's literary corpus is unorganized, random, or even unoriginal. This criticism is ubiquitous in the sparse secondary literature. In the introduction to their Italian translation of Peter's philokalic works, Benedetta Artioli and Francesca Lovato write that the works of Peter "do not require a particular introduction, because they are easy readings and do not present complex lines of development."[6] They then begin their summation with the judgments that "the writings present characteristics of disorder and approximation"; that "we are not dealing with writings of particular originality;"[7] and that the works consist of "editorial disorder and ... little originality."[8] After this disparaging summation, Artioli and Lovato turn their attention to

---

4 This "meandering" is most evident in those chapters that are disordered or in those chapters that claim to be dealing with a particular topic but then do not actually touch upon the stated topic. Some of these discrepancies may be the result of copyists or later editors, though, as Palmer, Sherrard and Ware observed, "Chapter headings sometimes refer only to the opening sentence or paragraph of the section, while the rest deals with other matters. But this outward lack of order would not greatly have troubled St Peter's monastic readers, who were interested not in abstract systems but in practical advice; and this the author has undoubtedly provided." G.E.H. Palmer, Philip Sherrard and Kallistos Ware, "Introductory Notes," in *Phil.*, 3: 72.

5 On Peter's relationship to his primary early Christian sources, see Greg Peters, "Peter of Damascus and Early Christian Spiritual Theology," *Patristica et Medievalia* 26 (2005): 89–109.

6 *La Filocalia: A cura di Nicodimo Aghiorita e Macario di Corinto*, trans. M. Benedetta Artioli and M. Francesca Lovato (Turin, 1985), 3: 9: "... non esigono una particolare introduzione, perché sono di facile lettura e non presentano linee di sviluppo complesse."

7 Ibid., 3: 9: "gli scritti presentano caratteristiche di disordine e approssimazione ... non si tratta di scritti particolarmente orginali."

8 Ibid. 3: 10: "il disordine redazionale e ... poca originalità."

some definite lines ... that surface continually along both works: First of all, a vivid sense of the continuous gratitude we owe to God ... Another characteristic of these writings is the insistence on humility ... Moreover, the Damascene has a very acute sense of the prevenience of grace ... as well as a profound conviction of the radical incapacity of man ... Another line that flows naturally from the previous is the one that draws attention to the necessity to bear with humble patience any event God lays out.[9]

They conclude that, "[W]e find in the writings of the Damascene an anthology of classical doctrines, not very well organized, but that in its kind, conserves a value of its own."[10]

Artioli and Lovato are echoing (perhaps simply repeating) similar conclusions reached by Jean Gouillard: "the work of Peter Damascene offers a *doctrinal ensemble* that is neither complete, nor original, but which, viewed from a certain angle, retains some interest [and that] the absence of a true originality does not have to be underlined: the work belongs to a genre that renews itself little; the anthological conception of the composition is a proof also, in its own way."[11] Gouillard characterizes the *Admonition* "as a memento of the spiritual life" since it,

[following] a "fundamental meditation" about the problem of salvation, reviews the aspects of interior progress according to the classic division of

9   Ibid., 3: 10–11: "alcune loro linee ben nette che affiorano continuamente lungo entrambe le opere ... Prima di tutto, un senso vivissimo della continua riconoscenza che dobbiamo al Dio ... Un'altra caratteristica di questi scritti è l'insistenza sull'umiltà ... Il Damasceno ha inoltre un senso molto acuto della prevenienza della grazia ... come pure una convinzione profonda dell'incapacità radicale dell'uomo ... Altra linea che scaturisce naturalmente dalle precedenti è quella che porta l'attenzione sulla necessità di sopportare con umile pazienza qualsiasi evento Dio disponga."

10   Ibid., 3: 12: "In conclusione, troviamo negli scritti del Damasceno un'antologia di dottrine classiche, organizzate in un insieme non sempre felice, ma che, conversa un suo valore."

11   Jean Gouillard, "Un auteur spirituel byzantin du XIIe siècle, Pierre Damascène," *Échos d'Orient* 38 (1939): 257–278, at 270: "l'oeuvre de Pierre Damascène offre un *ensemble doctrinal* qui n'est ni complet, ni original mais qui, vu de certain angle, retient quelque intérêt ... L'absence d'une originalité vraie n'a pas à être soulignée: l'oeuvre appartient à un genre qui se renouvelle peu; la conception anthologique de la composition est une preuve aussi, à sa manière."

πρᾶξις and θεωρία: the active life with its complementary set of bodily virtues and psychic virtues, the eight degrees of the contemplative life. This part takes half of the work ... The second part has the aim of fulfilling the lacuna by returning to the points that were only touched upon before: humility, discretion, reading, etc.[12]

In his final estimation, Gouillard judges the Petrine corpus as a whole to be "in the Evagrian current of interpretation, corrected and diffused by Maximus the Confessor."[13] Hans-Georg Beck reaches a similar conclusion when he says that Peter offers fundamentally a Maximian scheme of spiritual ascent that is expressed in less intellectual terms.[14]

Jacques Touraille's introduction to his translation of the Petrine corpus is the one exception to such negative evaluations.[15] In somewhat sensational language, Touraille describes Peter as a "man having God alone, who gathered all his life and gives us here his honey, sometimes mixed with wax, but always

---

12   Ibid., 266–267: "pour un memento de vie spirituelle ... une 'méditation fondamentale' sur le problème du salut ... déroule les aspects du progrès intérieur suivant la division classique en πρᾶξις et θεωρία: la vie active avec son jeu complémentaire de vertus corporelles et de vertus psychiques, les huit degrés de la vie contemplative. Cette partie remplit la moitié de l'ouvrage. ... La seconde partie a pour objet de combler la lacune en revenant sur les points qui n'ont été qu'effleurés plus haut: humilité, discrétion, lecture, etc." To support his thesis that Peter's spiritual program involves two stages Gouillard turns immediately to an external source saying that what "was written by Maximus the Confessor can in effect be applied to Peter Damascene." (The original French is "écrit de Maxime le Confesseur peut en effet être appliqué à Pierre Damascène."). Ibid., 272. I reject this bipartite division since it is a preconceived scheme formulated from earlier authors and imposed upon Peter. In light of this, Gouillard's discussion of Peter's spiritual theology must be used with caution.

13   Ibid., 277: "dans le courant évagrien interprété, corrigé et diffusé par Maxime le Confesseur."

14   Hans-Georg Beck, *Kirche und Theologische Litteratur im Byzantinischen Reich* (Munich, 1959), 644: "Petros bietet unter Benützung zahlreicher asketischer Quellen bis herauf zum Sinaiten Philotheos, Joannes von Karpathos und wahrscheinlich Symeon von Euchaita ein im Grunde maximianisches, wenn auch weniger intellektuell zum Ausdruck gebrachtes Schema des geistlichen Aufstieges."

15   *Philocalie des Pères Neptiques*, fasc. 2: *Pierre Damascène*, ed. Jacques Touraille (Bégrolles-en-mauges, 1980); the French translation of the Petrine corpus reprinted in *Philocalie des Pères Neptiques* (Paris, 1995), 7–11.

scented with blessed eternity."[16] He describes Peter's works as "neither source, nor current, but rather a lake where the readings ... [and] the testimony of the Byzantine liturgy and the experience of the monastic life come to display their waters."[17] Further, Peter "has nevertheless been able to transform the sap of the roots into one of the finest fruits of the tree."[18] In fact, the only negative assessment offered by Touraille concerns Peter's "comical enumerations of virtues and vices at the end of the first book."[19]

Thus it appears that of the few scholars who have ventured to comment on the teachings of Peter, most evaluate his thought negatively. Touraille's more complementary assessment is more the result of his personal subjectivity than an objective summary of Peter's spiritual theology. This is confirmed in Touraille's comment that "every one of us will be able to use to his profit and delight [Peter's texts], provided that he receive it into his life with piety."[20] The task, then, of the following exposition will be twofold: (1) to elucidate the spiritual theology of Peter of Damascus; and (2) to evaluate, critique and correct, when necessary, previously negative assessments of the Petrine corpus.

Of the two philokalic books, the *Admonition* is often characterized as less structured than the *Spiritual Alphabet*: "[The *Spiritual Alphabet*], with its *Twenty-Four Discourses* corresponding to the twenty-four letters of the Greek alphabet, possesses a more coherent structure than [the *Admonition*];"[21] "on the whole, [the *Spiritual Alphabet*] develops itself much more regularly;"[22] and "[t]he second book [i.e., the *Spiritual Alphabet*] ... is more structured."[23] Yet, Peter himself

---

16   Ibid., 8: "homme devant Dieu seul, qui a butiné toute sa vie et nous donne ici son miel, parfois mêlé de cire, mais toujours parfumé d'éternité bienheureuse."

17   Ibid., 8: "Ni source, ni courant, mais plutôt lac où les lectures ... le témoignage de la Liturgie byzantine et l'expérience de la vie monastique viennent étaler leurs eaux."

18   Ibid., 11: "Il a pourtant pu transformer la sève des racines en l'un des plus beaux fruits de l'arbre."

19   Ibid., 11: "inénarrables énumérations de vertus et de vices à la fin du premier livre."

20   Ibid., 11: "chacun de nous pourra faire son profit et ses délices, pourvu qu'il le reçoive dans sa vie avec piété."

21   Palmer, Sherrard and Ware, "Introductory Notes," 3: 72.

22   Gouillard, "Un auteur spirituel byzantin," 267: "[D]ans l'ensemble, il se développe beaucoup plus régulièrment."

23   Touraille, *Philocalie des Pères Neptiques*, fasc. 2: *Pierre Damascène*, 9: "Le second livre ... est plus structuré."

alludes to the fact that he has organized the *Admonition*.[24] In a discussion of those things that we will by ourselves, and are willed by the demons, he says that "[t]hese include battles, passions [τῶν παθῶν],[25] the whole range of sins from folly to despair and final destruction, *of which our treatise will speak as it goes on*" (76; 6.36–37; my italics). Furthermore, he writes that he "*will speak below* about how the [virtues][26] should be practised" (79; 9.23–24; my italics). In these two instances, it seems that Peter is hinting that he had thought out some of the direction that the book was going to take. What one must see is that while the *Spiritual Alphabet* may be more coherent and more developed, the arrangement of the *Admonition* was not thoughtless. More importantly, as will be argued below, the *Admonition* is organized in such a way as to highlight Peter's discussions of the passions and the virtues, as these are vital to his spiritual theology. His statements that he will speak of these matters later reveals that the book is more organized than previously judged.

A consideration of Peter's purpose for writing the *Admonition* also sheds light on Peter's organization of the treatise. Immediately, Peter states that he

---

24 Literary theorists recognize both a form (or shape/structure/style) and content (or substance). However, "[f]orm and substance are inseparable, but they may be analysed and assessed separately." J.A. Cuddon, *A Dictionary of Literary Terms and Literary Theory*, 4th ed., rev. C.E. Preston (Oxford, 1998), 327. More to the point, "[d]istinctions between form and content are necessarily abstractions made for the sake of analysis, since in any actual work there can be no content that has not in some way been formed, and no purely empty form." Chris Baldick, *The Concise Oxford Dictionary of Literary Terms* (Oxford; New York, 1990), 45.

25 The word πάθος and its derivatives have a long history in Christian spiritual writings. According to the editors of the English translation of the *Philokalia* "the word, signifies literally that which happens to a person or thing, an experience undergone passively; hence an appetite or impulse such as anger, desire or jealousy, that violently dominates the soul." G.E.H. Palmer, Philip Sherrard and Kallistos Ware, "Glossary," in *Phil.*, 3: 361. In Peter's spiritual theology, a passion results when "the soul dallies for a long time with an impassioned thought [ἐμπαθῆ λογισμὸν]" (207; 109.11–12). On the meanings of the term in Greek philosophy, see F.E. Peters, *Greek Philosophical Terms: A Historical Lexicon* (New York; London, 1967), 152–155. On the meanings of πάθος in early Christian literature, see Kallistos T. Ware, "The meaning of 'Pathos' in Abba Isaias and Theodoret of Cyrus," in *Studia Patristica*, ed. Elizabeth A. Livingstone (Leuven, 1989), 10: 315–322.

26 In the printed Greek edition this reads ἐντολῶν ("commandments"). However, both Paris, Bibliothèque Nationale, Ancien gr. 1134 and 1135 support ἀρετῶν. This is an important correction for the overall argument concerning Peter's organization of the *Admonition*.

wrote "this treatise as a rebuke to my unhappy soul, putting in it *whatever I have come across* from the lives and writings of the holy fathers" (74; 5.10–12; my italics). Later he says, "I am afraid that in my unawareness of my own limitations I will stray from the straight path, as St Isaac puts it. It is for this reason *that I have compiled* this present collection" (102; 28.8–10; my italics). Finally, "The questions and solutions that I propose here with regard to our common problems *are put forward* to help our understanding" (193; 98.36–37; my italics). In these three statements we can construct the process that Peter used to produce and disseminate the *Admonition*: (1) Peter read the lives and writings of the fathers and, likely, wrote down those sayings that he found beneficial to his own soul; (2) he then compiled these sayings in some form (perhaps by author or topically); and (3) he then put this collection forward to help others in understanding the spiritual life. In this process, specifically in the second step, we see Peter putting his materials into some form of organization. Artioli and Lovato suggest that Peter did not write down his quotations from their original sources but instead relied on his memory. They write, "As then for the patristic quotations, they are often extremely vague and demonstrate that the author, as he himself affirms, had to rely only on his memory because he had to return the books that he borrowed after he had read them."[27] However, the support that they provide seems tenuous at best. Simply because Peter "neither own[s] nor ever … owned any books" (74; 5.14) does not mean that he did not have the ability to go through borrowed books and take notes from these texts. Perhaps Peter did not possess whole copies of books but it seems that he did possess his own notes on these books. He says this much himself when he writes that "often a thought has spontaneously occurred to me, and it was by writing it down that I committed it to memory … Had I been negligent about writing it down, I would not have found it when I had need of it, and I would have been deprived of its help by the greatest of evils, forgetfulness" (182–183; 90.35–91.3). The importance of this lies in the fact that Peter, in some way, conducted research for his books. Instead of viewing Peter as an author who simply repeated quotations from previous spiritual theologians, some of which he stored improperly in his memory, it is imperative to see Peter as one who approached the writing of his books with a plan.

---

27 "Quanto poi alle citazioni patristiche, sono molte volte estremamente vaghe e mostrano bene che l'autore, come egli stesso afferma, doveva affidarsi all sola memoria perché restituiva i vari libri che gli prestavano subito dopo averli letti." *La Filocalia*, 3: 10.

Peter's statement concerning his methodology also leads to a similar conclusion regarding the presence of organization. He writes, "*I went through all these [books]* slowly and diligently, trying to discover the root of man's destruction and salvation, and which of his actions or practices does or does not bring him to salvation" (74; 5.25–27; my italics). From this quotation, it becomes obvious that Peter made an effort to organize the *Admonition*. He went through the books that he used, looking for particular teachings. Since Peter was looking for particular teachings, it seems reasonable to conclude that he had a sense of what he intended to write about. This implies, at least, that he likely had a sense of how he would organize the work.

It also seems, to some extent, that Peter was guided in the organization of the *Admonition* by the topics that he discovered in his sources. Peter augmented his thesis and its structure with quotations from other Christian authorities, employing them in a very specific manner. Peter's chapter "The Guarding of the Intellect"[28] contains many quotations from other Christian authorities. It is a series of quotations from John of Damascus, Hilarion, John Chrysostom, John Climacus and Philemon the Ascetic. As a result, it appears that this chapter is only in the *Admonition* because Peter had a desire to use some quotations that he recorded while going through the writings of the fathers. Yet, this chapter serves as a good example of how Peter assembled his book in light of his organizational plan. I suggest that there are two ways in which Peter composed the *Admonition*: Peter developed his spiritual theology and then searched his sources looking for quotations to support his views; and Peter read through his sources, then assembled them around particular topics, finally adding his own comments on the same topic. As one reads through the *Admonition*, it begins to become obvious that the structure of many of the chapters is similar. That is, there are comments that are original with Peter and then there are supporting quotations or allusions. In other words, there are teachings that are attributed

---

28   The chapter titles used in this thesis are those given in the text of the English translation that "are sometimes abbreviated or modified" from what is published in the Greek edition. See Palmer, Sherrard and Ware, "Introductory Notes," 72, n. 1. It is likely that the chapter divisions in the Greek *Philokalia* follow those given in the manuscript(s) used by Macarius and Nicodemus. In Paris, Bibliothèque Nationale, Ancien gr. 1134 each new chapter begins with a red capital, so it is probable that the manuscript(s) used as the basis for the Greek edition also divided chapters in this way. Macarius and Nicodemus, however, supplied the chapter titles themselves. although some chapter titles differ from the actual content of the chapter, the division itself most likely goes back to the original Greek manuscripts.

to another author and then there are those that are unattributed which I believe are Peter's particular contribution to the topic. Further, Peter draws broadly upon his sources with no one author preeminent. For example, as discussed in chapter One above, one sees the influence of John Climacus on Peter's thought throughout the *Admonition*. However, Climacus' overall spiritual theology is not simply adopted and repeated by Peter. Rather, Peter is unique despite his use of Climacus' thought. Like any well-read person, the thoughts and views of others stamped themselves on Peter's mind; therefore, Peter's own convictions will bear some resemblance to the convictions of those authors whom he read. A concrete example confirms this assertion.

As I stated above, "The Guarding of the Intellect"[29] contains many quotations from other Christian authors, yet Peter still says something unique. In the following quotation from that chapter, what is particular to Peter is italicized so that Peter's distinctiveness is seen visually.

As St John of Damaskos says, without attentiveness and watchfulness of the intellect we cannot be saved and rescued from the devil, who walks about "like a roaring lion, seeking whom he may devour" (1 Pet. 5:8). For this reason the Lord often said to His disciples, "Watch and pray; for you do not know at what hour your Lord is coming" (Matt. 26:41; 24:42). *Through them He was giving a warning to us all about the remembrance of death, so that we should be prepared to offer a defence, grounded in works and attentiveness, that will be acceptable to God.* For the demons, as St Hilarion has said, are immaterial and sleepless, concerned only to fight against us and to destroy our souls through word, act and thought. *We lack a similar persistence, and concern ourselves now with our comfort and with ephemeral opinion, now with worldly matters, now with a thousand and one other things. We are not in the least interested in examining our life, so that our intellect may develop the habit of so doing and may give attention to itself unremittingly.*

As Solomon says, "We walk among many snares" (Ecclus. 9:13); and St John Chrysostom has written about them, explaining what they are with great precision and wisdom. The Lord Himself, wishing to purge us of all worldly care, exhorts us not to bother about what we eat or wear, but to

---

29   The full title of this chapter in the Greek edition reads, "That it is impossible to be saved other than by rigorous attentiveness and the guarding of the intellect" [Ὅτι ἀδύνατον ἄλλως σωθῆναι εἰμή διά προσοχῆς ἀκριβοῦς καὶ τηρήσεως νοὸς] (30.1–3).

have only a single concern: how to be saved "as a roe from the snare and as a bird from the net" (Prov. 6:5. LXX), *in this way gaining the quick-sightedness of the roe and the soaring flight of the bird. It is truly remarkable that these things are said by King Solomon; and his father, too, said the same. Both of them lived in virtue and wisdom with great attentiveness and many ascetic struggles. Yet, after being granted so many gifts of grace and even the manifestation of God, they were overcome, alas, by sin: the first lamented both murder and adultery, while the second committed many terrible acts* (cf. 2 Sam. chs. 11–12; 1 Kings ch. 11). As St John Klimakos and Philimon the Ascetic put it, does this not fill anyone of understanding with fear and terror? *In our weakness, how can we not shudder and try to escape from the distractions of this life, we who are nothing and who are as insensate as brutes? Wretched as I am, would that I had been true to my nature, as animals are; for the dog is better than I.* (105–106; 30.1–35)

It looks as if Peter begins this chapter with the quotation from John of Damascus because he desires to connect this chapter textually to the previous chapter. Peter makes this textual connection through the use of "attentive [προσέχων]" (104; 29.28) at the end of the previous chapter, connecting it with John of Damascus' use of "attentiveness [προσοχῆς]" (105; 30.4) in the opening quotation cited above. More significantly, Peter's use of "attentive" in the former chapter occurs in a section that is particular to Peter. Thus it is his own understanding of attentiveness that causes him to quote John of Damascus and not the other way around. Peter is concerned that what leads the believer away from attentiveness is a loss of focus on death. By not contemplating death, writes Peter, the Christian will begin to fill his life with things that bring sensual pleasure so that he is caught up in too many things to reorder his focus.[30] Other obvious examples of this methodology and pattern are found in the chapters "Short discourse on the acquisition of the virtues and on abstinence from the passions" (162–164; 74.19–76.7); "On building up the soul through the virtues" (181–184; 90.1–92.8); and "The bodily virtues as tools for the acquisition of the virtues of the soul" (103–104; 28.25–29.31). In short, Peter organized the *Admonition*, and his comments, methodology, and use of sources demonstrate this fully.

---

30 The need to keep a remembrance of death before oneself is also found in John Climacus, *The Ladder of Divine Ascent*, Step 6; trans. Colm Luibheid and Norman Russell (New York, 1982), 132–135.

Almost immediately at the beginning of the *Admonition* Peter names his sources. His justification for this comes later in the *Admonition*: "I have given the names of books and saints at the beginning, so as not to overburden my work by specifying to whom each saying belongs" (103; 28.13–15). His sources are

> the Old and the New Testaments, that is, the Pentateuch [τὴν Παλαιάν], the Psalter, the Four Books of Kings, the Six Books of Wisdom, the Prophets, the Chronicles, the Acts of the Apostles, the Holy Gospels and the commentaries on all these; and then all the writings of the great fathers [Πατερικὰ][31] and teachers [Διδασκαλικὰ][32] – Dionysios, Athanasios, Basil, Gregory the Theologian, John Chrysostom, Gregory of Nyssa, Antony, Arsenios, Makarios, Neilos, Ephrem, Isaac, Mark, John of Damaskos, John Klimakos, Maximos, Dorotheos, Philimon, as well as the lives and sayings of all the saints. (74; 5.17–25)

To this list can be added John of Carpathos, Epiphanius, the Byzantine liturgy, the Clementine writings, John Cassian, Palladius, Paul Evergetinus, Cyril of Alexandria, Eustratius, Hilarion, Irene, Cronius, a bishop of Euchaïta (Symeon?) and, as discussed previously, Symeon Metaphrastes.[33] Gouillard says that "Severus of Gabala [is] cited implicitly" in the *Spiritual Alphabet*, that Peter borrows "from apocryphal writings like the 'Travels of John' by Prochorus" and

31   Usually used as an adjective as "a designation of hagiographical texts often of apophthegmatic type without special differentiation." Peter could be using the term generically to refer to the sayings of the fathers as a whole or to a specific work such as the *Evergetinon* of Paul Evergetinus. See *ODB*, s.v. "Paterika," by A.P. Kazhdan, 1595.

32   Διδάσκαλος is "a general term for laymen or clerics who were teachers of sacred or profane subjects; also, a technical term for those attached to the Patriarchal school at Hagia Sophia and engaged in instruction in the faith or exegesis of Holy Scripture." Peter, therefore, may be using the word in the most generic sense of teachings (as so translated in the English edition) or in reference to texts published by those who were διδασνκαλοι. See *ODB*, s.v. "Didaskalos," by R.J. Macrides, 619.

33   As noted previously, notably absent from this list is Symeon the New Theologian. Nowhere in the Petrine corpus is Symeon cited explicitly. Gouillard appears to suggest that this is because Symeon was not well known at this time. See Gouillard, "Un auteur spirituel byzantin," 278.

that the "influence of Philotheus the Sinaite should probably be accepted for the last chapter of [the *Admonition*]."[34] Moreover, the additional text in appendix 3 below draws inspiration from *Joseph and Aseneth*.[35] Finally, some of the references to Nilus are actually from Evagrius, even if Peter was unaware of this detail. Having suggested above that Peter may have made notes from his source material, this does not ignore the issue that in some places, as shown elsewhere, Peter misattributes his quotations. Concerning this Gouillard writes,

> One may well think that the treatment of citations in the Damascene does not sin by scrupulosity of exactness. Even his manner of citing often makes searching the texts difficult: it happens that the borrowings are absolutely insignificant, glossed and arranged without order, in part because the author has resorted to his memory. The materials are used sometimes second hand: for example, the words of Mark the Hermit ... were taken from a work of John Damascene. The attributions lack precision: these thoughts are alternatively attributed to one author or another (for example, τὸ οἴεσθαι οὐκ ἐᾷ γενέσθαι τὸ οἰόμενον at one time to Maximos ... and another time to Nilus) ... or simultaneously to two or three. They are sometimes false: ... Isaac is cited instead of Climacus ... In short, one stumbles everywhere over a very great freedom in the presentation of sources.[36]

34 Ibid., 268: "Sévère de Gabala cité tacitement ... des apocryphes comme les Voyages de Jean par Prochore. ... L'influence de Philotée le Sinaïte doit probablement être admise pour le dernier chapitre de A."

35 See Christoph Burchard, "Joseph and Aseneth" in *The Old Testament Pseudepigrapha*, ed. James H. Charlesworth (New York, 1985), 3: 176–247; and Marc Philonenko, *Joseph et Aséneth: Introduction, texte critique, traduction et notes* (Leiden, 1968).

36 Gouillard, "Un auteur spirituel byzantin," 269–270: "On pense bien que le traitement des citations dans Damascène ne pèche pas par scrupule d'exactitude. Sa manière même de citer rend souvent difficile la recherche des textes: il arrive que les emprunts sont absolument insignifiants, glosés et arrangés sans façon, en partie parce que l'auteur s'abandonne à sa mémoire. Les matériaux sont employés parfois de seconde main: v.g., les mots de Marc l'ermite ... ont été pris dans un opuscule de Jean Damascène. Les attributions manquent d'exactitude: telles pensées sont attribuées alternativement à un auteur ou à un autre (par exemple, τὸ οἴεσθαι οὐκ ἐᾷ γενέσθαι τὸ οἰόμενον tantôt à Maxime ... tantôt à Nil) ... ou simultanément à deux ou trois. Elles sont parfois fausses: ... Isaac est cité au lien de Climaque. ... Bref on se heurte partout à une très grande liberté dans la présentation des sources."

Gouillard ascribes some of Peter's incorrect attributions to the fact that he relied on his memory, but unlike Artioli and Lovato, Gouillard is less emphatic. For Gouillard, Peter's use of his memory only explains "in part" why he incorrectly cites his sources. I suggest that perhaps Peter's misattributions are the result of Peter's use of *florilegia*, which were incorrect in attribution. I also suggest that Peter likely would have used either the *Evergetinon* of Paul Evergetinus, or the *Interpretations of the Commands of the Lord* (or *Pandektes*) of Nikon of the Black Mountain.[37] An example taken from the *Evergetinon* shows that misattributions may be common in *florilegium*. A preliminary index of the sayings of Barsanuphius collected in the *Evergetinon* shows that Paul Evergetinus misattributes many of the sayings of John of Gaza and Dorotheus of Gaza to Barsanuphius.[38] That Peter does not use Barsanuphius is unimportant to the fact that *florilegia* may contain mistakes which could account for Peter's incorrect attributions. Ultimately, the final verdict on this matter must await a full study of the manuscripts containing Peter's works.

Destruction Versus Salvation: The Admonition's Critical Dialectic

The key to understanding Peter's spiritual theology and the organization of the *Admonition* is to be found in his introduction. After beginning the introduction with a brief statement concerning his own weakness and unworthiness, Peter then names his sources. Next he provides the key statement: "I went through all these [sources] slowly and diligently, trying to discover the root of man's destruction [ἀπωλείας] and salvation [σωτηρίας], and which of his actions or practices does or does not bring him to salvation" (74; 5.25–27). Here Peter sets up a dialectic around which the *Admonition* is organized: destruction versus salvation. Peter also uses this dialectic when discussing the types of monastic life, for he says that "[i]n each of these situations, some find salvation and oth-

---

37 For the Greek text of the *Evergetinon*, see Macarius of Corinth and Nicodemus of the Holy Mountain, eds., Εὐεργετινός ἤτοι Συναγωγή τῶν θεοφθόγγων ῥημάτων καὶ διδασκαλιῶν τῶν θεοφόρων καὶ ἁγίων πατέρων (Venice, 1783). There is still no critical Greek edition of the *Pandektes*. For a list of manuscripts containing the *Pandektes*, see Marcel Richard, "Florilèges spirituals grecs," in *Dictionnaire de spiritualité ascétique et mystique: Doctrine et histoire*, ed. Marcel Viller, F. Cavallera and A. Solinac (Paris, 1964), 5: col. 504.

38 Savas Zambillas compiled this preliminary index for the Theotokos Evergetinus Project of the Queen's University of Belfast. Robert Jordan, one of the Project directors, made a copy of this index available to me.

ers perish" (75; 6.2). Similarly, the dialectic serves as bookends to Peter's introduction to the *Admonition*. He concludes the introduction by writing, "All Scripture is inspired by God and profitable (cf. 2 Tim. 3:16), and no one can thwart someone who wishes to be saved. Only God who made us has power over us, and He is ready to help and protect from every temptation those who cry out to Him and want to do His holy will" (89; 17.5–10). Since it is the giving in to temptation that leads to destruction, Peter has again combined the concepts of salvation and destruction, further emphasizing their importance to his thought and organization. In a similar way, Peter says that "man stands at the crossroads between righteousness and sin, and chooses whichever path he wishes. But after that the path which he has chosen to follow ... will lead him to the end of it, even if he has no wish to go there" (79–80; 9.40–10.4). Though Peter does not quote it explicitly, it seems (from the standpoint of vocabulary and tone) that Peter received inspiration for this organization from Philippians 1:27–30 and 3:19:

Only let your manner of life be worthy of the gospel of Christ, so that whether I come and see you or am absent, I may hear of you that you stand firm in one spirit, with one mind striving side by side for the faith of the gospel, and not frightened in anything by your opponents. This is a clear omen to them of their destruction, but of your salvation, and that from God. For it has been granted to you that for the sake of Christ you should not only believe in him but also suffer for his sake, engaged in the same conflict which you saw and now hear to be mine ... Their end is destruction, their god is the belly, and they glory in their shame, with minds set on earthly things.[39]

---

39 "Revised Standard Version," in *The Layman's Parallel New Testament* (Grand Rapids, 1970), 699 and 706–707. Greek text in *The Greek New Testament*, 4th rev. ed., edited by Barbara Aland, Kurt Aland and Barclay Moon Newman (Stuttgart, 1994), 674: "Μόνον ἀξίως τοῦ εὐαγγελίου τοῦ Χριστοῦ πολιτεύεσθε, ἵνα εἴτε ἐλθὼν καὶ ἰδὼν ὑμᾶς εἴτε ἀπὼν ἀκούωτὰ περὶ ὑμῶν, ὅτι στήκετε ἐν ἑνὶ πνεύματι, μιᾷ ψυχῇ συναθλοῦντες τῇ πίστει τοῦ εὐαγγελίου καὶ μὴ πτυρόμενοι ἐν μηδενὶ ὑπὸ τῶν ἀντικειμένων, ἥτις ἐστὶν αὐτοῖς ἔνδειξις ἀπωλείας, ὑμῶν δὲ σωτηρίας, καὶ τοῦτο ἀπὸ θεοῦ· ὅτι ὑμῖν ἐχαρίσθη τὸ ὑπὲρ Χριστοῦ, οὐ μόνον τὸ εἰς αὐτὸν πιστεύειν ἀλλὰ καὶ τὸ ὑπὲρ αὐτοῦ ἐμοὶ καὶ νῦν ἀκούετε ἐν ἐμοί."

That a biblical passage may be the inspiration for Peter's overarching organizational scheme in the *Admonition* should not come as a surprise since Peter's spiritual theology relies heavily on Scripture, as do most Byzantine spiritual theologies. In fact, he quotes from or alludes to the letter to the Philippians seven other times throughout his literary corpus. In addition to Peter's continuity with Christian tradition, his spiritual theology, just like the spiritual theology of his predecessors, is firmly rooted in the Christian Scriptures. The rest of this chapter will detail Peter's spiritual theology using the same organizational grid that Peter uses in his introduction. Each section will introduce a teaching taken from the introduction to the *Admonition*. I will then flesh this teaching out using the whole of the *Admonition*.

Before continuing, it is important to note that Peter believes in the pervasiveness of both sin and the grace of God in the formulation of his spiritual theology. Such a strong emphasis on grace is unusual in Byzantine writers of the period c. 850–1204, though common in the Latin church. For example, Bernard of Clairvaux (1090–1153) wrote a treatise *On Grace and Free Will*, and Anselm of Canterbury (ca. 1033–1109) wrote a treatise entitled *On the Harmony of the Foreknowledge, Predestination, and Grace of God with Free Will*. As well, there are the encyclopedic works of Peter Abelard, Peter Lombard and Hugh of St Victor, all of which discuss the doctrine of grace.[40] Given the heightened interest in the topic of grace among Western theologians and spiritual writers, and Peter's own striking emphasis on grace in the *Admonition*, the question naturally arises whether or not Peter had some exposure to those currents of thought.[41]

---

40 See Jaroslav Pelikan, *The Growth of Medieval Theology (600–1300)* (Chicago, 1978), 114–116, 204–214.

41 Augustine of Hippo, the western church's theologian of grace, was known in the east around the same time that Peter was active. The *acta* of the Council of Constantinople in 1166 inserted Τοῦ ἁγίου Αὐγουστίνου into the *florilegia* between Gregory of Nyssa and John of Damascus. This paraphrase of Augustine's *In Evangelium Johannis tractatus* 78.3 states that of the twofold substance of Christ, the divine makes him equal with the Father, whereas the Father is greater than Christ's human substance. See PG 140: 217A; and George E. Demacopoulos and Aristotle Papanikolaou, "Augustine and the Orthodox: 'The West' in the East," in their *Orthodox Readings of Augustine* (Crestwood, NY, 2008), 12–13. It is uncertain, however, if Peter had any knowledge of Augustine's literary corpus, including his theology of grace.

From the beginning of the age of the Crusades, Latin theologians found themselves in the Byzantine capital and its environs in increasing numbers, some on official diplomatic missions, and others as private travelers. Some examples of this trend include Peter Chrysolanus (also known as Peter Grossolano, archbishop of Milan), an early and very important Western thinker who visited Constantinople in 1112 and was involved in public debates about the procession of the Holy Spirit and the primacy of Peter. Grossolano, apparently Greek by birth, disputed with the heretical Byzantine monk named John Phournes before Emperor Alexius I Comnenos and Patriarch of Constantinople Eustratios of Nicea.[42] In 1135, Anselm of Havelberg was chosen by the western emperor Lothair III to head an embassy of Latin clerics and theologians to Constantinople to discuss how the eastern emperor could assist Lothair in taking military action against Roger II of Sicily. Barmann writes, "When in Constantinople Anselm was invited by the emperor and the patriarch [of Constantinople] to take part in a public debate on the questions which currently caused disagreement between the eastern and western Churches."[43] Thus in April 1136 Anselm and Nicetas, archbishop of Nicomedia, had a lengthy discussion on the *filioque*, the azymes question and papal primacy that drew a lot of public attention in the Byzantine capital.[44] In 1150, Pope Eugenius asked

<hr>

42 Kenneth M. Setton, "The Byzantine Background to the Italian Renaissance," *Proceedings of the American Philosophical Society* 100, no. 1 (1956), 21. Extant documents from this exchange can be found in A.K. Demetrakopoulos, Ἐκκλησιαστικὴ Βιβλιοθήκη (Leipzig, 1866), I:36–127; PG 127: 911–920; and *Bibliotheca Casinensis seu codicum manuscriptorum* (Montecassino, 1880), 4:351–358.

43 Lawrence F. Barmann, "Reform Ideology in the *Dialogi* of Anselm of Havelberg," *Church History* 30 (1961): 379–395, at 380. See also Jay T. Lees, *Anselm of Havelberg: Deeds into Words in the Twelfth Century* (Leiden; New York, 1998), 40–47.

44 Anselm of Havelberg, *Dialogi*, Prologue: "Et ipse quidem nonnullis auctoritatibus sanctarum Scripturarum ad suum sensum violenter retortis, universa in quibus Graeci a Latinis discordant tanquam recta visus est affirmare; ea vero, in quibus Latini a Graecis discrepant, tanquam non recta visus est infirmare: illud nimirum quod suum erat, quia suum erat, non quia verum erat, per omnem modum probando; hoc autem quod nostrum, quia nostrum et non suum erat, omnino improbando. Inter quae maxime, sicut dixistis, *de processione Spiritus sancti* disputavit, quem Graeci quidem a Patre tantum, Latini vero a Patre et Filio procedere credunt et dicunt; et [de] ritu sacrificii in altari, quod Latini quidem in azymo, Graeci vero in fermentato celebrant, nec non de quibusdam aliis satis argumentose in quaestionem positis" (italics mine). Latin text in PL 188:1139–1140.

Anselm for a written account of this debate, the result of which was Anselm's *Dialogi* (or, in Greek, the *Antikeimenon*), perhaps the best extant summary of theological discussion between Latin and Greek theologians. Four years later, Anselm was once again in the East where he discussed the procession of the Holy Spirit with Basil of Ohrid. In turn, Basil of Ohrid appears to have held a disputations with Henry, archbishop of Beneveto, who was in Constantinople in 1161 and 1165–66. In September 1153, Anselm was sent by Emperor Frederick Barbarossa to Constantinople to ask Emperor Manuel I Comnenos for the hand of his daughter, Maria, in marriage. On his return trip from Constantinople in October 1154, Anselm discussed the procession of the Holy Spirit with Basil of Ohrid while passing through Thessaloniki.[45] Between these visits to the Byzantine capital, in 1150, Pope Eugenius III asked Anselm for a written account of his debate with Nicetas of Nicomedia, resulting in Anselm's *Dialogi* (or, in Greek, the *Antikeimenon*), perhaps the best extant summary of theological discussion between Latin and Greek theologians.[46] Basil of Ohrid appears to have also held a disputation with Henry, archbishop of Benevento, who was in Constantinople in 1161 and 1165–1166.[47] Though many more examples could be provided, it is clear that despite the emphasis placed on grace in the West during the twelfth century and the increased opportunities for Latin and Greek theologians to learn from each other it is not fully known where Peter may have learned his theology of grace. There is at least one possible source, however.

It is likely that Peter learned his theology of grace from the writings of Mark the Monk/Hermit, whom he references as one of his sources (74; 5.23).[48]

---

45   Barmann, "Reform Ideology in the *Dialogi* of Anselm of Havelberg," 380–381. See also Francis Dvornik, *The Photian Schism* (Cambridge, 1948), 379; and Norman Russell, "Anselm of Havelberg and the Union of the Churches," *Sobornost* 1.2 (1979): 19–41 and 2.1 (1980): 29–41. See Beck, *Kirche und theologische Literatur im Byzantinischen Reich*, 312–317, 611–626 for further discussion of the East-West theological exchange.

46   Anselm of Havelberg, *Anticimenon: On the Unity of the Faith and the Controversies with the Greeks*, trans. Ambrose Christe and Carol Neel (Collegeville, MN, 2010). For an English translation of the *Dialogi*, see Anselm of Havelberg, *Anticimenon: On the Unity of the Faith and the Controversies with the Greeks*, trans. Ambrose Criste and Carol Neel (Trappist, KY, 2010).

47   Joseph Hergenröther, *Photius, Patriarch von Constantinopel: Sein Leben, seine Schriften und das griechische Schisma* (Regensburg, 1869), 3: 807–808.

48   See Mark the Monk, *Counsels on the Spiritual Life*, trans. Tim Vivian and Augustine Casiday (Crestwood, NY, 2009), 34–44.

Further, Mark's theology of sin and grace has been compared to Augustine of Hippo's,[49] thereby perhaps helping to explain the Latin-like nature of Peter's theology. Mark insists that through sin humankind inherits from Adam the state of being alienated from God, a kind of spiritual death that results in physical decay and physical death. Because of this state, we live in sin and experience guilt. The answer to this dilemma in Mark's theology is grace, which comes by way of baptism. Mark has an extremely high view of baptismal efficacy, so much so that once the believer is baptized, he has the same freedom that prelapsarian Adam had in choosing freely whether to sin or not to sin. Neither God nor Satan can force someone's free will towards goodness or sin once they have been baptized. It is now up to the baptized, grace-filled believer to choose to either follow the commandments or not. Post-baptismal sin is not something inherited from Adam but rather the result of neglecting the commandments:

> If sin is destroyed by baptism, someone will say, why does it continue to work in the heart? We have stated the cause many times: it is not because sin has been left to do its work after baptism but because sin is cherished by us because we have neglected the commandments. Holy Baptism provides the perfect release; to bind oneself again because of one's evil inclinations or to be freed from them because one keeps the commandments is a matter of choice and free will.[50]

It would appear then that Peter's theology of sin and grace, though sharing many similarities with western theologians, was acquired through his reading of Eastern Christian texts. Just as Mark the Hermit/Monk, as a spiritual theologian, focused attention on sin and grace so too does Peter. In both cases it kept the authors from postulating a spirituality that was overtly works-based, helping them present a spiritual theology that was not only ascetical and monastic-like but one rooted in the very graciousness of God.

---

49 Kallistos Ware, "The Sacrament of Baptism and the Ascetic Life in the Teaching of Mark the Monk," in *Studia Patristica*, vol. 10: *Papers presented to the Fifth International Conference on Patristic Studies held in Oxford 1967*, pt 1: *Editiones, Critica, Philologica, Biblica, Historica, Liturgica et Ascetica*, ed. F.L. Cross (Berlin, 1970): 441–452, at 444, 449.

50 Mark the Monk, *On Baptism*, reply to question 3; in *Counsels on the Spiritual Life*, 295. Greek text in *Marc le Moine: Traités*, ed. Georges-Matthieu de Durand (Paris, 1999), 1: 296–396.

Exposition of the Admonition

I. SIN

Following Peter's key statement about the dialectic between salvation and destruction, he next turns to the reality of sin. Beginning with the recollection of the fall of Satan, "that erstwhile angel in heaven" (75.6.3), Peter develops a theology of sin throughout the *Admonition*. According to Peter, "since Adam's transgression we are all subject to the passions" (77; 8.1–2) and "[s]ome of us do not even perceive our desperate plight" (77; 8.9). Yet, our path to sin follows an explicit order. One is first faced with "provocations [προσβολή], in other words, conceptions of either good or evil, which in themselves are neither commendable nor reprehensible. What follows on these is known as 'coupling' [συνδυασμός]; that is to say, we begin to entertain a particular thought and parley with it, so to speak; and this leads us either to give assent [συγκατάθεσιν] to it or to reject it" (207; 109.3–6). Further, "We do not sin against our will, but we first assent [συγκατατιθέμεθα] to an evil thought and so fall into captivity. Then the thought itself carries the captive forcibly and against his wishes into sin" (83–84; 13.8–10). Peter later defines this "assent" as "a pleasurable inclination of the soul towards what it sees; and it leads to the state of seduction, or captivity, in which the heart is induced forcibly and unwillingly to put the thought into effect" (207; 109.9–11). At first, a person assents to something small and insignificant that then grows into a greater sin. Peter insists that when the enemy "wants to plunge a person into some great sin, the enemy prepares the ground by making him negligent in trivial, unnoticed things. For example, before adultery, there are frequent licentious glances; before murder, moments of anger; before the clouding of the mind, small distractions" (153; 67.32–36).[51] For Peter, at its root, the propensity to sin is inherent in humanity and the act of sinning is the daily reality for all human persons. In fact, Peter writes that we "deliberately and willfully choose to do evil" (80; 10.19–20). Our sinfulness is so extensive that Peter can only describe humanity as "nothing but a slight, short-lived stench, baser than any other created being" (96; 22.39–23.2). In Peter's estimation, humanity is so sinful that the only option is to cry out to God, saying, "Woe is me, a sinner!" (110; 34.7).

---

51   See also 187; 94.18–19.

2. GRACE

Peter tempers the harsh reality of sin with the pervasive presence of God's grace. As Artioli and Lovato observed, Peter "has a very acute sense of the prevenience of grace."[52] From the start of the *Admonition*, Peter insists that it is by grace that any good is accomplished. According to Peter, it is only by "God's grace" that he has been able to write anything concerning the spiritual life (74; 5.6) and that it is "through God's grace" that he came upon the answers to his questions (76; 7.12). Furthermore, according to Peter, salvation is by the grace of God (149; 64.8–9) and prayer is only possible because of the presence of grace (80; 10.9, 32). Like the apostle Paul, Peter sees grace as a gift of God (84; 13.21), though God may deprive a person of this gift (120; 42.37). Perhaps it is the concluding paragraph to Peter's introduction to the *Admonition* that most vividly illustrates the role of grace in Peter's spiritual theology. He writes,

> But the evil that we commit ourselves is our own responsibility and arises from our own laziness with the help of the demons. On the other hand, all knowledge, strength and virtue are the grace of God, as are all other things. And through grace He has given all men the power to become sons of God (cf. John 1:12) by keeping the divine commandments. Or, rather, these commandments keep us, and are the grace of God, since without His grace we cannot keep them. (89; 17.12–18)

Throughout the *Admonition*, Peter returns repeatedly to the significance of grace in the spiritual life. In fact, Peter has such a "high" theology of grace that twice he personifies grace as a mother: "God's grace, our universal mother [ἡ χάρις τοῦ Θεοῦ καὶ κοινὴ πάντων Μήτηρ]" (94; 21.31–32); and "the grace of God, the common mother of us all [ἡ χάρις τοῦ Θεοῦ καὶ κοινὴ πάντων μήτηρ]" (197; 101.38). Continuing with the motherhood analogy, we conclude that for Peter, grace is the gift of God that gives birth to salvation, and by extension, the spiritual life.

Of the more than one hundred references to grace in the *Admonition*, most pertain to God's "enabling" grace. Of these, Peter frequently makes the connection between God's grace and the acquisition of knowledge. Since Peter's overall spiritual theology relies heavily on the appropriation of knowledge, it is imperative to grasp fully his teachings on the grace of God and its role in the attainment of knowledge. He writes,

---

52 "[U]n senso molto acuto della prevenienza della grazia." *La Filocalia*, 3: 10.

... through God's grace, I came upon the answers I sought for. (76; 7.11–12)

For God is the God of salvation, bestowing on us ... the knowledge ... that we cannot have without the grace of God. (80; 10.7–9)

[I]n His grace He has created our prayer, our knowledge. (80; 10.30–31)

[H]e has been found worthy of knowing and enduring these things by the grace of God. (85; 14.28–29)

[S]piritual knowledge is not acquired simply through study but is given by God through grace to the humble. (92; 19.15–16)

[T]he grace of the Holy Spirit reigns in their soul and leads it where it will, bestowing the divine knowledge. (98; 24.13–14)

[W]hen you possess ... an intellect that apprehends, through the grace and the wisdom of the Holy Spirit. (100; 26–17–18)

[H]im who through grace has learned from God. (101; 27.1–2)

[T]o possess all knowledge, or, rather, to receive it from God by grace. (101; 27.19–20)

[G]race begins to open the eyes of our soul and we come with astonishment to understand thoughts and words. (109; 33.26–28)

[T]hrough Thy grace I have begun to perceive. (116; 39.19–20)

[T]he knowledge [of God] is not mine ... for it is Thy grace. (129; 49.33–34)

Having grasped, through grace, a knowledge of the higher powers. (141; 58.2)

[I]f grace has raised him to the sphere of divine knowledge. (155; 68.37)

[T]he grace of God who has given to all men spiritual knowledge. (177; 87.5)

According to Peter, knowledge is a gift of God's grace, bestowed upon humankind. Spiritual or divine knowledge (πνευματικὴ γνῶσις/θείαν γνῶσιν)[53] comes not through simple reading and study but through an endowment of God's grace. Once a person receives this gift of divine knowledge through the grace of God, they are then able to study and struggle to understand the Holy Scriptures (192; 97.18–20). In summary, all knowledge of uncreated things, including God, is ultimately a gift of God's grace.

Peter also emphasizes that theosis is the result of God's grace. The *Admonition* contains six references to theosis, and Peter connects five of these with grace:

> If we succeed in doing this, there is no object, no activity or place in the whole of creation that can prevent us from becoming what God from the beginning has wished us to be: that is to say, according to His image and likeness, gods by adoption through grace [καὶ θέσει Θεὸς κατὰ χάριν]. (76; 7.21–24)

> Through the wisdom and indwelling of the Holy Spirit and through adoption to sonship, we are crucified with Christ and buried with Him, and we rise with Him and ascend with Him spiritually by imitating His way of life in this world. To speak simply, we become gods by adoption through grace [καὶ ἁπλῶς θέσει Θεὸς κατὰ χάριν γίνεται], receiving the pledge of eternal blessedness. (79; 9.16–20)

---

53 The phrase πνευματικὴ γνῶσις is sometimes understood in early Christian literature as referring to that knowledge granted by God whereby one is able to penetrate to a deeper understanding of the biblical text, traditionally understood as the allegorical sense of Scripture. However, according to Columba Stewart, "Evagrius uses the term for Christian knowledge generally." Throughout his corpus, Peter appears to have a more Evagrian understanding of spiritual knowledge since he does not say that it leads to deeper insight into the Bible. Rather, Peter understands πνευματικὴ γνῶσις as that gift of God that makes *any* understanding of the Scriptures possible. See Columba Stewart, *Cassian the Monk* (New York; Oxford, 1998), 91, 194, n. 39.

In the end [the seven commandments] make man a god [ἄχρις ἂν Θεὸν ποιήσωσι τὸν ἄνθρωπον], through the grace of Him who has given the commandments to those who choose to keep them. (93; 20.8–10)

All the Beatitudes make man a god by grace [Πάντες γὰρ οἱ μακαρισμοὶ Θεὸν κατὰ χάριν ποιοῦσι τὸν ἄνθρωπον]. (98; 24.17–18)

In that realm one's thoughts are at peace and one becomes a son of God by grace [υἱὸς Θεοῦ κατὰ χάριν γίνεται], initiated into the mysteries hidden in the Holy Scriptures. (142; 58.31–33)

Similarly, the ability to proceed through the eight stages of contemplation is possible only by the grace of God (109; 33.14).[54]

Finally, acquisition of the virtues is only through God's grace: "To acquire all of [the virtues] is possible only through the grace of Him who grants us victory over the passions" (204; 107.6–8). For example, he writes, "If by the grace of God you have received the gift of discrimination" (158; 71.33) and, more explicitly, "for even if the ability and the desire to do good are one's own, the grace to do it comes from God" (162–163; 75.11–12). Significantly, all good things, says Peter, including the virtues are the result of the graciousness of God (176; 86.4–6). To state the same truth negatively, a person can "be delivered from the passions through the grace of Christ" (208; 109.23). In Peter's spiritual theology, grace is omnipresent and is responsible for all good. Without grace, he says, humankind is destined for eternal separation from God. It is only by the grace of God that anyone, whether monk or not, has "the strength to do anything" (147; 63.9). In short, Peter's spiritual theology is centered on, and fully dependent on, the grace of God.[55]

---

54 See below (pp. 109–116) a discussion of the stages of contemplation.
55 Peter's emphasis on grace here is reminiscent of Maximus the Confessor. Maximus, in a treatise on the Lord's Prayer, gives a concise summary of his spiritual theology: "The Logos bestows adoption on us when He grants us that birth and deification which, transcending nature, comes by grace from above through the Spirit. The guarding and preservation of this in God depends on the resolves on those thus born: on their sincere acceptance of the grace bestowed on them and, through the practice of the commandments, on their cultivation of the beauty given to them by grace." *On the Lord's Prayer*, lines 96–102, in Andrew Louth, "Introduction," in his *Maximus the Confessor* (Crestwood, NY, 1996), 3–70, at 33–34. Notice that both salvation and deification come to the believer by grace. See also Josef Loosen, *Logos und Penuma im begnadeten Menschen bei Maximus Confessor* (Münster, 1940).

3. NATURAL KNOWLEDGE (φυσικὴ γνῶσις [7.14])

Peter says little about natural knowledge in either the *Admonition* or the *Spiritual Alphabet*, but it seems that in Peter's thought the term "natural knowledge" refers to both knowledge in keeping with nature (φύσις) and knowledge of nature. In Byzantine thought, φύσις

> is everything in the world that belongs to the realm of matter insofar as it is provided for man, and not something created by man (through his *techne*, or culture, customs, and laws). Therefore, it also includes everything that actually exists, the totality of objects and the state of affairs to which any judgment must exactly conform. The term not only designates everything that exists, that grows or takes place in the 'natural world' apart from human intervention, but it can also be used to designate the process of production itself.[56]

In light of this, it looks as though Peter understands natural knowledge as that which is the opposite of spiritual or divine knowledge (γνῶσις), since he conceives of spiritual or divine knowledge as knowledge in keeping with God and knowledge of God. He does say, however, that humankind is given two gifts by God, natural knowledge and free will. Peter writes, "First, we must recognize that the starting-point of all our spiritual development is the natural knowledge given us by God ... Then, alongside this knowledge, there is our capacity to choose" (76; 7.13–14, 18–19). It is the natural knowledge given by God that gives birth to a person's "ordinary initial faith [ἡ πρώτη καὶ κοινὴ πίστις]" (166; 78.10–12). For Peter, natural knowledge may come "through the Scriptures by human agency, or by means of ... divine baptism" (76; 7.14–15). It will be instructive to now consider these two sources of natural knowledge, and how they function in Peter's spiritual theology.

3a. The Divine Scriptures

In the *Admonition*, Peter has much to say concerning the Scriptures. He first devotes a chapter to the consistency of Holy Scripture. Peter writes that only an unenlightened (ἀφώτιστον) person thinks that there are contradictions in the

---

56   *ODB*, s.v. "Nature," by Karl-Heinz Uthemann, 1440–1441.

Scriptures.[57] On the contrary, "Whenever a person even slightly illumined [φωτισθεὶς μικρόν] reads the Scriptures or sings psalms he finds in them matter for contemplation and theology, one text supporting another" (144; 60.8–10). For Peter, the appearance of contradiction is due to human ignorance and therefore, we can only read them to the "limit of our capacity" (144; 60.16). A person must approach the Scriptures with humility so that improper meanings are not forced from them; rather, one allows the Holy Spirit to direct him/her to a proper understanding: "What kind of knowledge can result from adapting the meaning of the Scriptures to suit one's own likes and from daring to alter the words? The true sage is he who regards the text as authoritative and discovers, through the wisdom of the Spirit, the hidden mysteries to which the divine Scriptures bear witness" (145; 60.34–61.4).[58] Peter then holds up Basil the Great, Gregory Nazianzen and John Chrysostom as the outstanding examples of proper scriptural interpreters, "for what they understand and expound comes from the Holy Spirit" (145; 61.9–10).

Peter returns to his teaching on the Holy Scriptures in a chapter entitled, "That the Frequent Repetition Found in Divine Scripture is Not Verbosity," which could more accurately be entitled "On the Interpretation of Scripture." In Peter's spiritual theology, the Scriptures are not always easily understood, for "in the Holy Scriptures some things are obvious and easy to grasp, while others are unclear and difficult to grasp." The reason for this is that:

> Through the first category God draws the slower amongst us towards faith and towards the investigation of more difficult things; and in this way He ensures that we do not fall into despair and lose our faith because of our utter failure to understand what is said. Through the second category He preserves us from incurring even greater condemnation by disdaining the passages that we can understand. He desires that those who want to do so should labour willingly to search out and put into effect what is unclear –

---

57 It is possible that Peter's reference to an unenlightened person is a reference to someone who is not baptized. The point of Peter's statement is that only a non-Christian, that is, a pagan, would suggest that there are contradictions in the Scriptures. As early as Justin Martyr baptism was called illumination: "And this washing [in baptism] is called illumination (φωτισμός)." *The First Apology* 61.12, in Justin Martyr, *The First and Second Apologies*, trans. Leslie William Barnard (New York, 1997), 67. "Illumination" became a technical term for baptism in the second century.

58 See also 123; 44.30–31, 45.9–10; 132; 51.33–34 and 194; 99.20.

and for this they shall receive praise, as St John Chrysostom says. (187–188; 94.32–39)[59]

Since the Scriptures can be difficult to comprehend, God offers assistance by often repeating the same words. In this way, those who labour slowly expose themselves repeatedly to the same truths while those who are quicker or busier do not forget particular sayings (188; 95.3–8). There are many "mysteries hidden in the divine Scriptures" and what may appear as a contradiction at first is due to one's failure "to understand the meaning disclosed by a spiritual interpretation [ἐκ τῆς θεωρίας] of divine Scripture" (189; 95.18 and 26–27). In Peter's estimation, all scriptural passages and even every word of God "refers in a hidden way to the purpose of created things" (190; 96.11–13), but only those who keep God's commandments can understand these passages and words (190; 96.27–29).

For Peter, though, keeping the commandments is only one part of being able to understand God's Word. In addition to obeying the commandments, "we ought to search the Scriptures assiduously, in humility and with the counsel of experienced men, learning not merely theoretically but by putting into practice what we read ... For the Lord commands that we should search the Scriptures above all by means of bodily and moral actions" (191; 97.6–8, 14–15). As well, the study of the Scriptures should not cease once one has advanced in the spiritual life but rather, one is to continually study them "with deep dedication, humility, attention and fear of God" (192; 97.20–21). He who is truly spiritual will best understand the meaning of the Scriptures (154; 68.16–19).

3b. Baptism
In the teaching of Peter, natural knowledge comes through the Scriptures and baptism, or, more appropriately, through "the angel that is given in divine baptism to guard the soul of every believer, to act as his conscience and to remind him of the divine commandments of Christ" (76; 7.14–17).[60] A person is to

---

59   This quotation is actually from the last paragraph of Peter's preceding chapter entitled "The Great Value of Love and of Advice Given with Humility."

60   On angels in eastern Christian thought, see Martin Jugie, *Theologia dogmatica christianorum orientalium ab Ecclesia catholica dissidentium*, vol. 2: *Theologiae dogmaticae Graeco-Russorum expositio de theologia simplici, de oeconomia* (Paris, 1933), 549–567; and Lothar Heiser, *Die Engel im Glauben der Orthodoxie* (Trier, 1976). Michael Psellos, a near contemporary of Peter (having died in the late eleventh century), wrote two treatises on angels, though both concern demons: Περὶ ἐνεργείας δαιμόνων and Περὶ δαιμόνων δοξάζουσιν ἕλληνες. Greek text in PG 122: 819–882C. This may suggest that there was a renewed interest in angelology during Peter's lifetime.

keep those commandments of Christ, revealed in the Holy Scriptures, and baptism, for Peter, makes such fidelity to Christ's mandates possible. He writes,

> It is now that the devil, having failed in all his other schemes, tempts us with thoughts of despair: he tries to persuade us that in the past things were different and that the men through whom God performed wonders for the strengthening of the faith were not like us. He also tells us that there is now no need for such exertion. For are we not all of us Christians and all baptized? "He who believes and is baptized shall be saved" (Mark 16:16). What more do we need? But if we succumb to this temptation and remain as we are, we will be completely barren. We will be Christians only in name, not realizing that he who has believed and been baptized must keep all Christ's commandments; and even when he has succeeded in doing this, he should say, "I am a useless servant" (Luke 17:10), as the Lord told His disciples when He instructed them to carry out all He had laid down for them. (82; 11.29–12.1)

Peter understands baptism as the point at which one's Christian life (and by extension one's spiritual life) begins, for by baptism "you were called a Christian" (114; 38.6).[61] As well, in his thought, the baptismal state involves an aspect of sinlessness, or at least the ability to keep the commandments of Christ fully: "Yet if from the start we had wanted to keep the commandments and to remain as we were when baptized, we would not have fallen into so many sins or have needed the trials and tribulations of repentance" (84; 13.18–20). Nonetheless, since people do fall into sin, God provides a way to renew the baptismal state – repentance (178; 87.7–8). As discussed below, it appears that the first three stages of contemplation involve a restoration of this baptismal state, since they deal explicitly with repentance.

4. FREE WILL

Peter immediately connects free will to an individual's salvation. He writes that free will "is the beginning of our salvation; by our free will we abandon our own wishes and thoughts and do what God wishes and thinks" (76; 7.19–21). Furthermore, Peter views free will as inherently good, though it can also lead one to destruction and many "have perished" as a result of freely choosing their

---

61 See also 208; 110.8.

"own thoughts and wishes" (76–77; 7.21–32). Likewise, he says that free will has been given to us so that God will not condemn us "as incapable of doing anything" (208; 109.23–27). In a brilliant analogy, Peter anthropomorphizes humankind's free will as an eye that can choose to either receive or reject the knowledge that "comes like light from the sun" (79; 9.25–26). According to Peter, "God made both the sun and ... eyes, but how man uses them depends on himself" (78; 8.35–36). Only a "foolish man through lack of faith or laziness deliberately closes his eye – that is, his faculty of choice – and at once consigns the knowledge to oblivion because in his indolence [ῥαθυμίας] he fails to put it into practice" (79; 9.26–28). In fact, no other person or thing is to blame for one's destruction except one's own free will, since no one is forced into evil but instead chooses freely (80; 10.6–7, 15–16). This truth is repeated twice more in the *Admonition*:

> But the evil that we commit ourselves is our own responsibility and arises from our own laziness [ῥαθυμίας] with the help of the demons. (89; 17.12–13)

> For I am the cause of my own destruction. I have been honoured with free will and no one can force me. (112; 35.32–36.1)

For Peter, then, free will is a gift from God that places humankind on the road to salvation. Yet, each person then freely chooses to either use this gift for salvation or for destruction.

Peter has much to say about a person using free will to do evil things; however, he does not dwell on this reality. Peter chooses instead to use an array of vivid metaphors to communicate the action that should be taken against our "own will." Like all good things, he says that we overcome the sinful inclination of our will through the grace of God (84; 13.38–39). Thus it is by the grace of God that we are then able to "relinquish [ἀρνησώμεθα] our own will and thought" in order to keep Christ's commandments (82; 12.6–8). To follow Christ, one must "keep the commandments, thereby cutting off [ἐκκοπῇ] all pleasure or personal will" (84; 14.1–2) since this is characteristic of a spiritual person who "restrains [κατέχει] his own will" (85; 14.11–12). Moreover, spiritual persons are to renounce their own thoughts and will (87; 15.39–16.1). God assists the believer in this process of destroying the will. He gives to each person universal and particular gifts. These gifts are given so that each person "may voluntarily abstain from pleasure and may readily embrace hardship through the eradication [ἐκκοπῆς] of his own will" (172; 82.35–83.1). One such example is stillness: "by withdrawing into complete stillness all of these men cut off [ἔκοπτον] their own wills" (196; 100.33). This relinquishing, renouncing, eradicating and cutting off the will all result in spiritual progress. In fact, Peter says that nothing contributes to our spiritual progress like "the excising [ἐκκοπὴ] of our own will" (162; 74.24–25); and, ultimately, "if for God's sake we amputate [κόπτη] our own will, God will enable us to reach, with inexpressible joy, a perfection that we have never known" (149; 64.31–32). More importantly, if a person abandons his/her will then they will receive salvation (83; 12.32.33).[62] According to Peter, then, God gives humankind the free will with which they are capable of choosing either goodness or evil. By choosing the good one advances in spiritual progress, but choosing to commit evil results in trials and sufferings.

5. VOLUNTARY AND INVOLUNTARY TRIALS/SUFFERINGS

Since God endowed humankind with both natural knowledge and free will, and in spite of God's graciousness, humankind is subject to trials and temptation, some of which are "conducive to repentance" (75; 6.20). Some of these trials are involuntary, bestowed upon us by God with the purpose of helping us, "[f]or it is to help us that He increases our tribulation, both through the sufferings we willingly embrace in our repentance and through the trials and punishments not subject to our will" (77; 8.18–21).[63] Other trials are voluntary, bestowed upon us by ourselves or by the demons or our enemies with the purpose of hurting us. Peter writes, "Other things are willed not by God but by ourselves or by the demons" (76; 6.35); and "the trials imposed by spiritual fathers in order to discipline and instruct their spiritual children are one thing; but the trials brought on by our enemies for our destruction are another" (140; 57.13–15). More pointedly, "Sufferings produce devotion to God and a recognition of His gifts and our faults" (78; 9.6–7).

Nonetheless, though trials and temptations can have such a good outcome, the extent of the sufferings of humankind overwhelmed Peter. He writes, "When from my laborious study of the Scriptures I became aware of all these things, and many more, my soul was shattered and often I felt quite helpless, like spilt water" (76; 7.6–8). According to Peter, examples of involuntary sufferings include hunger, grief, labours, fear of death, "and in addition to these, the

---

62 See also 194; 99.7–8.
63 See also 140; 57.18–19.

various agelong punishments, the useless lamenting and the ceaseless tears; the unrelieved darkness, the fear, the pain, the exile, the dismay, the oppression, the throttling of the soul in this world and in the next" (75; 6.28–31). Examples of voluntary sufferings include "battles, passions, the whole range of sins from folly to despair and final destruction [and] the attack of demons, wars, the tyranny of the passions; the derelictions, dislocations and vicissitudes of life; the anger, slander and all the affliction" (76; 6.35–7.3). Regardless of their source, these sufferings are for our good. Peter believes that "we need trials, and toils of repentance … so that we may regain our former health of soul and shake off the sickness which our folly has induced" (77; 8.13–16).

Peter diffuses his teaching on the presence of trials and sufferings in the spiritual life throughout the *Admonition*, but he joins most of the references to two specific teachings: salvation and humility. According to Peter, "God did not create us for wrath but for salvation (cf. 1 Thess. 5:9), so that we might enjoy His blessings; and we should therefore be thankful and grateful towards our Benefactor" (84; 13.24–27). This salvation, or healing, by God comes through trials and sufferings:

> For it is to help us that He increases our tribulation [ὀδυνηρά], both through the sufferings we willingly embrace in our repentance and through the trials and punishments [πειρασμῶν καὶ κολάσεων] not subject to our own will. In this way, if we voluntarily accept affliction, we will be freed from our sickness and from the punishments to come, and perhaps even from present punishments as well. Even if we are not grateful, our Physician in His grace will still heal us, although by means of chastisement and manifold trials. (77–78; 8.18–24)

Continuing with the medical theme, Peter also says that "[e]very trial and temptation is permitted by God as a cure for some sick person's soul" (95; 22.21–22). Yet, merely suffering trials and temptations does not automatically lead to salvation. These trials must be accepted in a spirit of thankfulness or they are ineffectual (136; 54.32–34). Salvation is not simply a result of one's existence but also of one's attitude and response to God's gracious initiative. To put it briefly, "Those who love God are saved through the trials and temptations" (179; 87.36–37); and "we must endure either temporary trials and temptations, or else agelong punishment" (179; 88.5).

Peter writes that "[n]o passion is so hateful as pride" (161; 73.35). Therefore, it must be true that no virtue is so lovely as humility, a virtue resulting

ultimately from trials and suffering, for "[h]umility is born of spiritual knowledge, and such knowledge is born of trials and temptations" (85; 14.30–31). In
turn, when humility is combined with patience, knowledge results: "If a person's purpose is fixed in God with all humility and he patiently endures the
trials that come upon him, God will resolve for him any question that perplexes
him and perhaps even leads him into delusion" (139; 56.30–33). A sign of our
humility, according to Peter, is that we are "to be extremely troubled and
afflicted" if we are "not suffering any such trial [πάθη]" (147; 63.1–2). Not only
are trials a sign of our humility but they may also be a means of acquiring
humility. Peter writes, "Sometimes God allows a person [who is suffering tribu-
lation] to be defeated by his enemies so that he may acquire humility" (146–
147; 62.18–19).

6. PATIENT ENDURANCE (ὑπομονή)

In Peter's spiritual theology, a person patiently endures voluntary and involuntary trials. The significance of this concept for Peter's spirituality is obvious
since there are nineteen references to the patient endurance of trials or temptations in the *Admonition*:

> [W]e ... learn how to endure our sufferings patiently. (78; 9.5–6)

> From knowledge, or understanding, is born self-control and patient
> endurance. (85; 14.10–11)[64]

> [H]e first suffers many temptations of soul and body, and gains experience
> by enduring them patiently. (86; 15.14–15)

> [W]e should patiently endure all that God allows to happen to us. (92;
> 19.29–30)

> For through patient endurance we may be granted forgiveness for many
> sins. (95; 22.13–14)

---

64   The connection of trials to patient endurance is not obvious in this quotation. However, Peter says in another place that "[h]umility is born of spiritual knowledge,
and such knowledge is born of trials and temptations" (85; 14.30–31). Therefore, the
knowledge that leads to self-control and patient endurance must also be the result
of trials and temptations.

Once we have purified the soul through patient endurance. (138; 56.15–16)

If a person's purpose is fixed in God with all humility and he patiently endures the trials that come upon him, God will resolve for him any question. (139; 56.36–38)

Every tribulation that we accept patiently is good and profitable ... he suffers affliction. Consequently, he patiently awaits for God to release him, and when this happens he rejoices and gratefully endures whatever comes. (140; 57.18–23)

[I]f you defeat your assailants you should endure with all patience. (156; 69.27–30)

[W]e must endure every trial imposed by our enemies and by our many and various thoughts. (164; 76.12–14)

So long as you do not surrender yourself willingly to the enemy, your patient endurance, combined with self-reproach, will suffice for your salvation ... either through trials and temptations ... He will accept your patient endurance. (170; 81.4–11)

Better than them all, however, is the patient endurance of afflictions. (172; 82.30–31)

For it is better to take refuge in God by patiently enduring whatever befalls us than to turn away from Him in fear of facing the trials and temptations He may send ... Nor is there ... any swifter path to the forgiveness of sins than the patient endurance of evil [ἀνεξικακία]. (179; 88.1–2, 20–21)

According to Basil the Great, the chief thing that every man needs is endurance. (181; 90.2–3)

We should begin by patiently enduring what befalls us. (195; 100.5)

Consequently, in Peter's view, the proper response to trials and temptations is to withstand them. Since trials are part of the spiritual life, one should not seek to avoid such suffering. Rather, one must patiently endure them through the grace of God. It is trials and temptations that continually remind spiritual persons that they are still in need of God's assistance and that they have not yet reached the end of the spiritual ascent. Peter also holds that patient endurance is a necessary component in attaining salvation. Peter bases this on Matthew 10:22, which reads, "He who endures to the end will be saved" (156; 69.28). Further, Peter illustrates the importance of patient endurance is his spiritual theology by placing it near the top of his list of virtues (203; 106.5).

7. DISCRIMINATION (διάκρισις, "discernment")[65]

In his introduction to the *Admonition*, Peter lays out his understanding of the spiritual life. After stating his unworthiness to write such a work and after naming his sources, Peter establishes the salvation and destruction dialectic that forms the core of his spiritual program. He continues by saying that each person suffers voluntary and involuntary trials and temptations that are the result of natural knowledge, given by God through the Scriptures and baptism, and free will. He next abruptly states, "This, then, is the general picture [Καὶ ταῦτα μετὰ οὕτως]" (77; 7.32). Peter is making a deliberate move to a new topic, indicating that he has reached the conclusion to the previous discussion. Peter brings the reader to the fulcrum of his salvation/destruction dialectic: discrimination. Having been gifted by God with both natural knowledge and free will, and patiently enduring voluntary and involuntary sufferings, the Christian is now faced with a decision – either to choose good, leading to salvation, or to choose evil, leading to destruction. To make this decision, God has bestowed discrimination upon each person:

> But situations and pursuits vary, and one needs to acquire discrimination, either through the humility given by God or through questioning those who possess the gifts of discrimination. For without discrimination nothing that comes to pass is good, even if we in our ignorance think that it is. But when through discrimination we learn how it lies in our power to

---

65 I agree with Theodore Stylianopoulos that "discernment" is a more accurate English equivalent of διάκρισις. However, when quoting from the English translation of the *Philokalia* I retain the translation "discrimination" for the sake of consistency. See Theodore G. Stylianopoulos, "*The Philokalia*: A Review Article," *The Greek Orthodox Theological Review* 26 (1981): 252–263, at 263. See also G.W.H. Lampe, ed., *A Patristic Greek Lexicon* (Oxford, 1961), 354.

attain what we wish, then what we do begins to conform to God's will. (77; 7.32–38)

For Peter, discrimination comes through either humility or from questioning those who have the gift of humility. This likely accounts for Peter's emphasis on the need for a "spiritual director."

As said beforehand, Peter chose a form of monastic life where he was subject to a spiritual father.[66] Yet, Peter also says that all Christians, including those outside of the monastic life, should have someone who directs them spiritually. In fact, if necessary, if one cannot find a spiritual father, a person should have Christ as spiritual director. Peter writes, "If we do not have anyone to advise us, we should take Christ as our counsellor" (149; 64.24–25).[67] More significantly, one's spiritual director assumes the role of Christ in the spiritual life by "setting our spiritual father in the place of Christ and referring every idea, thought and action to him, so that we have nothing we can call our own" (150; 65.6–7). When choosing a director, Peter stresses that "not every man can be trusted when giving advice to those who seek it. We can trust only him who has received from God the grace of discrimination" (183; 91.11–13). In a passage that sets a high standard for both spiritual directors and their disciples, Peter warns about the possible dangers of a poorly matched spiritual father and his disciple. He writes,

> For he who wishes to admonish someone or to give him advice ... should first be purified of the passions, so that he may truly understand God's purpose and the state of the person who asks for his counsel. For the same medicine is not suited for all, even when the illness is the same. Then we

66   On spiritual direction in the Byzantine church, see chapter 5 below as well as Irénée Hausherr, *Direction spirituelle en Orient d'autrefois* (Rome, 1955), with English translation in Anthony P. Gythiel, *Spiritual Direction in the Early Christian East* (Kalamazoo, 1990). See also H.J.M. Turner, *St. Symeon the New Theologian and Spiritual Fatherhood* (Leiden, 1990).

67   This sentiment is also found in Symeon the New Theologian: "If by the grace of God you have found a spiritual father, tell him your thoughts, to him alone; if you have not, raise your eyes constantly to Christ and always view Him as one spectator of your despondency and affliction." Symeon the New Theologian, *Ethical Discourses* 7, cited in Basil Krivocheine, *In the Light of Christ: St. Symeon the New Theologian – Life, Spirituality, Doctrine* (Crestwood, NY, 1986), 93. Greek text in Symeon the New Theologian, *Traités théologiques et éthiques*, ed. Jean Darrouzès (Paris, 1966).

must ascertain from the person who is seeking advice whether he does this because he has once and for all committed himself to obedience in soul and body; or whether he has made his request spontaneously and with fervent faith, seeking counsel from us before questioning his own teacher; or whether there is something else that forces him to pretend that he longs for such counsel. For if this last is the case both teacher and disciple will succumb to falsehood and idle talk, deceitfulness and many other things. The disciple, forced by his supposed teacher to speak against his will, feels ashamed and tells lies, pretending that he wants to do good; and the teacher who acts deceitfully, flattering his disciple in order to discover what is hidden in his mind, and in general employing every kind of trick and speaking at length, in spite of the fact that Solomon has said, "Through talkativeness you will not escape sin" (Prov. 10:19) ... All this has been said, not so that we should refuse to advise those who come to us readily and with firm faith, especially if we have attained a state of dispassion; it is said so that we should not, out of self-esteem, presumptuously teach those who do not express the wish to hear us either through their actions or through their fervent faith. (185–186; 93.1–21)

In light of the responsibilities and dangers for both the spiritual director and the disciple, it may seem that Peter would shy away from making this a feature of his spiritual theology. For Peter, however, it is necessary for a Christian to be under the guidance of someone who has attained discrimination. For those who place themselves under spiritual direction, Peter says that God will bless them (103–104; 29.5–11).

In Peter's estimation, discrimination "gives us spiritual insight and makes it possible for the intellect in its purity to foresee coming faults and to forestall them through its experience and recollection of what happened in the past; in this way it can protect itself against stealthy attacks" (78; 9.9–12). Discrimination is absolutely necessary in the spiritual life because, though there are good thoughts, they too require discrimination from those with experience "for without discrimination even those thoughts that seem good are not in fact good" (82; 12.13);[68] and "[e]verything ... demands discrimination if it is to be used for the good; without discrimination we are ignorant of the true nature of things" (119; 42.5–7). Since Peter places such a high importance on the gift

---

68   See also 208; 109.28–29.

of discrimination, he devotes two chapters of the *Admonition* specifically to the topic.

The chapter entitled "Discrimination" contains eighty-nine lines of text in the Greek edition, but only eighteen of these lines deal specifically with discrimination. The remaining lines appear to form part of the following chapter on spiritual reading.[69] In these few lines Peter says several things about discrimination: (1) "We need discrimination in all things so that we may rightly assess every form of action"; (2) "[t]hen discrimination reveals the nature of things, their use, quantity and variety, as well as the divine purpose and meaning in each word or passage of Holy Scripture"; and (3) "[d]iscrimination clarifies all these things and also the significance of the interpretation given by the fathers [to Holy Scripture]" (152; 66.33–67.14). Peter's first statement in this chapter shows that discrimination is all-encompassing and all-pervasive in the spiritual life. The second statement corresponds to what he says elsewhere but adds that it is discrimination that brings forth meaning from the Scriptures. Since God gives natural knowledge through the Scriptures, we can conclude that a proper understanding of natural knowledge is ultimately the result of discrimination. This proves the centrality and the importance of discrimination in Peter's spiritual theology. Finally, he says that we must also place under the microscope of discrimination the interpretations given to the Scriptures in tradition. That a certain church father interprets a particular scriptural text in one way does not mean that his understanding is beyond scrutiny. The gift of discrimination confirms that the fathers of the church have understood the passage properly.

In his chapter "True Discrimination," Peter writes that it is "by the grace of God" that a person receives discrimination (158; 71.33), and that "[d]iscrimination is born of humility" (158; 72.3). Peter further clarifies the relationship between discrimination and humility when he says that God gives discrimination and then the believer does everything possible to guard it (158; 33–34). This is essential since humility is the "mother of discrimination" (159; 72.12.13). In this chapter he says that "[d]iscrimination is characterized by an unerring recognition of what is good and what is not, and the knowledge of the will of

---

69 This anomaly may be the result of the improper division of chapters in the manuscript(s) from which Macarius of Corinth and Nicodemus of the Holy Mountain worked. Perhaps the scribe failed to begin what should have been a new chapter with a red capital. It is also possible that Macarius and Nicodemus failed to begin a new chapter despite the presence of a red capital indicating a division in the text.

God in all that one does" (158–159; 72.7–9).[70] In a striking analogy illustrating the centrality and the all-encompassing nature of discrimination in the spiritual life, Peter writes: "Discrimination is not only called light; it truly is light. We need this light before we say or do anything ... Let it be said again: discrimination is light; and the spiritual insight it generates is more necessary than all other gifts" (159; 72.22–28). Just as light is essential to physical life, so discrimination is essential to spiritual life. Without discrimination humankind would be lost and would never be able to choose to do that which leads to salvation.

8. DESTRUCTION

At the heart of Peter's spiritual theology is the fact that some actions and practices lead to salvation and some lead to destruction. Those that lead to destruction manifest themselves as passions. One sees this most clearly in Peter's misnamed chapter "Spiritual Reading":[71]

> Everything not strictly necessary is a hindrance to salvation – everything, that is to say, that does not contribute to the soul's salvation or to the body's life. For it is not food, but gluttony, that is bad; not money, but attachment to it; not speech, but idle talk; not the world's delights, but dissipation; not love of one's family, but the neglect of God that such love may produce; not the clothes worn only for covering and protection from cold and heat, but those that are excessive and costly; not the houses that also protect us from heat and cold, as well as from anything human or animal that might harm us, but houses with two or three floors, large and expensive; not owning something, but owning it when it has no vital use for us; not the possession of books on the part of those who have embraced total poverty, but the possession of books for some purpose other than spiritual reading; not friendship, but the having of friends who are of no benefit to one's soul; not woman, but unchastity; not wealth, but avarice; not wine, but drunkenness; not anger used in accordance with nature for the chastisement of sin, but its use against one's fellow-men.

---

70   Peter appears to be indebted to John Climacus on this point. For Climacus, discrimination "is ... a solid understanding of the will of God in all times, in all places, in all things." John Climacus, *The Ladder of Divine Ascent*, Step 26; trans. Colm Luibheid and Norman Russell (New York, 1982), 229.

71   This peculiarity is the result of Macarius and Nicodemus' poor naming of a chapter.

Again, it is not authority that is bad, but the love of authority; not glory, but the love of glory and – what is worse – vainglory; not the acquisition of virtue, but to suppose that one has acquired it; not spiritual knowledge, but to think that one is wise and – worse than this – to be ignorant of one's own ignorance; not true knowledge but what is falsely called knowledge (cf. 1 Tim. 6:20); not the world, but the passions; not nature, but what is contrary to nature; not agreement, but agreement to do what is evil and does not contribute to the soul's salvation; not the body's members, but their misuse ... I marvel at God's wisdom, at how the most indispensable things – air, fire, water, earth – are readily available to all. And not simply this, but things conducive to the soul's salvation are more accessible than other things, while soul-destroying things are harder to come by.

None the less, it is not the thing itself, but its misuse [παράχρησις], that is evil. (156–157; 69.31–71.13)

Again, Peter's dialectic of salvation versus destruction comes to the foreground of his spiritual theology. Also, this extended quotation shows that Peter is a spiritual theologian of moderation and balance. Peter does not reject material objects or natural relationships outright, rather he writes that how one uses them or views them is the criteria by which one decides what actions he/she needs to modify or what possessions he/she needs to renounce. As Peter himself writes, "All these things, even if they are opposed to each other, are nevertheless good when used correctly; but when misused, they are not good, but are harmful for both soul and body" (172; 82.28–30).

The passions have their source in – and receive assistance from – the devil and the demons. Peter has a developed understanding of the devil and demons that plays an important part in his spiritual theology. He repeatedly reminds his readers that the devil is an angel of God who has fallen into sin. He writes,

... I was astonished also by the fall of that erstwhile angel in heaven, immaterial by nature, clothed with wisdom and every virtue, who suddenly became a devil, darkness and ignorance, the beginning and end of all evil and malice. (75; 6.2–5)

For the Lord has established this as the basic commandment, knowing that without this even living in heaven would be profitless, for one would still possess the same madness through which the devil, Adam and many others have fallen. (93; 20.24–27)

I see how Satan, the angel who once rose as the morning star (cf. Isa. 14:12), has now become the devil, as we call him. (110; 34.26–27)

For example, the fall of the devil was not God's will. (137; 55.27–28)

It was precisely this lack of humility on Lucifer's part that was enough without any other sin to turn him into darkness. (177; 86.15–16)

He who humbles himself is illumined all the more, while he who refuses to humble himself remains in darkness, as was the case with him who was the Morning-star and is now the devil. (187; 94.9–11)

Without a doubt, Peter understands that originally Satan was an angel who, through pride, rebelled against God and, as a result, fell from heaven. Having fallen from heaven, Satan spends his time tempting believers with God's permission, "[f]or the devil is permitted to tempt the elect" (137; 55.28–29). Yet, the devil cannot compel a believer to sin (80–81; 10.34–39). The devil can only tempt humankind; it is through free will that humankind commits sin. As a visible sign of this limited ability of the devil, each believer renounces Satan at his/her baptism. Peter says that "[e]veryone who is baptized renounces the devil, saying, 'I renounce Satan and all his works, and I join myself to Christ and all His works" (83; 12.2–4).[72]

Like Satan, the demons are immaterial (105; 30.10–11)[73] and they tempt believers "so that we may be humbled and have recourse to God, thus being saved from self-elation and delivered from negligence" (173; 83.30–32). Peter says that demons "hate God's works, and they commit evil deliberately" (171; 81.36–37). In two places, Peter connects the activity of the demons with the

---

72 See also 114; 38.4. This is the formula said by the baptizand in the Byzantine baptismal liturgy that has its source in the baptismal instructions of John Chrysostom. For a translation of the Byzantine baptismal liturgy, see Isabel Florence Hapgood, *Service Book of the Holy Orthodox-Catholic Apostolic Church*, 3rd ed. (New York, 1956), 271–285. For the Greek texts of the baptismal instructions of John Chrysostom, see *Jean Chrysostome: Huit catéchèses baptismales inédites*, ed. Antoine Wenger (Paris, 1957); PG 49: 225–240; and Athanasios Papadopoulos-Kerameus, ed., *Varia graeca sacra* (St Petersburg, 1909), 154–183. For an English translation, see John Chrysostom, *St. John Chrysostom: Baptismal Instructions*, trans. Paul W. Harkins (Westminster, MD; London, 1963).

73 See also 111; 35.14–15.

passions. He says that "[b]oth St Makarios and Abba Kronios say that there are ruling demons and demons that are subordinate. The ruling demons are self-esteem, presumption and so on; the subordinate demons are gluttony, unchastity and similar things" (180; 88.32–35). After listing the passions he insists that "all that the demons produce is disorderly" (206; 108.29). Peter says that the source of the passions is the demons and since the demons are Satan's ministers then all the passions have their source in Satan. Related to this are Peter's categories of thought: human, demonic and angelic.[74] He writes,

> Demonic thought consists in a conceptual image compounded with passion. One thinks, for example, of a human being, but this thought is accompanied by mindless affection, that is to say, by the desire for a relationship not blessed by God but involving unchastity; or else it is accompanied by unreasoning hatred, that is to say, by rancour or spite. Again, one thinks of gold avariciously or with the intention of stealing or seizing it; or else one is roused to hatred and blasphemy against God's works, thus causing one's own perdition. (134; 53.3–9)

In summary, the passions have their origin and existence through the activity of Satan and the demons. These passions lead the spiritual person to destruction; therefore, it is necessary for each Christian to know what the passions are so that they can avoid them.

Peter provides a list of passions at the end of the *Admonition* (205–206; 107.9–108.36). According to him, "These, then, are the passions which I have found named in the Holy Scriptures. I have set them down in a single list, as I did at the beginning of my discourse with the various books I have used. I have

---

74   As the editors of the English translation of the *Phil.*, 134. Evagrius writes, "After lengthy observation we have learned to recognize this difference between angelic and human thoughts, and those that come from the demons. Firstly, angelic thoughts are concerned with the investigation of the natures of things and search out their spiritual principles ... The demonic thought neither knows nor understands these things, but without shame it suggests only the acquisition of sensible gold and predicts the enjoyment and esteem that will come from this. The human thought neither seeks the acquisition of gold nor is concerned with investigating what gold symbolizes; rather, it merely introduces in the intellect the simple form of gold separate from any passion of greed." Evagrius of Pontus, "On Thoughts 8" in *Evagrius of Pontus: The Greek Ascetic Corpus*, trans. Robert E. Sinkewicz (Oxford, 2003), 158.

not tried, nor would I have been able, to arrange them all in order; this would have been beyond my powers" (206; 108.25–27). Peter does not systematically discuss the passions but chooses to scatter his teaching on them throughout his textual corpus. Unquestionably, pride is the worst passion in Peter's thought since "[n]o passion is so hateful as pride" (161; 73.35). In the introduction to the *Admonition*, Peter explains how the passions come about as well as providing a list of the "eight ruling passions":[75]

The foolish man through lack of faith or laziness deliberately closes his eyes – that is, his faculty of choice – and at once consigns the knowledge

75   The exact origin of the "eight ruling passions" is difficult to trace. Some scholars believe that early Christian theologians of the fourth century borrowed a list of seven or eight sins from heretical and pagan religions, which were then considered the principal sins of the Christian faith and purged of their unorthodox associations. In some pagan religions these sins were linked to the (then known) seven planets and the aerial demons that inhabit them or, in Hellenistic sects, a soul, after death, had to journey through the seven zones of heaven while aerial spirits (ἄρχοντες, κοσμοκράτορες, τελώνια) attempted to hinder its passage. See Morton W. Bloomfield, "The Origin of the Concept of the Seven Cardinal Sins," *Harvard Theological Review* 34 (1941): 121–128. Early texts that provide lists of principal sins include the pseudepigraphal *Testament of the Twelve Patriarchs* 2:1–3:6 (πορνεία, γαστριμαργία, μάχη, κενοδοξία, ὑπερηφανία, ψεῦδος and ἀδικία), ibid.; Horace, *Epistles* 1.33–40 (*avaritia, cupidine, laudis amore, invidus, iracundus, iners, vinosus* and *amator*), ibid.; and Poimandres, the Shepherd of Men, from *Corpus Hermeticum* 25; A.-J. Festugière and A.D. Nock, eds, *Corpus Hermeticum* (Paris, 1946), 1: 15-16: (τὴν αὐξητικὴν ἐνέργειαν καὶ τὴν μειωτικήν, τὴν μηχανὴν τῶν κακῶν, τὴν ἐπιθυμητικὴν ἀπάτην, τὴν ἀρχοντικὴν προφανίαν ἀπλεονέτητον, τὸ θράσος τὸ ἀνόσιον καὶ τῆς τόλμης τήν προπέτειαν, τὰς ἀφορμὰς τὰς κακὰς τοῦ πλούτου and τὸ ἐνεδρεῦον ψεῦδος). Peter, however, certainly learned about the eight passions from Evagrius of Pontus. In "On the Vices Opposed to the Virtues 1," Evagrius writes, "render it to me as well that we may make a brief submission on the vices opposed to the virtues, indicating what is gluttony against which abstinence is opposed, what is fornication and chastity, what is avarice and freedom from possessions, sorrow against which there is joy, what is anger and patience, acedia and perseverance, what is vainglory and freedom from it, jealousy and freedom from it, pride and humility." Likewise, in "Praktikos 6," he says that "All the generic types of thoughts fall into eight categories in which every sort of thought is included. First is that of gluttony, then fornication, third avarice, fourth sadness, fifth anger, sixth acedia, seventh vainglory, eighth pride." Finally, in "On the Eight Thoughts," Evagrius gives his list of the eight passions as gluttony, fornication, avarice, anger, sadness, acedia, vainglory and pride. For preceding quotes, see Evagrius of Pontus, *Evagrius of Pontus: The Greek Ascetic Corpus*, 62, 73–90 and 97 respectively.

to oblivion because in his indolence he fails to put it into practice. For folly leads to indolence, and this in turn begets inertia and hence forgetfulness. Forgetfulness breeds self-love – the love of one's own will and thoughts – which is equivalent to the love of pleasure and praise. From self-love comes avarice, the root of all evils (cf. 1 Tim. 6:10), for it entangles us in worldly concerns and in this way leads to complete unawareness of God's gifts and of our own faults. It is now that the eight ruling passions take up residence: gluttony, which leads to unchastity, which breeds avarice, which gives rise to anger when we fail to attain what we want – that is, fail to have our own way. This produces dejection, and dejection engenders first listlessness and then self-esteem; and self-esteem leads to pride. From these eight passions come every evil, passion and sin. (79; 9.26–38)

Peter later adds "craftiness and thoughtlessness; ... obduracy and licentiousness; ... overbearingness and cowardice; ... over-frugality and greed" (101; 26.31–34) to this list. Regardless of the number of passions, Peter teaches that they are the result of the fall of humankind into sin. He writes, "And then there was Adam, who enjoyed such honour and so many blessings, such familiarity with God, who was adorned with wisdom and virtue, alone in paradise with Eve: he suddenly became an exile, filled with passions, mortal, forced to labour with sweat and affliction" (75; 6.5–9). Further, "since Adam's transgression we are all subject to the passions" (77; 8.1–2). Thus in Peter's spiritual theology it is the passions that lead to destruction and the devil and the demons assist in this process. The way to avoid these passions is to practice the virtues that lead to salvation.

9. SALVATION

According to Peter, "God did not create us for wrath but for salvation (cf. 1 Thess. 5:9), so that we might enjoy His blessings" (84; 13.24–26). Since this is the purpose for the creation of humankind, it is logical for Peter to conclude that salvation is possible for all persons. He writes, that "if someone wants to be saved, no person and no time, place or occupation [ἐγχείρημα] can prevent him" (83; 13.3–5);[76] "no one can thwart someone who wishes to be saved" (89;

---

76 On the concept that one may have a particular occupation in life, see Symeon the New Theologian, *Hymn* 14: "This then is inexpressible, this then is supernatural, the work and the undertaking that I have been ordered to accomplish; it induces me always to keep before my eyes the picture of death." Symeon the New Theologian,

17.6–7); and "He is able and willing to save all men, myself included, as He wishes" (149; 64.12–14). In Peter's thought, salvation is available to all persons, and since salvation reveals itself in the attainment of virtues, then everyone can acquire salvation. Therefore, Peter intends his spiritual program to be for all people, not just monks, "[f]or we should all, as Christians, keep the commandments, since in order to acquire the virtues of the soul we need, not bodily effort, but simply probity of intention and the desire to receive what is given," (195; 100.7–10) and that "all should be detached and should devote themselves to God" (107; 32.12–13).

This openness to non-monastics is seen most clearly in the introduction to the *Admonition*, where Peter writes that "there is no object ... that can prevent us from becoming what God from the beginning has wished us to be ... whether we are rich or poor, married or unmarried, in authority and free or under obedience and in bondage – in short, whatever our time, place or activity" (76; 7.21–27).[77] Yet, Peter believes that the monastic life, or at least the solitary life, is preferable:

> Yet bodily asceticism [σωματικῶν πράξεων] does help in the acquisition of the virtues, especially in the case of those who lead a life of stillness and are completely undistracted [ἀπερισπάστου] and detached [ἀμεριμνίας]. For a man cannot see his own habits and correct them unless he is free from worry about worldly things. Hence we ought first to acquire dispassion by withdrawing from worldly affairs and human society. (195; 100.11–16)

Similarly, "if one does not first flee from distraction and acquire complete quietude, one will never be dispassionate with regard to anything, or be able to say what is right and good. In short, this total flight from distraction is of prime importance in all things" (147; 62.21–25). As well, "nothing so quickly

---

Hymns of Divine Love by St. Symeon the New Theologian, trans. George Maloney (Denville, NJ, 1976), 48. Unlike the Latin church in the west, the Byzantine church did not have a strong conception of *ordines*, that is, a division of society into different classes, ranks, or grades. On *ordines*, see Giles Constable, *Three Studies in Medieval Religious and Social Thought: The Interpretation of Mary and Martha, the Ideal of the Imitation of Christ, the Orders of Society* (Cambridge, 1995), 251–360.

77   See chapter 4 for further discussion of this point.

fosters the acquisition of virtue as the solitary life [μόνωσις] and meditation" (162; 74.27–28). Peter sees the world as a hindrance to one's acquisition of the virtues and, ultimately, one's salvation (87; 16.2–3). Therefore, one must flee the world, or at least renounce the expectations of the world. Peter's teaching on possessions clearly shows this perspective of renouncing the expectations of the world.

Peter views possessions as a cause of trials in the spiritual life (125; 46.11–24). Consequently, the goal is to use them properly since the "[l]ove of possessions consists not merely in owning many things, but also in attachment to them, or in their misuse or excessive use" (87; 15.32–34).[78] However, since many cannot use possessions properly, it is best to renounce them voluntarily. He writes that "[t]hose, however, who choose to shed all their possessions will be crowned with glory" (136; 54.34–35) since such an action is "in imitation of Christ and His holy disciples" (158; 71.18–19). In Peter's spirituality, "the total shedding of possessions is far superior to giving alms" since possessions "are a great weakness" (97; 24.5–6 and 23.38). In summary, while Peter's spiritual program is open to all persons, both monastics and non-monastics, the most effective approach is either to renounce the world (through the monastic life), or to live above the "fashion of the world" (through a non-monastic, spiritual life; 104; 29.12). More importantly than the form of life that one lives is the attainment of the virtues "possible only through the grace of Him who grants us victory over the passions" (204; 107.6–8).[79] Since, in Peter's teaching, a person acquires the virtues through doing them instead of simply talking about them (183; 91.3–4),[80] it is imperative to know what the virtues are.

9a. Salvation and the Virtues

Just as he provides a list of the passions, Peter also provides a list of the virtues that he learned "from the fathers" (203; 105.36–37). According to Peter there are "altogether 228 virtues" (204; 107.6) but this list is incomplete due to his "lack of knowledge" (203; 105.39). Elsewhere, in a chapter entitled "The Four Virtues of the Soul," Peter discusses and gives distinction to the first four virtues in his

---

78   See also 172; 82.15–30.
79   See also 163; 75.21–22.
80   See also 78; 8.38–39; and 184; 92.14–19.

list (moral judgment, self-restraint, courage and justice).⁸¹ In this chapter, Peter describes each of them:

> [F]irst, moral judgment [φρόνησις], or the knowledge of what should and should not be done, combined with watchfulness of the intellect; second, self-restraint [σωφροσύνη], whereby our moral purpose is safeguarded and kept free from all acts, thoughts and words that do not accord with God; third, courage [ἀνδρεία], or strength and endurance in sufferings, trials and temptations encountered on the spiritual path; and fourth, justice [δικαιοσύνη], which consists in maintaining a proper balance between the first three. (100; 26.21–26)

He continues by saying that these four virtues arise from the three powers of the soul: moral judgment and justice come from the intelligence (λογισμός) or intellect (νοῦς); self-restraint comes from the desiring power (ἐπιθυμητικός); and courage from the incensive power (θυμικός).⁸² These four virtues, says Peter, "constitute an image of the heavenly man" (101; 26.34–35). Nevertheless, though Peter devotes a short chapter to these four virtues, it becomes apparent throughout the *Admonition* that humility is the greatest virtue.

Peter says that the "humble person must possess every virtue and yet truly think himself the greatest of debtors and inferior to everything else in creation ... For even a true angel possessing so many virtues and so much wisdom cannot conform to the Creator's will unless he also possesses humility" (159; 72.13–19). Yet Peter dedicates only one short chapter to humility in which he pro-

---

81 These four virtues, of course, correspond to Plato's enumeration in the *Republic*, Book IV and are often translated as prudence, temperance, fortitude and justice. These virtues were adopted and discussed by the earliest Christian theologians. In time, the theological virtues of faith, hope and love were added to the four natural virtues to total seven virtues. For Plato, see *Republic* in *Plato: Complete Works Republic*, ed. John M. Cooper, trans. G.M.A. Grube with revisions by C.D.C. Reeve (Indianapolis; Cambridge, 1997), 1061–1064.

82 On these "appetitive aspects" of the soul in early Christian thought, see Lars Thunberg, *Microcosm and Mediator: The Theological Anthropology of Maximus the Confessor*, 2nd ed. (Chicago, 1995), 169–207. Though this tripartite division is important in the history of spiritual theology and prominent in other writers, this is the only mention of them in the *Admonition*. The tripartite division itself, like the four natural virtues, entered Christian thought primarily through Plato's *Republic*. See Plato, *Republic*, 1071–1072.

vides a list of the "signs of humility" (147; 62.30–63.6).[83] In another poorly entitled chapter, "How it is Impossible To Be Saved Without Humility," Peter couples humility with salvation.[84] Peter begins this chapter by reminding his readers about the dangerousness of the passions. He says that "[b]ecause of the great obscurity produced by the passions, a person may become so demented as to imagine in his lack of humility that he is the equal of the angels, or even greater than they" (177; 86.13–15). He then asks, "What, then, will be the fate of a man who is without humility, since he is but dust and mortal, not to say a sinner?" (177; 86.16–17). Apparently, Peter viewed the question as rhetorical, since he does not attempt to answer it. In fact, the chapter does not return to humility.

Peter also has a chapter entitled "The Great Value of Love and of Advice Given With Humility." Here he writes that

> we all need to humble ourselves before God and before each other, in that we have received from God our being and all other things, and from one another, through Him our knowledge. He who humbles himself is illumined all the more, while he who refuses to humble himself remains in darkness, as was the case with him who was the Morning-star and is now the devil. (187; 94.7–11)

In Peter's spiritual teaching humility is the result of believers realizing who they are in light of who God is. Each Christian must see that any good that they do is the result of God's working in them, through his grace. Yet, a believer is not to sit idly expecting God simply to impart the virtues. A believer exercises his/her free will in cooperation with God's grace in the attainment of the virtues:

> Thus God in his unutterable goodness has arranged all things in a marvellous way for us; and if you want to understand this and to be as you should, you must struggle to acquire the virtues so as to be able to accept with gratitude everything that comes, whether it is good or whether it appears to be bad, and to remain undisturbed in all things. And even when the demons suggest some pride-provoking thought in order to fill you with self-elation, you should remember the shameful things they have said to

---

83 See also 139; 57.4–7.
84 See also 160; 73.8–10.

you in the past and should reject this thought and become humble. And when they again suggest to you something shameful, you should remember that pride-provoking thought and so reject this new suggestion. through the co-operation of grace and by means of recollection, you make the demons cast out the demons, and are not brought to despair because of their shameful suggestions, or driven out of your mind because of your own conceit. On the contrary, when your intellect is exalted, you take refuge in humility; and when your enemies humble you before God, you are raised up through hope. In this way until your last breath you will never become confused and fall, or through fear succumb to despair. (174; 84.11–25)

In Peter's spiritual theology, then, God gives the virtues by his grace. Yet, one helps to attain them through prayer, spiritual reading, bodily discipline and by keeping the commandments.

Peter accepts that attaining the virtues is "helped by prayer and the study of the divine Scripture" (203; 105.34–35), that is, by spiritual reading. In light of this, Peter has a very developed doctrine of prayer. First, prayer is a gift of God (80; 10.31–32) and, as the apostle Paul commands in 1 Thessalonians 5:17, it should be unceasing, "that is, be mindful of God at all times, in all places, and in every circumstance" (173; 83.14–15).[85] Second, he sets out that each person should have a "rule of prayer [ὡρισμένον ... κανόνα]" (107; 31.28).[86] Those in a monastery will pray at the canonical hours but not only at the fixed times. Peter says that "[a]fter the service of Compline [μετὰ τὴν τοῦ ἀποδείπνου] each of us should recite the Creed and the Lord's Prayer, and then repeat 'Lord, have mercy' many times" (199; 102.24–36).[87] Third, he pre-

---

85 See also 154; 68.18–19.

86 See also 121; 43.34; and 198; 102.6.

87 Peter's employment of the prayers used in the liturgy occurs in his teaching on the eight stages of contemplation. Therefore, I say more about liturgical prayers below. The *typikon* from the Stoudios monastery in Constantinople (composed after 842) and the "Rule" of Athanasius for the Great Lavra on Mount Athos (dated 963) regulated that the office of Compline include the "Lord, have mercy." The *typikon* of Nikon for the Black Mountain monastery regulated the saying of the Creed at Compline. See *BMFD*, 101, 386. I am unaware of any *typika* which regulate that the Creed, the Lord's Prayer and the "Lord, have mercy" all be said at Compline.

scribes particular postures during prayer: "We should sit facing east,[88] like someone mourning for the dead, moving our heads backward and forward with pain in our souls and with a grieving heart" (199; 102.36–38); at other times, prayers should be said while standing (119; 41.29); and sometimes during prayer a person "falls unbidden to his knees, his hands outstretched and his eyes gazing at Christ's Cross" (120; 42.14–16). Fourth, as discussed below, prayer is to be imageless. Fifth, there is a purpose for praying and an order to prayer. In a summary statement concerning this doctrine of prayer, Peter states that

> [t]he purpose of what we say in our prayers is as follows. The thanksgiving is in recognition of our incapacity to offer thanksgiving as we should at this present moment, of our negligence in doing so at other times, and of the fact that the present moment is a gift of God's grace. Our confession of sins proclaims that God's gifts are measureless and that we are unable to understand them all or even to recognize them: we have only known of them from hearsay, and then not of them all. It also proclaims that we are constantly being benefited, visibly and invisibly, and that God's restraint in the face of our many sins cannot be put into words ... And we should briefly confess all the various types of sin into which we fall, so as to recall them and to grieve for them, acknowledging our own weakness so that the power of Christ may come upon us, as St Paul says (cf. 2 Cor. 12:9), and so that our many evil actions may be forgiven ... We pray for those whom we have distressed, and for those who have distressed us, or who will distress us ... We then pray for the departed, that they may receive salvation and so as to remind ourselves of our own death ... We also pray to be directed by

---

88   See also 109; 33.34–35. Praying while facing eastward has its foundation in 2 Chronicles 5:13 when the Levitical singers stood to the east of the altar at the dedication of the Solomonic temple. The *Apostolic Constitutions* (compiled in the late fourth century) legislated that a catechumen was to "pray towards the east." Also, in the late fourth century, Basil of Caesarea in his *On the Holy Spirit* 66 asks, "What writing has taught us to turn to the East at the prayer?" It appears that it was a common practice from at least the late fourth century for Christians to pray facing east. For the Greek text of the *Apostolic Constitutions* legislation, see *Les Constitutions apostoliques*, ed. Marcel Metzger (Paris, 1987), 3: 106; and with English translation in Alexander Roberts and James Donaldson, eds., *Ante-Nicene Fathers*, rev. A. Cleveland Coxe (1885–96; repr. Peabody, MA, 1995), 7: 477. Greek text of Basil of Caesarea's *On the Holy Spirit* in PG 32: 188B; trans. Blomfield Jackson in *Nicene and Post-Nicene Fathers*, ed. Philip Schaff and Henry Wace (1886–89; repr. Peabody, MA, 2004), 8: 41.

God and to become what He wishes us to be; and to be united with others, so that through their prayers we may receive mercy, all the while regarding them as superior to ourselves. (199–200; 103.5–104.2)

This extended quotation shows that prayer occupies a central place in Peter's spiritual theology. One expects this, of course, from a monk, though Peter has a doctrine of prayer applicable also to non-monastics, as distinct from a monastic-only rule of prayer. This again, in a subtle way, demonstrates that Peter's spiritual program was open to all believers.

Related to his doctrine of prayer is Peter's teaching on meditation. For Peter, meditation should follow immediately upon the completion of one's rule of prayer (107; 31.28–29). This meditation should be either on the Scriptures or on the life and sufferings of Jesus Christ (126–127; 47.27–22) . Concerning the Scriptures, Peter writes, "And we, too, who do no more than listen to the Scriptures, should devote ourselves to them and meditate on them so constantly that through our persistence a longing for God is impressed upon our hearts" (123; 44.33–35). Once the Scriptures have been impressed upon the heart, one can acquire the virtues. In Peter's thought, the Scriptures are not the only texts that a believer should read. Peter viewed his own books as a simple distillation of the teachings of the fathers – one gained through reading their writings and studying their lives (74; 5.11–12).[89] In a chapter dedicated to the topic, Peter writes that the "purpose of spiritual reading is to keep the intellect from distraction and restlessness" (155; 69.9–10). To do this, one should seek the proper environment in which to read so that one fixes the mind on the text. (For a monk, this means keeping "to your cell" [155; 69.13].) Having placed oneself in the proper environment, one must now fight the temptation of listlessness (ἀκηδία). In Peter's spiritual theology, to "get rid of your listlessness, you should give up all talk with other people and all sleep beyond what is necessary, allowing the listlessness to smelt you in body and soul, until such time as it grows exhausted and retreats in the face of your patient uninterrupted devotion to God, your reading, and the purity of your prayer" (156; 69.20–25). In the remainder of the chapter, Peter strays from the topic of spiritual reading, arguing that it is the misuse of things that is evil (157; 71.13–14). In another chapter, however, Peter connects proper spiritual reading to stillness, the ultimate result of a proper environment and freedom from listlessness (162; 74.22–23).

---

89   See below, Peter's sixth form of bodily discipline.

In his chapter "That Stillness Is of Great Benefit to Those Subject to the Passions," Peter laments the poor state of spiritual reading that he apparently sees around him. He writes,

> The fathers, says the *Gerontikon*, kept the commandments; their successors wrote them down; but we have placed their books on the shelves. And even if we want to read them, we do not have the application to understand what is said and to put it into practice; we read them either as something incidental, or because we think that by reading them we are doing something great, thus growing full of pride. We do not realize that we incur greater condemnation if we do not put into practice what we read, as St John Chrysostom says ... Thus reading and spiritual knowledge are good, but only when they lead to greater humility. (169; 80.16–24)[90]

In summary, Peter says that to help acquire the virtues each believer should be praying, meditating and reading the Scriptures and the writings and the lives of the holy fathers.

9b: Salvation and the "Bodily Disciplines"

Peter also says that the body "co-operates [συνεργὸν] in the acquisition of the virtues" (151; 66.5–7). In his spirituality, this is done through the "bodily disciplines." In his chapter on "The Seven Forms of Bodily Discipline," Peter begins with stillness (ἡσυχία).[91] Stillness consists in "living a life without distraction, far from all worldly care" (89; 17.26–27). This, says Peter, makes it possible for believers to avoid inner turmoil so that they can be concerned about how to do God's will: to prepare their souls for death, and to learn about both "the snares of the demons" and their own faults, which are as numerous as the sands of the sea[92] and often unrecognizable (89–90; 17.28–34).

---

90 Perhaps Peter viewed the writing of his books as an attempt to solve part of this problem regarding spiritual reading. If people were not reading the fathers themselves, perhaps they would read a text that synthesized the thought of the fathers.

91 The concept of ἡσυχία has a long history in Eastern Christian spiritual theology. For general comments on what ἡσυχία is, see G.E.H. Palmer, Philip Sherrard and Kallistos Ware, "Introductory Note," in *Phil.*, 14–16. For a history of ἡσυχία, see Irénée Hausherr, "L'hésychasme: Étude de spiritualité," *Orientalia Christiana Periodica* 32 (1956): 5–40 and 247–285.

92 See also 92; 19.37.

The second form of bodily discipline is moderate fasting, where a person only eats "once a day and then not to the point of satiety" (90; 18.6–7). Food should be simple, easily accessible, and not the kind that is desirable. Through this fasting, a person overcomes "gluttony, greed and desire" and lives without distraction (90; 18.8–9). Peter continues his discussion by steering a middle course between complete rejection of some foods and the goodness of God's creation. As well, one should also eat food in a properly paced way and with restraint. Peter says that only one type of food should be eaten each day and that wine is allowed, though more liberally to the sick and elderly than to the healthy and young, since "thirst is the best of all bodily disciplines" (90; 18.17).

Sleeping "for half the night" and devoting the other half to psalmody, prayer, compunctive sorrow and tears (90; 18.18–20) characterizes moderate vigils, the third form of bodily discipline. Peter believes that "[t]hrough this judicious fasting and vigil the body will become pliable to the soul, healthy and ready for every good work; while the soul will gain in fortitude and illumination, so as to see and to do what is right" (90–91; 18.20–22). Having said that, Peter now writes that the recitation of psalms is the fourth form of bodily discipline. This is not simple recitation, though, but "prayer expressed in a bodily way through psalms and prostrations" (91; 18.23–24).[93] He says that this is the way to goad the body and humble the soul. These actions lead to the flight of our enemies (i.e., the demons) and prepare the way for "our allies the angels" (91; 18.25).

The fifth form of discipline "consists in spiritual prayer [προσευχή πνευματική], prayer that is offered by the intellect and free from all thoughts [ἐννοίας]" (91; 18.29–30). Expounding on this, Peter writes that

---

93 Making prostrations during the psalmody was a feature of earliest Christian monasticism. Stewart sums up the Egyptian Pachomian practice when he writes: "The Pachomian texts present an elaborate choreography for *oratio* in the communal liturgical gatherings. After a soloist had finished reciting, the brothers would rise from their seated position and make the sign of the Cross. They would then kneel and prostrate for silent prayer, standing after a signal from the superior and again making the sign of the Cross. Together they would pray the Lord's Prayer (probably with their arms outstretched in the *orans* position), followed by another sign of the Cross. Then they would sit for another text recited by the soloist." In Stewart, *Cassian the Monk*, 103. This is a summary of *The Regulations of Horsiesios* 8–10 and *Precepts of Pachomius* 4–6 whose English translations are in *Pachomian Koinonia*, vol. 2: *Pachomian Chronicles and Rules*, trans. Armand Veilleux (Kalamazoo, 1981).

[d]uring such prayer the intellect is concentrated within the words spoken and, inexpressibly contrite, it abases itself before God, asking only that His will may be done in all its pursuits and conceptions. It does not pay attention to any thought [λογισμὸν], shape, colour, light, fire, or anything at all of this kind; but, conscious that it is watched by God and communing with Him alone, it is free from form, colour and shape. Such is the pure prayer appropriate for those still engaged in ascetic practice [πρακτικῷ]; for the contemplative [θεωρητικῷ] there are yet higher forms of prayer. (91; 18.30–36)[94]

According to Peter, the "sixth form of discipline consists in reading the writings and lives of the holy fathers, paying no attention to strange doctrines, or to other people, especially heretics" (91; 18.37–38). In this way, one learns how to conquer the passions and acquire the virtues because the thoughts of the Holy Spirit fill a person's intellect. This will help to drive out "unseemly words and conceptions" that remain in one's memory (91; 19.1–2). Since prayer is helped by this reading, it is important not to read carelessly as we "cannot properly understand the full significance of what we read because of the darkness induced by the passions" (91; 19.6–7). Further, Peter believes that reading and listening are not enough to attain knowledge of God, rather we need to put into practice what we read and hear. In an impressive analogy, Peter writes that "[o]ne cannot become a craftsman simply by hearsay: one has to practice, and watch, and make numerous mistakes, and be corrected by those with experience, so that through long perseverance and by eliminating one's own desires [ἰδίων θελημάτων] one eventually masters the art" (92; 19.11–15). More importantly, knowledge of God comes through God's grace to the humble person. Those "at the stage of ascetic practice [μάλιστα πρακτικὸς ὑπάρχῃ]" (92; 19.18) often think that they understand what they are reading, but they are actually only hearing the words of those who do, in truth, possess such knowledge of God. Becoming personal, Peter confesses that he is like those in the first stage of ascetic practice because he has "collected material from the Holy Scrip-

---

94 Peter also discusses "imageless prayer" at 81; 11.21–27; 117; 40.2–3; 119; 42.2–4; 135; 53.38–40 and 166–167; 78.20–23. The concept comes from Evagrius' *De oratione* 66–67, 114 and 117. See Evagrius of Pontus, *The Praktikos, Chapters on Prayer*, trans. John Bamberger and John Eudes (Kalamazoo:, 1972), 66, 74–75; and Columba Stewart, "Imageless Prayer and the Theological Vision of Evagrius Ponticus," *Journal of Early Christian Studies* 9 (2001): 173–204.

tures, but [has] not been found worthy of learning directly from the Holy Spirit; [he has] learnt only from those who did learn directly from the Holy Spirit" (92; 19.21–24).[95]

The seventh and final form of bodily discipline is "questioning those with experience about all our thoughts and actions" (92; 19.25–26). A person should do this because of inexperience and because, if they do not, they may think that they are doing one good thing after another "and so become presumptuous, imagining that we know as we should, although we still know nothing" (92; 19.27–28). In addition to these seven forms of discipline, Peter says that a person should patiently endure all that happens to him/her in order to gain experience and knowledge. As well, believers are to "always meditate on God's name" (92; 19.33–34) and continually abase themselves before God. Using the image of a ladder, Peter writes that the seven bodily disciplines have been established by God "and we cannot miss one out and go on to the next: as with steps, we must go from the first to the second, from the second to the third, and so on" (93; 20.5–8).[96]

Peter's seven forms of bodily discipline are important enough that he returns to the topic in two later chapters: "The Bodily Virtues as Tools for the Acquisition of the Virtues of the Soul," and "A Further Analysis of the Seven Forms of Bodily Discipline." The former is simply a series of quotations from church fathers concerning the bodily virtues; the latter contains Peter's own views. Since his chapter on "The Seven Forms of Bodily Discipline" did not contain any quotations from early Christian authors, Peter is likely trying to compensate for this absence. It is also significant that the current chapter follows one of Peter's statements about his methodology related to his use of the church fathers. He begins by saying, "[i]t is good to be reminded of certain things frequently, and so I will begin by quoting for the most part from the writings of others. For what I say is not my own invention but comes from the words and discernment of the divine Scriptures and the holy fathers" (103; 28.27–29). He then references writings by John of Damascus, a "prophet of

---

95 It is unlikely here that Peter is actually saying that he is in the beginning stages of ascetic practice. Rather, this passage should be seen as a rhetorical device stressing Peter's humility, akin to the opening statement of the *Admonition* where he claims that he has "never done anything good" (74; 5.6–7).

96 See also 88–89; 17.1–5.

God," King David, Job, John Chrysostom and Basil the Great. In "A Further Analysis of the Seven Forms of Bodily Discipline" Peter writes that "[w]e should always carry out what was said at the beginning of this work with regard to the seven forms of bodily and moral discipline, not doing either more or less than was recommended there" (150; 65.24–26).[97] Next, he turns to the issue of those who are too weak to do the seven bodily disciplines. He writes that "exceptions may be made in cases of bodily frailty" but the "relaxation must be no more than is necessary as a remedy for the sickness" (151; 65.28–31). However, Peter also believes that there will be those who possess excessive bodily strength "which requires a correspondingly severe degree of discipline" (151; 65.27–28). He then proceeds to give examples of those who fall into this latter category: Basil the Great, Maximus the Confessor, Sisoes, a "certain elder living in the desert," and Ephrem the Syrian. Thus Peter concludes his teaching on the forms of bodily disciplines by giving examples of those who excelled in the performance of the disciplines.

9c: Salvation and the Seven Commandments

At the end of his chapter entitled "The Seven Forms of Bodily Discipline," Peter writes, "In the end [the bodily disciplines] make man a god [Θεὸν ποιήσωσι τὸν ἄνθρωπον], through the grace of Him who has given the commandments to those who choose to keep them" (93; 20.8–10). He then begins the next chapter on the seven commandments by saying that "[i]f we want to make a start, we must concentrate on the practice of these seven forms of bodily discipline and on nothing else" (93; 20.14–15).[98] These serve as Peter's transition statements into his discussion of the seven commandments that he sees as intimately connected to the seven forms of bodily discipline. In light of this, Peter understands that the observance of these commandments also leads to the acquisition of the virtues.

The first commandment, says Peter, is to have the fear of the Lord (φόβου Θεοῦ) for "if we do not begin with fear, we can never ascend to the rest" (93; 20.16–17). This fear, Peter writes, comes mainly through meditation on God's blessings, God's provisions, and God's patience. Furthermore, a person should meditate on the example that Christ and his followers exhibit:

97 This quotation further suggests that Peter's work is organized since he refers to his previous discussions of the seven forms of bodily discipline.
98 This chapter is in actuality an exposition on the Beatitudes from the Gospel of Matthew, chapter five.

Moreover, we should not only recall the sufferings and struggles of the saints and martyrs, but should also reflect with wonder on the self-abasement of our Lord Jesus Christ, the way He lived in the world, His pure Passion, the Cross, His death, burial, resurrection and ascension, the advent of the Holy Spirit, the indescribable miracles that are always occurring every day, paradise, the crowns of glory, the adoption to sonship that He has accorded us, and all the things contained in Holy Scripture and so much else. (94; 21.6–13)

A person does these things so that his/her soul fills with contrition and so that he/she fears God. The second commandment is inward grief (πένθος).[99] For Peter, this involves mourning as if for a dead person, "because we perceive the terrible consequences that the things we have done before our death will have for us after we are dead; and we weep bitterly, from the depths of our heart and with inexpressible sorrow" (94; 21.26–28).

The third commandment is gentleness, given by grace so that one can imitate Christ. Gentleness produces stability in the spiritual life, a recognition that "what happens, happens" (95; 22.4).

The fourth commandment is a "longing to acquire the virtues [πόθου πρὸς τὴν κτῆσιν τῶν ἀρετῶν]" (96; 23.5–6). For "he who has tasted the sweetness of the commandments, and realizes that they lead him gradually towards the imitation of Christ, longs to acquire them all" (96; 23.10–12).

Mercy, the fifth commandment, is characterized by giving to others what one has himself received from God, "whether it be money, or food, or strength, a helpful word, a prayer, or anything else" (97; 23.22–25). Merciful persons consider themselves debtors, since they receive more than God asks them to give. One's willingness to die for another person just as Christ died for humankind is evidence, Peter believes, of perfect mercy.

The sixth commandment is detachment, or purity of heart. It is evidenced in those "who have accomplished every virtue reflectively and reverently and have come to see the true nature of things" (97; 24.8–9).

---

99 On the significance of πένθος in Eastern Christian spirituality, see Irénée Hausherr, *Penthos: La doctrine de la compunction dans l'orient chrétien* (Rome, 1944). Translated into English as *Penthos: The Doctrine of Compunction in the Christian East*, trans. Anselm Hufstader (Kalamazoo, 1982).

The seventh and final commandment is peace. The peacemakers are "those who have set soul and body at peace by subjecting the flesh to the spirit, so that the flesh no longer rises against the spirit" (97–98; 24.11–13).

To summarize, one obtains the virtues in a number of ways, including through the bodily disciplines and by obeying the commands of God. In addition, Peter views humility as the greatest virtue though his total list of virtues numbers over two hundred. Of these, Peter dedicates only three other chapters to specific virtues.[100] For Peter, like much of the Christian spiritual tradition, there is a strong balance between the sin of pride and the virtue of humility. Pride was traditionally seen as *the* Satanic sin, the vice that caused the angel Lucifer to fall from heaven. In order then not to commit such an insidious sin, one needs to cultivate its opposing virtue: humility.

Having looked at Peter's thought concerning the bodily disciplines, virtues and commandment, we return to his theology of salvation. In Peter's articulation, salvation is acquired by faith; therefore, one needs to know how to acquire faith. In "How to Acquire True Faith," faith is described as "the foundation of all blessings, the door to God's mysteries, unflagging defeat of our enemies, the most necessary of all the virtues, the wings of prayer and the dwelling of God within our soul" (164; 76.9–12). Through the patient endurance of trials and temptations, one acquires faith. At this point Peter elaborates on the connection between faith and the eradication of the passions. He writes,

> But we should take courage; because if we forcibly triumph over the trials and temptations that befall us, and keep control over our intellect so that it does not give in to the thoughts that spring up in our heart, we will once and for all overcome all the passions; for it will not be we who are victorious, but Christ, who is present in us through faith. (164; 76.15–20)

It is through the keeping of the commandments of God, assisted by faith, that a person sees beyond the tricks of the devil. In fact, it is not the believer who fights the enemy, but God, "who watches over him on account of his faith" (165;

---

100 The chapter entitled "That Stillness is of Great Benefit to Those Subject to the Passions" deals only in passing with ἡσυχία. Peter writes, "Stillness and withdrawal from men and human affairs are of benefit to all, but especially to those who are weak and subject to the passions" (167; 79.3–4). Varieties of topics discussed elsewhere in this book occupy the remainder of the chapter.

77.1). Peter also writes that it is through faith, and not free will, that someone acts according to God's will. He concludes the chapter by explaining that there are two kinds of faith: initial faith (ἡ πρώτη καὶ κοινὴ ... πίστις) and great faith (ἡ μεγάλη πίστις). Quoting Isaac of Nineveh, Peter writes that "[t]he former is the faith of hearsay, the latter is the faith of contemplation" (166; 78.9–10). Therefore, those progressing in the spiritual life "should persist in [their] ascetic practice [ἀσκήσει]" so that they, through faith, will draw towards God (167; 78.31–33).

In "The Great Benefit of True Repentance" Peter succinctly elucidates the core of his teaching on repentance. He begins positively by reminding his readers that "[i]t is always possible to make a new start by means of repentance" (170; 81.2). He then does not return to the topic again in the chapter[101] but elsewhere says that someone who does not repent after sinning should regard themselves as "the lowest of creatures" (160; 73.10–12). In fact, God punishes believers when they do not repent (207; 109.14–15). Employing Isaac of Nineveh again, Peter writes that the fear of God brings about repentance (199; 102.32–33), and using John Chrysostom we learn that "repentance, properly speaking, is the eradication of evil ... while what are called acts of repentance or prostrations are a bending of the knees, which expresses the fact that the person who bows sincerely before God and man after having offended someone assumes the attitude of a servant" (202; 105.3–6). In sum, for Peter, repentance gives the Christian a new start after they sin and can possibly lead to the removal of all evil. Further, anyone who does not repent is almost sub-human, and God will punish him or her. Yet, fear of God brings about the necessary repentance in order to avoid these undesirable consequences.

For Peter, then, the virtues lead to salvation aided by prayer and the study of the Holy Scriptures. Of the many virtues, the greatest is humility. Attainment of all the virtues comes through a variety of means but especially through the seven forms of bodily disciplines and obedience to the commandments of God. Further, the acquisition of the virtues, and ultimately salvation, is open to both monastics and non-monastics though the monastic life, according to Peter, is in some measure preferable. Peter now turns to the immediate results of overcoming the passions and acquiring the virtues: dispassion and spiritual knowledge.

---

101 This misnaming, like the chapter entitled "Spiritual Reading," is the result of Macarius and Nicodemus' poor designation of a chapter title.

10. DISPASSION (ἀπάθεια)

Teaching on dispassion has a long history in early Eastern Christian spiritual theology;[102] Peter's *Admonition* continues this tradition, albeit with less scrutiny. In his chapter entitled "Dispassion," Peter writes that the signs of dispassion are "to remain calm and fearless in all things ... [to be] unconcerned about [one's] material life ... [to be] in thought and practice ... found worthy of [the eternal world]" (147–149; 63.8–10, 27–28). Next, Peter explains how this is accomplished:

> In order to attain all this we must focus our attention on God, have no concern for this world, and must not be dismayed by any trial or temptation. Starting from this world, we must continually advance, ascending to a higher level of reality. We should not be distracted by anything: neither by dreams, whether evil or seemingly good, nor by the thought of anything, whether good or bad, nor by distress or deceitful joy, nor by self-conceit or despair, nor by depression or elation, nor by a sense of abandonment or by illusory help and strength, nor by negligence or progress, nor by laziness or seeming zeal, nor by apparent dispassion or passionate attachment. Rather with humility we should strive to maintain a state of stillness, free from all distraction, knowing that no one can do us harm unless we ourselves wish for it. (148; 63.29–64.3)

In Peter's view, the spiritual person longs for dispassion in an attempt to imitate God, who is himself dispassionate (83; 12.36).[103] In three places, Peter goes into greater detail about how to achieve dispassion. First, dispassion is the result of God's grace and one's establishment in the virtues. This results in the working of the Holy Spirit, given by God the Father, in the life of each believer. He writes,

> For unless we are dispassionate God in his holiness does not send down the Holy Spirit [Πανάγιον Πνεῦ`μα] upon us, lest we violate His indwelling because out of habit we are still drawn towards the passions, and so incur

---

102 For the use of the term up until the time of Maximus the Confessor, see Gustave Bardy, "Apatheia," in *Dictionnaire de spiritualité ascétique et mystique: Doctrine et histoire*, ed. Marcel Viller, F. Cavallera and A. Solinac (Paris, 1937), 1: cols. 727–746.

103 See also 168; 79.29–30; and 100; 26.5.

greater condemnation. But when we are established in virtue, and are no longer friendly with our enemies or pulled this way and that by our impassioned habits, then we receive grace and are not liable to condemnation for receiving it. (168; 79.31–37)

Second, the attainment of dispassion is the result of participation in the liturgy, knowledge of the Scriptures and knowledge of the writings of the fathers:

> The troparia to be found in the liturgical books are intended to assist us in understanding these books as well as other texts. In addition, as St John Klimakos says, they stimulate compunction in people whose intellect is still weak. For the melody, says St Basil the Great, draws the mind where it will, whether to grief or longing, to remorse or joy. Moreover, we should search the Scriptures in accordance with the Lord's commandment, so that we may find eternal life in them (cf. John 5:39); and we should pay attention to the meaning of the psalms and troparia, becoming in this way totally aware of our ignorance. For if one does not taste of knowledge, says St Basil the Great, one does not know how much one lacks. To promote this experience and knowledge I have described the origins of the virtues and the passions; for thereby others may come to recognize them, and so struggle to acquire what engenders the virtues and to expel by retaliatory action that which produces the passions. We should also and at all times keep a watch over our bodily activities as if they were plants, and should always give attention to the virtues of the soul and study how we can acquire each virtue. We should learn about this from the divine Scriptures and from saintly men. (194–195; 99.25–100.1)

By doing these things, one comes to acquire the virtues and to dispel the passions leading ultimately to dispassion. Third, as discussed above, "bodily asceticism does help in the acquisition of the virtues" (195; 100.11–12), and by extension dispassion, but Peter says elsewhere that one "cannot attain dispassion by means of ascetic practice alone" (167; 79.5). Therefore, for Peter, God ultimately gives dispassion through grace to those who are participating in the liturgy, studying the Scriptures and reading the holy fathers. As well, bodily asceticism assists in the attainment of dispassion but is not a requirement for its reception. This view is consistent with Peter's emphasis that the spiritual life is open to both monastics and non-monastics. Finally, quoting John Climacus, Peter says that dispassion is not the equivalent of salvation since "all can be saved and reconciled" but "[i]t is not possible for all to achieve dispassion" (207; 109.18–19). This distinction is important since it is often tempting to categorize dispassion as the height of the spiritual life. In Peter's spiritual theology, however, salvation is the highest good. This is additional evidence that the salvation/destruction dialectic is at the core of Peter's spirituality.

11. CONTEMPLATION (θεωρία)

As I argue throughout this chapter, Peter's introduction to his first book provides the organizational structure of the *Admonition*. After discussing the passions, and the destruction that ultimately results from these passions, Peter moves to a discussion of the virtues and salvation. Coupled with this he writes about the monastic lifestyle that he terms the "royal way" and uses this discussion to move into his understanding of dispassion which is the result of acquiring the virtues. Finally, just before he concludes his introduction with a paragraph re-emphasizing the role of God's grace in the spiritual life, he mentions "the different stages of spiritual contemplation [that] are given to the believer" (89; 17.4–5). Peter, realizing the level of advancement in the spiritual life necessary to reach the contemplation of God, warns his readers that they should not seek such an experience prematurely. He writes, "For this reason we should not try, through contempt or arrogant zeal, to attain this kind of contemplative knowledge prematurely" (138; 56.12–13). Further, "In all this ... one should keep a proper order, and one should work on whatever one understands. For what one cannot understand one should give silent thanks, as St Isaac says, but should not presumptuously assume that one has understood it" (140; 57.30–34).

In Peter's understanding, there are eight stages of contemplation (108; 32.26).[104] The first stage is

---

104 See also 145; 61.17; and 197; 101.30. Peter attributes his own understanding of the eight stages of contemplation to Isaac of Nineveh, who writes: "Sunday is the symbol of true knowledge which is not received by flesh and blood, and which is elevation above [mere] opinion. In this world, however, there is no eighth day; but neither is there a true Sabbath ... Six days are accomplished in the service of life; the seventh is accomplished in the grave; the eighth in departing from it." Isaac of Ninevah, *Mystic Treatises*, trans. from Bedjan's Syriac text with an introduction and registers by A.J. Wansinck (Amsterdam, 1923), 136–137. See Basil of Caesarea's "On the Hexaemeron 2.8": "For, Scripture knows as a day without evening, without succession, and without end, that day which the psalmist called the eighth, because it lies outside this week of time." In Basil of Caesarea, *Exegetic Homilies*, trans. Agnes Clare Way (Washington, 1963), 35. See also Maximus the Confessor, "*Capita 200*

knowledge of the tribulations and trials of this life ... The second is knowledge of our own faults and of God's bounty ... The third is knowledge of the terrible things that await us before and after death ... The fourth is deep understanding of the life led by our Lord Jesus Christ in this world, and of the words and actions of His disciples and the other saints, the martyrs and the holy fathers ... The fifth is knowledge of the nature and flux of things ... The sixth is contemplation of created beings, that is to say, knowledge and understanding of God's visible creation ... The seventh is understanding of God's spiritual creation ... The eighth is knowledge concerning God, or what we call 'theology.' (108–109; 32.28–33.11)

According to Peter, the first three stages "are suitable for one still engaged in ascetic practice [πρακτικῷ]" and the last five stages "pertain to the contemplative or gnostic [θεωρητικῷ, ἤτοι γνωστικῷ]" (109; 33.12, 15). Therefore, writes Peter,

the man engaged in ascetic practice begins to enter the path of spiritual knowledge by way of the first three stages; and by concentrating on his task and by meditating on the thoughts produced within him, he progresses in them until they are established in him. In this way the next stage of knowledge enters automatically into his intellect. The same happens with all the remaining stages.

To make things quite clear, I will speak, despite my incompetence, about each stage of contemplation, and about what is understood and said at each stage. In this way we can discover how we ought to act when grace begins to open the eyes of our soul and we come with astonishment to understand thoughts and words that instill in us fear of God, in other words, contrition of soul. (109; 33.17–30)

---

theologica et oeconomica 1.54–55": "He who after the example of God has completed the sixth day with fitting actions and thoughts, and has himself with God's help brought his own actions to a successful conclusion, has in his understanding traversed the condition of all things subject to nature and time and has entered into the mystical contemplation of the aeons and the things inherent in them ... He experiences the blessed life of God, who is the only true life, and himself becomes god by deification ... The eighth day is the transposition and transmutation of those found worthy into a state of deification." In *Phil.*, 2: 125.

With this, Peter begins his discussion of each stage of contemplation, dedicating a chapter to each level. It is important to note, however, that Peter again places the emphasis on the role and absolute necessity of grace when he says that "grace begins to open the eyes or our soul." For Peter, all upward movement in the spiritual life is due to grace.

Those at the first stage of contemplation, writes Peter, should seat themselves in a posture of prayer and meditate on "the damage done to human nature through sin" (108; 32.30).[105] Using liturgical texts and scriptural examples, he then prescribes what one is to say at this level of contemplation. First, one begs for God's mercy. Second, one grieves "with all his soul and shaking his head" (110; 34.5) over the depravity of humanity. By doing these two things, "the soul is made contrite, if it has at least some sensibility. By persisting in this way, and growing accustomed to the fear of God, the intellect begins to understand and meditate on the second stage of contemplation" (111; 35.20–24).

At the second stage of contemplation, the believer turns to his/her own sin. Yet, this is not a sorrowful self-loathing. Again using the liturgy as a guide, believers at this stage confess their great sinfulness but consistently seek God's mercy through repentance.[106] God, in his φιλανθρωπία responds to this request for forgiveness and the believer "gradually advances to the third stage of contemplation" (114; 37.21–22).

The third stage also begins with lamentation for sin and again uses the texts of the liturgy as the basis for this expression of sorrow. As in the second stage, repentance characterizes these cries for God's assistance. Peter writes that

---

105 Regarding a particular posture, Peter says that the person engaged in the first stage of contemplation "should seat himself facing the east" (109; 33.34–35). He suggests this same posture later in the *Admonition* when he writes that during prayer one "should sit facing east, like someone mourning for the dead" (199; 102.36–37). On this practice, Louth writes: "Christians ... turned to face East, whence the sun rose and when they expected the coming of the Messiah. Three treatises on prayer survive from the pre-Constantinian period – by Origen, Tertullian, and Cyprian – and for all these writers prayer is to be made by Christians, standing up, with hands raised, facing East." See Andrew Louth, "The Body in Western Catholic Christianity," in *Religion and the Body*, ed. Sarah Coakley (Cambridge, 2000), 113. The later Byzantine hesychasts, in addition to a particular posture, recommended a particular form of breathing during prayer, earning them the derogatory name ὀμφαλόψυχοί, that is, "people-whose-soul-is-in-their-navel." See Gregory Palamas, *The Triads*, ed. John Meyendorff, trans. Nicholas Gendle (Mahwah, NJ, 1983), 8.

106 In this short chapter, Peter speaks of repentance five times.

God's grace kindles a "deep penitence in the heart" (119; 41.32–33).[107] Once one is finished with liturgical praying, Peter recommends that one

> should begin the psalms, reciting the *Trisagion* after each subsection of the Psalter [ποιῶν κατὰ ἀντίφωνον Τρισάγιον] ... After the *Trisagion* say "Lord, have mercy" forty times; and then make a prostration and say once within yourself, "I have sinned, Lord, forgive me". On standing, you should stretch out your arms and say once, "God, be merciful to me a sinner". After praying in this way, you should say once more, "O come, let us worship ... " three times, and then another sub-section of the Psalter in the same way. (118–119; 41.25–32)

At last, Peter explains why such extensive singing is good:

> Yet, because of the feebleness of our intellect, the Church is right to commend the singing of hymns and troparia; for by this means those of us who lack spiritual knowledge may willy-nilly praise God through the sweetness of the melody, while those who possess such knowledge and so understand the words are brought to a state of compunction ... Thus hymns and troparia are remedies for our weakness. (120; 42.21–25, 31–32)

Finally, Peter concludes his discussion of the third stage of contemplation. In this final section, Peter connects his teaching on repentance and compunction to an intellect that "has attained the level of good thoughts" (120; 42.35–36). Peter believes that when God-given thoughts increase in the mind, one should give thanks, since this is the result of God's grace. Nonetheless, if these good thoughts darken again, it is likely the result of a loss of inward grief. Restoration of the good thoughts, says Peter, comes through devotion to God, reading the Scriptures and keeping the intellect free from vain thoughts during prayer (121; 43.21–24). With all of this accomplished, a believer can now "go forward to the further stages" (122; 43.41).

"The fourth stage of contemplation consists in the understanding of our Lord's incarnation and His manner of life in this world," writes Peter (122; 44.2–3). Once a believer receives this knowledge of the incarnation through the virtues, he "will never lose his longing or cease from shedding the tears that

---

107 Notice again Peter's emphasis on grace.

come to him unbidden" (123; 44.31–33). After speaking briefly about the Scriptures and the mysteries contained therein, Peter returns to his thoughts on the incarnation, saying that Christ is the "primary goal" of the Christian (125; 46.3; πρῶτος ... σκοπός). For

> who can partially understand the grace of the Holy Gospel and the things
> that are in it – that is to say, the actions and teachings of the Lord, His com-
> mandments and His doctrines, His threats and His promises – knows what
> inexhaustible treasure he has found ... For Christ is hidden in the Gospel,
> and he who wishes to find Him must first sell all that he has and buy the
> Gospel (cf. Matt. 13:44). It is not enough merely to find Christ through
> one's reading, but one should also receive Him in oneself by imitating His
> way of life in the world ... Like Christ we should become sinless in body
> and soul, in so far as a human being can do this. (126; 46.35–47.5)

According to Peter, the whole purpose for Christ's incarnation is to be conformed to God, and the God-man provides the example. Realizing the significance of the incarnation leads one to exclaim God's greatness by performing the liturgy, culminating in the Eucharistic presence of Jesus Christ himself (127; 47.23). In addition, understanding the importance of the incarnation leads to praise, by way of the liturgical prayers, of the "Blessed Queen of the universe" since she is the mother of God (129; 49.35–36). Next, knowledge of the weight of the incarnation results in the liturgical praise of the "Holy apostles and disciples of the Saviour, eyewitnesses of His mysteries" (131; 50.26–27). Finally, understanding of the incarnation leads one to pray for one's own deliverance (132; 51.24–27).

Peter devotes little space in the *Admonition* to the fifth stage of contemplation, in which "one comes to understand, as the final Beatitude indicates, the changeable nature of visible created things: how they derive from the earth and return again to the earth" (133; 52.18–20). Contemplation upon these things simply leads one to agree with the author of Ecclesiastes, John of Damascus, and the psalmist that all is vanity. In Peter's thought, this is why the liturgy says that "[b]y the time we have gained the whole world we shall be in the grave, where king and pauper are one" (133; 52.26–28).[108]

---

108 As the editors of the English translation note, this quotation is from the funeral
liturgy. See Hapgood, *Service Book of the Holy Orthodox-Catholic Apostolic Church*,
381, 385.

Describing the sixth stage of contemplation, Peter writes, "When a person has acquired the habit of detachment, then he is granted access to the sixth stage of contemplation, that known as 'strength' (cf. Isa. 11:2). At this stage, one begins to look without passion on the beauty of created things" (134; 52.30–32). This, then, leads Peter into his discussion of the three categories (human, demonic and angelic) of thought mentioned above. Of the three categories of thought, it is angelic thought that the sixth stage of contemplation is attempting to acquire. For "[a]ngelic thought [Ἀγγελικός], finally, consists in the dispassionate contemplation of things ... It is the knowledge taught by those earthly angels [ἐπιγείοις Ἀγγέλοις] who have made themselves dead to the world, so that their intellect has grown dispassionate and hence sees things as it should" (134–135; 53.13, 19–22). With this kind of thought one is able to look upon humankind "with wonder, conscious that [their] intellect, being infinite, is the image of the invisible God" (135; 53.32–34) and to marvel at the body considering "the way in which the eyes, ears and tongue are used externally according to the soul's wish" and that it has a "noetic and deiform soul [νοερᾷ καὶ λογικῇ ψυχῇ]" (135; 54.6–11). In Peter's spirituality, believers marvel at these things as well as other aspects of human nature. In addition, a believer "contemplates the beauty and use of gold, and marvels at how such a thing has come out of the earth for our sake" (136; 54.30–31). In short, those at the sixth stage of contemplation are to marvel at all of God's creation, "By thus contemplating dispassionately the beauty and use of each thing, he who is illumined is filled with love for the Creator" (136; 54.39–40). Once a person is aware of the beauty of creation, he/she recognizes that God created all things for a particular purpose and that all things are "'wholly good and beautiful' (Gen. 1:31)" (138; 55.36). In conclusion, Peter writes that "he who is strong enough to attain understanding apprehends the spiritual from the sensible, and the invisible and eternal from what is visible and transient" (141; 57.40–28.2). This, ultimately, is the goal and the result of the sixth stage of contemplation.

Peter begins his exposition of the seventh stage by writing that a "person given grace to attain the seventh stage of contemplation marvels at the multitude of incorporeal powers: authorities, thrones, dominions, seraphim and cherubim, the nine orders mentioned in all the divine Scriptures" (141; 58.10–12).[109] The sixth stage involves the visible creation, whereas the seventh stage

---

109 That there are nine orders of angels comes from Pseudo-Dionysius the Areopagite: "The word of God has provided nine explanatory designations for the heavenly

now involves the invisible creation of God. The remainder of this short chapter is, in effect, a brief treatise on the angels. Peter quotes from John Chrysostom, Gregory of Nazianzus, Athanasius the Great, the liturgy, and Cosmas the Hymnographer to explain the existence and nature of the angelic orders.

In the eighth stage of contemplation, "we are led upwards to the vision of what pertains to God by means of the second kind of prayer, the pure prayer proper to the contemplative [θεωρητικῷ]" (142; 59.9–10). Yet, Peter says that[110]

> God in Himself is not among any of the things that the intellect is capable of defining, for He is undetermined and undeterminable. In theology we can speak about the attributes of God but not about God in Himself ... It is indeed more correct to speak of God in Himself as inscrutable [ἀκατάληπτον], unsearchable [ἀνεξιχνίαστον], inexplicable [ἀνερμή-νευτον], as all that it is impossible to define. For He is beyond intellection [νοῦν] and thought [ἔννοιαν], and is known only to Himself, one God in three hypostases, unoriginate, unending, beyond goodness, above all praise. All that is said of God in divine Scripture is said with this sense of our inadequacy, that though we may know that God is, we cannot know what He is; for in Himself He is incomprehensible to every being endowed with intellect and reason. (143; 59.21–31)

Along these same lines, Peter says that the same lack of knowledge concerning the essence of God applies to the incarnation of Jesus Christ. He writes, "We can only marvel at the way in which the flesh He assumed from us is taken up into His divinity" (143; 59.32–33).

Thus in Peter's spiritual theology, progression through the eight stages of contemplation is the result of one's acquisition of the virtues, especially dispassion, and salvation. It would be wrong to see these eight stages as Peter's scheme for the spiritual life. In other words, Peter's spiritual plan does not consist of eight stages culminating in contemplation of God's being. In fact, Peter

---

beings" ("The Celestial Hierarchy 6.2"). Though Pseudo-Dionysius says here that it is a biblical designation, he indicates elsewhere in his corpus that it comes from his teacher Hierotheus. See Pseudo-Dionysius, *Pseudo-Dionysius: The Complete Works*, trans. Colm Luibheid (New York, 1987), 160, n. 68.

110 Here Peter is relying heavily on Pseudo-Dionysius and Basil of Caesarea and anticipates his own later arguments concerning the essence and energies of God.

is at his most uninspired when discussing the eight stages of contemplation. This may be a result of Peter's own lack of experience of the higher levels of contemplation. Throughout the *Admonition*, Peter places an emphasis on the importance of first-hand experience in the spiritual life. For example, he believes that a person should seek "the counsel of experienced men" so that the knowledge that a person gains is not merely theoretical (191; 97.6–8). Peter, as will be shown in the next chapter, argues the same point throughout the *Spiritual Alphabet*. Yet there he explains that knowledge of such inexperienced events can come from those who have, in fact, the necessary first-hand experience. In this context, it seems that Peter reaches the limits of his own personal experience but likely felt that it was necessary to comment anyway on the place of contemplation in the spiritual life since it holds such an important position in the tradition of spiritual teaching, even if everyone does not attain this summit. His extensive use of quotations from liturgical texts and from the theological writings of the church fathers to describe the experience of contemplation is an indication of his own inexperience with this stage in the spiritual life. Contemplation, in Peter's spirituality, is the result of the acquisition of the virtues, leading to dispassion that then allows one to contemplate God. Peter proves this textually in the first lines of his exposition of the sixth stage where he speaks twice of dispassion as a necessary prerequisite for contemplating God. The eight stages of contemplation are a result of someone's salvation and not the process by which one attains salvation. This is obvious in Peter's introduction to the *Admonition* where he writes that "the different stages of spiritual contemplation are given to the believer" (89; 17.5). In other words, contemplation is for the person who possesses salvation.[111]

Concluding Remarks

In the introduction to the *Admonition*, Peter presents his understanding of the spiritual life. He insists on his unworthiness to write such a work and then, after naming his sources, Peter establishes the salvation/destruction dialectic that forms the core of his spiritual program. Next, he says that each person suffers voluntary and involuntary trials and temptations that are the result of natural

---

111 This is an important detail to further demonstrate, contra Gouillard, that Peter's spiritual theology cannot simply be understood as a division into πρᾶξίς and θεωρία.

knowledge, given by God through the Scriptures, baptism, and free will. One, however, must endure these trials patiently. Peter then discusses discrimination, the fulcrum of his salvation/destruction dialectic. The purpose of discrimination, says Peter, is to help the believer make the right decision between destruction and salvation. Destruction manifests itself as the passions and receives assistance from the devil and demons. Salvation manifests itself as the virtues and receives assistance from prayer, spiritual reading, bodily discipline and keeping the commandments. After discussing the passions, Peter moves to a discussion of the virtues and their accompanying salvation. Included in this discussion of salvation is the fact that Peter's spiritual program is open to all persons, though those living a monastic lifestyle, or at least solitary lifestyles, more readily acquire the virtues. Peter then moves into his understanding of dispassion that is the result of acquiring the virtues. Lastly, Peter discusses the eight stages of contemplation that are possible only by those who possess dispassion. Peter himself provides a summary of his spiritual program in the *Admonition*. He writes,

> Yet let no one think that he himself brings about these gifts of grace. Rather, he has received much more than he deserves, and he should be deeply grateful, and should go in fear lest he incur greater condemnation because of what has been given to him; for without labouring he has been granted the fruits for which the angels strive. Knowledge is given to anoint the intellect, to strengthen us in the keeping of the commandments, and to help us in the practice of the virtues. It is also given so that we may know how and why we practise the virtues, and what we should do and what we should not do, so as to avoid condemnation. For borne on the wings of knowledge, we strive joyfully and receive yet greater knowledge, strength and gladness through our striving; and, when this happens, we are enabled by grace to give thanks to Him who has bestowed these great blessings on us, knowing whence we have received them. For when God is thanked, He gives us still further blessings, while we, by receiving His gifts, love Him all the more and through this love attain that divine wisdom whose beginning is the fear of God (cf. Prov. 1:7). Fear brings about repentance, says St Isaac, and through repentance comes the revelation of hidden things. (198–199; 102.19–33)

To conclude, the *Admonition* shows that not only is Peter's spiritual program a combination of both distinctive and traditional themes, but that it is also a highly developed and well-thought-out spiritual theology.

CHAPTER FOUR

The Spiritual Theology of Peter of Damascus II:
The Spiritual Alphabet (Λόγοι κατ᾽ ἀλφαβῆτον)

In the meager secondary literature on the Petrine corpus, scholars conclude that the *Spiritual Alphabet* is more organized than the *Admonition to His Own Soul*. For example, in his introduction to the English translation of Peter's works, Kallistos Ware says that "[the *Spiritual Alphabet*], with its *Twenty-Four Discourses* corresponding to the twenty-four letters of the Greek alphabet, possesses a more coherent structure than [the *Admonition*]."[1] Similarly, Jean Gouillard writes that "on the whole, [the *Spiritual Alphabet*] develops itself much more regularly."[2] In the introduction to the French translation of Peter's works, Jacques Touraille also says that "[t]he second book [that is, the *Spiritual Alphabet*] ... is more structured."[3] It seems that these authors base their conclusions on the fact that the structure of the book follows the Greek alphabet, thereby containing twenty-four λόγοι. Once one reads the book, however, it appears at first that the conclusions of these scholars are, in some ways, without foundation. Since these same authors reached the conclusion that the *Admonition* lacked organization, it is surprising that they would consider the *Spiritual Alphabet* better organized just because Peter arranged the book around the Greek alphabet. At first, the *Spiritual Alphabet* appears as topically "unorganized" as the *Admonition*. In this chapter, though, I will show that not only is the *Spiritual Alphabet* a compendium of the spiritual theology found in the *Admonition*, but that Peter's purpose for writing the book was to distill highlights of his teaching in a more structured plan that would likely be more accessible to a larger

---

1 *Phil.*, 3: 72.
2 See Jean Gouillard, "Un auteur spirituel byzantin du XIIe siècle, Pierre Damascène," *Échos d'Orient* 38 (1939), 267: "dans l'ensemble, il se développe beaucoup plus régulièrement."
3 *Philocalie des Pères Neptiques*, fasc. 2: *Pierre Damascène*, ed. Jacques Touraille (Bégrolles-en-mauges, 1980), 9: "Le second livre ... est plus structuré."

audience. In view of this, I conclude that Peter's purpose in the *Spiritual Alphabet* is to summarize his spiritual theology as given in the *Admonition*.[4]

Spiritual alphabets are a well-known literary genre in the Byzantine empire and are most often in the form of either a κοντάκιον, a sermon in verse usually celebrating major feasts and saints, or a κανών, a set of verse phrases.[5] Others exist in the form of short penitential works in both "prose and verse and in the vernacular as well as the learned languages."[6] The *Spiritual Alphabet* of Peter is an example of a prose alphabet and appears unique during the twelfth century. It is likely that Peter used this genre for the *Spiritual Alphabet* as a way of making his spiritual theology more accessible.[7] Furthermore, at the beginning of each discourse Peter includes four or more lines of verse that summarize the teaching found in the λόγος.[8] These lines of verse reveal the topic(s) of each λόγος, making it easier to remember Peter's progression of thought throughout the *Spiritual Alphabet*.[9] I find nothing, however, in the Petrine corpus itself, the meager secondary literature on Peter, nor in the manuscript of the *Spiritual Alphabet* that I consulted (i.e., Paris, Bibliothèque Nationale, Ancien gr. 1135) that indicates conclusively that these verses are not original to Peter.

---

4   For a comparison of the contents of the *Admonition to His Own Soul* with the *Spiritual Alphabet*, see appendix 1.

5   See Willhelm Weyh, "Die Akrostichis in der byzantinischen Kanonesdichtung," *Byzantinische Zeitschrift* 17 (1908): 1–69.

6   *ODB*, s.v. "Acrostic," by Elizabeth M. Jeffreys, 15. See also Karl Krumbacher, A. Ehrhard and Heinrich Gelzer, *Geschichte der byzantinischen Literatur von Justinian bis zum Ende des Oströmischen Reiches (527–1453)*, 2nd ed. (Munich, 1897), 697–705, 717–720.

7   John Climacus also provides a summary of the spiritual life in alphabet form twice in *The Ladder of Divine Ascent*, Step 26. The first is provided "for everyone" whereas the second is "a measure, rule, and law for those in the flesh aiming at perfection in spirit and body." See John Climacus, *The Ladder of Divine Ascent*, Step 26; trans. Colm Luibheid and Norman Russell (New York, 1982), 232.

8   See appendix 2 for a translation of these verses. Jacques Touraille translated these verses into French in *Philocalie des Pères Neptiques*, 228–325.

9   Byzantine society was a culture of memory. Individuals often learned the Psalms and other biblical and liturgical texts by memory. A.P. Kazhdan writes that "Even the works of contemporary writers were memorized." It is plausible, though impossible to prove without doubt, that Peter's *Spiritual Alphabet* was one of these "contemporary writers" that people memorized. See *ODB*, s.v. "Memory," by A.P. Kazhdan, 1338. Note also that the translators of the English edition of Peter's works chose not to translate the introductory verses.

Concerning the literary form of the *Spiritual Alphabet*, a definitive conclusion is impossible. In the Byzantine era, λόγος, as a literary term, had two distinct meanings. It could refer to either a written treatise or a sermon.[10] Thus the question concerning the *Spiritual Alphabet* is: Did Peter deliver these λόγοι as sermons or were they, from the start, intended to be written treatises only? Though scholars recently began turning their attention to the study of preaching in the early Byzantine church, "preaching in the later Byzantine period needs a study of its own."[11] Thus determining the literary form of Peter's *Spiritual Alphabet* is made more difficult due to the lack of a comprehensive study of homiletical practice in the later Byzantine church, including the twelfth century. Comparing the *Spiritual Alphabet* to other Byzantine texts does not provide the answer either. Since I am unaware of any contemporaries of Peter that include verse epigrams before ascetical discourses, I am unable to compare Peter with another author of whom we know more about. Though Peter ends each λόγος with a benediction that reads – "to whom belongs all glory, honour and dominion throughout the ages. Amen." (216; 116.33–35) – or something similar, this is found in both written treatises and homilies of the Byzantine period. For example, the *Ethical Discourses* of Symeon the New Theologian (949–1022) each end with a benediction, and these discourses were written treatises.[12] Similarly, the homilies of Photius, the Patriarch of Constantinople from 856–867 and 877–886, also conclude with a benediction.[13] The same is

---

10   G.W.H. Lampe, ed., *A Patristic Greek Lexicon* (Oxford, 1961), 807. See also E.A. Sophocles, *Greek Lexicon of the Roman and Byzantine Periods (From B.C. 146 to A.D. 1100)* (New York, n.d.), 2: 719.

11   Mary B. Cunningham and Pauline Allen, "Introduction" in *Preacher and Audience: Studies in Early Christian and Byzantine Homiletics*, ed. Mary B. Cunningham and Pauline Allen (Leiden, 1998), 1.

12   See, for example, Symeon the New Theologian, *Symeon the New Theologian, On the Mystical Life: The Ethical Discourses*, vol. 2: *On Virtue and Christian Life*, trans. Alexander Golitzin (Crestwood, NY, 1996), 80: "[T]hrough the grace and love for humanity of our Lord Jesus Christ, to whom be glory, honor, and worship, together with the Father and the Holy Spirit, now and ever, and unto ages of ages. Amen." The Greek text of the *Ethical Discourses* is in Symeon the New Theologian, *Syméon le Nouveau Théologien: Traités théologiques et éthiques*, ed. Jean Darrouzès (Paris, 1966), 1: 308.

13   See, for example, Photius I of Constantinople, *The Homilies of Photius Patriarch of Constantinople*, trans. Cyril Mango (Cambridge, MA, 1958), 73: "to whom be glory and power for ever and ever. Amen." Greek text in Photius I of Constantinople, Φωτίου Ὁμιλίαι. Ἔκδοσις κειμένου, εἰσαγωγὴ καὶ σχόλια, ed. B. Laourdas (Thessaloniki, 1959).

true of Patriarch Nicholas I (852–925).[14] This issue is complicated further through the introduction of Cunningham and Allen's "'desk-homily', which was written in homiletic form but was intended for private reading or study."[15] Unfortunately, Peter's inclusion of the verse epigrams does not assist in identifying the *Spiritual Alphabet*'s literary form since it is impossible to determine if the verses were added after Peter completed the λόγοι, or if he used the verses to guide the content of the λόγοι. Since each of the verses ends with "now, O Father, bless the beginning," we can conclude that Peter viewed them as prayers. Yet, whether they were prayers introducing a sermon, a written treatise, or used as a conclusion to the reading of a text within a monastic gathering remains uncertain.

Regardless, the layout of the *Spiritual Alphabet* may further suggest the universality of Peter's spiritual program for both monastics and non-monastics, since the *Admonition* is an extended discussion of his spiritual program given in great detail, whereas the *Spiritual Alphabet* is the same spiritual program given in less detail. Perhaps the *Admonition* would likely be read by monastics who dedicated their entire life to achieving theosis, while the *Spiritual Alphabet* would be read by a literate non-monastic audience. As well, the introductory verses to each λόγος would make Peter's spiritual theology easily memorable for both illiterate monastics and non-monastics. It is most likely that the *Spiritual Alphabet* appealed to a larger audience since its alphabetical structure and introductory verses made it easier to understand and to memorize.

※ ❧

Exposition of the Spiritual Alphabet

Λόγος Α´

Peter begins this chapter by stating that "the first of all the virtues is spiritual wisdom [πνευματικὴ σοφία], though it is also their consummation [τέλος ὑπάρχη πάλιν]" (211; 112.22–23). Interestingly, Peter does not place "spiritual wisdom" in his list of virtues in the *Admonition* but only speaks of "wisdom." It

---

14 See Nicholas I of Constantinople, *Miscellaneous Writings*, ed. and trans. L.G. West-erlink (Washington, 1981), 17: "may we enjoy the kindness so dear to Him, now and always and for ever and ever, amen" (with Greek text at 16. 129–130).

15 Cunningham and Allen, "Introduction", 1.

seems, rather, that Peter is referring here to the eighth stage of contemplation since spiritual wisdom is the consummation of all the virtues. If this is true, then spiritual wisdom is the "vision of what pertains to God" (142; 59.9). Yet, he continues by saying that spiritual wisdom comes "by grace" and serves as the foundation for all of our learning. For just as "the alphabet is something elementary, unless we learn it we cannot proceed to any more advanced study. In the same way, although our first steps in spiritual knowledge [γνώσεως] may be very slight, unless we make them we will not acquire any virtue at all" (211; 112.26–113.2). Therefore, for Peter, spiritual wisdom equates to spiritual knowledge, which he says is the tenth virtue (according to his list in the *Admonition*).

Peter now turns his attention to a related topic, the intellect, or more properly, to how one learns to say something. In his thought, there are

> four things which make the intellect articulate: first, supranatural grace and blessedness; second, the purity that comes from the practice of the virtues and that restores the soul to its pristine beauty; third, experience of the lower forms of teaching, through human education and secular learning; fourth, the accursed and satanic delusion that works in us through pride and demonic cunning, and distorts our nature. (211; 113.3–9)

First, the intellect is enlightened by God with divine understanding. Second, understanding is a characteristic of a pure soul and the practice of the virtues restores the soul so that it can employ this insight. Third, intelligence comes through human schooling and learning. Fourth, understanding, or more properly, misunderstanding, is the result of demonic delusion. In his humility, Peter states that he shares in none of these four categories. In other words, he has no knowledge. So, Peter asks, how did he write this book? He answers,

> Perhaps the faith of you who in your devotion to God urge me to write will bring grace to my pen; for my intellect and my hand are unworthy and impure. I know from experience that this can happen. For, fathers, whenever I have wanted to write something I have not been able to formulate it in my intellect until I have actually picked up my pen. Frequently it was some small thought suggested by Scripture, or something I had heard or seen in this world, that set my mind to work; but as soon as I took up my pen and began to write, at once I discovered what I needed to say. It is as if someone is forcing me to write the thing down; and when this hap-

pens I begin to write freely and without anxiety for as long as my hand holds out. If God puts something into my darkened heart, I write it down without thinking. (211–212; 113.11–23)

In his answer, Peter provides several interesting fragments of information related to his own intellectual formation, the process used in writing the *Spiritual Alphabet*, and for whom he composed the book. Peter insists in this chapter that he is intellectually unable to write this book. However, this must be accepted with caution since he also claimed his unworthiness to write the *Admonition* (74; 5.6–13), and expressions of humility are typical in Byzantine spiritual writings,[16] though this does not make them mere *topoi*. According to Peter, he received "inspiration" and it was only after he began to write that he understood what the content should be. Ware says that this writing occurred "almost automatically" but this is likely going too far.[17] It is more likely to see this process as a sign of Peter's humility and his attempt to take no credit for the work. Finally, Peter alludes to why and for whom he wrote this work. It appears that he wrote the *Spiritual Alphabet* at someone's request since he writes, "you who in your devotion to God urge me to write." Further, it appears that those who persuaded Peter to write were in a relationship to Peter so that he referred to them as "fathers." We know from the *Admonition* that Peter was a monk who lived the "royal way," likely at the monastery at Areia, which involved "leading a life of silence with one or two companions: these had one another as counsellors in doing God's will. And those who, after being subject to a spiritual father, were then appointed by him to take charge of other brethren, carried out their task as if they were themselves still under obedience, keeping the traditions of their own spiritual fathers" (87; 16.8–12). "Fathers" may refer either to Peter's spiritual directors, assuming that he had more than one, or to his companions in the monastic life. Since the time of the Egyptian desert ascetics of the fourth century, people have called monks "fathers." Even the desert monks used this term themselves. For example, the alphabetical collection of the *Apophthegmata patrum* records that "[i]t was said concerning Abba Daniel, that when the barbarians invaded Scetis and the Fathers fled away, the old man said, 'If God does not care for me, why still live?'"[18] It seems, then, that Peter was

---

16 Cf. John Climacus, *The Ladder of Divine Ascent*, Step 1, 73.
17 *Phil.*, 71.
18 Benedicta Ward, trans., *The Sayings of the Desert Fathers: The Alphabetical Collection* (Kalamazoo, 1975), 51. Greek text in PG 65: 153.

asked to write the *Spiritual Alphabet* by either (or both) his spiritual fathers and/or his monastic companions.

To conclude Λόγος A΄, Peter defends his process of "inspiration" when writing. Using Isaac of Nineveh, Peter says that those who have attained a state of stillness have thoughts come to them spontaneously and are "free from discursive thought [σκέψεως]" (212; 113.27). This is good since discursive thought is subjective and individualistic, Peter believes (212; 113.28–29). Lastly, he says that it is in the spirit of Balaam's ass that he writes "in order to reprove [his] unhappy soul" (212; 113.32). With this, we see that Peter begins the *Spiritual Alphabet* in much the same way that he began the *Admonition*, with a statement about his unworthiness.

Λόγος B΄

This λόγος begins with Peter discussing two types of faith.[19] The first type of faith is that which is "the basis of all actions that conform to God's will, and that we received it through holy baptism" (213; 114.15–17). This faith generates fear

---

19 The schema of virtues found in λόγοι B΄–Z΄ (faith, fear of God, self-control, patient endurance and hope) form a unit that is indebted to Evagrius of Pontus who, in turn, is indebted to Clement of Alexandria. Clement wrote in his *Stromata*: "I affirm, that faith, whether founded in love, or in fear, as its disparagers assert, is something divine; which is neither rent asunder by other mundane friendship, nor dissolved by the presence of fear. For love, on account of its friendly alliance with faith, makes men believers; and faith, which is the foundation of love, in its turn introduces the doing of good; since also fear, the pædagogue of the law, is believed to be fear by those, by whom it is believed. For, if its existence is shown in its working, it is yet believed when about to do and threatening, and when not working and present; and being believed to exist, it does not itself generate faith, but is by faith tested and proved trustworthy. Such a change, then, from unbelief to faith – and to trust in hope and fear, is divine. And, in truth, faith is discovered, by us, to be the first movement towards salvation; after which fear, and hope, and repentance, advancing in company with temperance and patience, lead us to love and knowledge." Alexander Roberts and James Donaldson, eds., *Ante-Nicene Fathers*, rev. A. Cleveland Coxe (1885–96; repr. Peabody, MA, 1995), 2: 354. In his *Praktikos*, Evagrius writes that "[t]he fear of God, my child, strengthens faith, and abstinence in turn strengthens fear of God, and perseverance and hope render abstinence unwavering, and from these is born impassibility of which love is the offspring." Evagrius of Pontus, "Praktikos, Prol. 8," in *Evagrius of Pontus: The Greek Ascetic Corpus*, trans. Robert E. Sinkewicz (Oxford, 2003), 96. In the Evagrian corpus this schema is repeated in "Praktikos 81"; "To Monks 3–5"; and "To Monks 67–69". Evagrius of Pontus *Evagrius of Pontus: The Greek Ascetic Corpus*, 110, 122, 126, respectively. For Antoine

that leads a believer to keep the commandments and to patiently endure "trials and temptations" (213; 114.19). The second type of faith "is born in us, the great faith of contemplation" (213; 114.20–21). Therefore,

> there is, first, the ordinary faith of all Orthodox Christians [ἡ πίστις ἡ κοινὴ τῶν ὀρθοδόξων], that is to say, correct doctrinal belief concerning God and His creation, both visible and invisible, as the Holy Catholic Church, by God's grace, has received it; and there is, second, the faith of contemplation or spiritual knowledge, which is not in any way opposed to the first kind of faith; on the contrary, the first gives birth to the second, while the second strengthens the first. (213; 114.22–27)

This sets Peter up now to give an extended summary of his spiritual program. For, in fact, the two types of faith appear to be referring to two kinds of believers: those with a knowledge of the faith that is available to all Christians through baptism and the teaching of the church, and those with a knowledge of God obtained through contemplation. Or, to say it another way, there are Christians and then there are believers who are progressing in their spiritual life. Regarding the spiritual life Peter writes that

> [w]e acquire the first kind of faith through hearing about it, inheriting it from devout parents and teachers of the Orthodox faith; but the second is engendered in us by our true belief and by our fear of the Lord in whom we have come to believe. For because of this fear we have chosen to keep the commandments and so have resolved to practise the virtues that pertain to the body – stillness, fasting, moderate vigils, psalmody, prayer, spiritual reading, and the questioning of those with experience about all our thoughts, words, or undertakings. We practise these virtues so that the body may be purified of the worst passions – gluttony, unchastity and superfluous possessions – and so that we may be content with what we have, as the apostle puts it (cf. Heb. 13:5). (213; 114.28–115.3)

Guillaumont's argument that Evagrius is dependent on Clement, see Antoine Guillaumont, "Étude historique et doctrinale" in *Évagre le Pontique: Traité pratique or le moine*, ed. Antoine Guillaumont and Claire Guillaumont (Paris, 1971), 1: 21–126, at 52–55.

The results of this spiritual life, says Peter, are devotion to God, knowledge of God's doctrines and commandments and rejection of the eight leading passions.[20] These, in turn, lead to a fear of God that results in the keeping of the commandments with the help of God's grace and a belief that the Orthodox faith is "truly glorious [ὄντως μεγάλη]" (214; 115.12).

Peter uses Basil of Caesarea to say that the acquisition of the second kind of faith is open only to those who do not worry about life or death. This worry-free state comes from one's knowledge that all things come from God, though humans and demons have free will that they often attempt to use in harmful ways but are prevented from doing so by God. In spite of this, a person "should not be at all afraid, since he knows that they are all the creatures of a single Creator [Δημιουργοῦ] and are co-servants with him" (214; 115.18–19). Since God is all-powerful and controls all things "[t]he trials and temptations of righteous and holy men take place with God's consent and contribute both to the perfecting of their souls and to the shaming of their enemies, the demons" (215; 115.39–116.2). This leads the believer to conclude that all things are possible with God and, therefore, he/she tries to do God's will always.

To complete this chapter, Peter again launches into a recollection of his unworthiness. He claims that he is "worse than the infidel, for [he is] unwilling to make efforts to find that greater faith" (215; 116.11–12), that he deliberately breaks God's law and that "at other times [he is] blinded by forgetfulness and enter[s] a state of total ignorance" (215; 116.14–15). These aspects do not characterize the one "who has faith that God is close at hand and not far off" (215; 116.24–25). This person is like a swimmer, writes Peter, since he/she makes progress and does not beat the air (215; 116.27). This person "aspires to the realm above ... So he gains, or rather he is given, the power to ascend from the practice of the virtues to the state of contemplation, through the grace and love of our Lord Jesus Christ" (215–216; 116.28–33). Having begun the *Spiritual Alphabet* with a statement and defense of his methodology in the first chapter, Peter moves directly in Λόγος Βʹ to a summary of his spiritual theology. We should view this chapter, therefore, as the equivalent to Peter's introduction in the *Admonition*.

---

20 These passions as given in the *Admonition* as gluttony, unchastity, avarice, anger, dejection, listlessness, self-esteem and pride (79; 9.34–37) and are discussed in chapter 3, above.

Λόγος Γ´

Having talked about the two kinds of faith, Peter now moves to a discussion of the two kinds of fear. The first is the fear of God and the second is the fear that grows in a person as he/she "struggles to do good" (217; 118.3). The fear of God, "which is the first commandment" (216; 117.9),[21] defeats all eight of the ruling passions, writes Peter, of which gluttony is the first (216; 117.8). He believes that this fear of God leads one to a state of love, whether one realizes this or not. Yet, "[s]hould someone say that he has reached the state of love by some other path, he has been taken captive either by spiritual joy or by his own obduracy" (216; 117.13–15). The proper response is astonishment at "the many blessings that God in His grace has bestowed on him, and he loves his Benefactor" (216; 117.16–17). The obdurate person thinks that if someone who has fear still suffers trials and temptations, then this is the result of sin. This just proves, Peter believes, that the obdurate person lives in a delusion and "is totally unaware of God's forbearance towards him" (216; 117.24). This person will be defenseless on the day of judgment and, unfortunately, there "are many non-believers of this type ... who live comfortably in the present life" (216–217; 117.27–30).

Returning to the topic of the two fears, Peter says that "the first is introductory, while the second, which grows out of the first, is perfect" (217; 117.31–32). The first grows out of a fear of God's punishments and the second results in showing believers their "slightest faults" (217; 118.4). Thus "[w]hen fear in this way has become perfect, he himself becomes perfect through inward grief; he no longer desires to sin but, fearing the return of the passions, he remains in this pure fear invulnerable" (217; 118.6–8). According to Peter, a person continues to fear, not because of sin, but because "the further he advances through the acquisition of the virtues, the more he fears" (217; 118.11–12). Peter believes that what he says applies to all persons regardless of how far advanced in the spiritual life since everyone sins in some small way and "such a person's thoughts need to be corrected, so that he may learn what kind of fear he is subject to, and through the deepest grief and by patiently enduring affliction may purify himself of sins, and in this way through God's grace may attain perfect fear" (218; 118.20–23). In short, "in every situation throughout this present life we ought always to be afraid of falling" (218; 118.25–26).

---

21 On the seven commandments, see 93–100; 20.11–26.19; and my discussion of them in chapter 3.

Λόγος Δ΄

The next eight λόγοι deal with specific virtues, with Λόγος Δ΄ considering self-control (ἐγκράτεια). Before beginning his exposition on the virtues, however, Peter begins with a discussion of true piety (εὐσέβεια), which he sees as, in a way, an all-encompassing term for the acquisition of the virtues. In Peter's spirituality, "true piety consists not in the possession of a single virtue alone, but in the keeping of all the commandments" (218; 119.14–15). According to him, the Greek word for true piety has the meaning of "'to serve well' [καλῶς δουλεύειν]" (218; 119.15). He then insists that serving well is not the same as faith. This is an important distinction for Peter since he has just said in the last chapter that there are two kinds of faith: that present in all believers and that present in those moving forward in the spiritual life. It seems, therefore, that for Peter, true piety is a synonym for the second kind of faith or, in more general terms, the acquisition of the virtues. This is confirmed when he writes that "faith gives rise to fear, and from fear comes true piety" (219; 119.18). Next, Peter progresses into his fuller discussion of the virtues that will encompass the remainder of this λόγος and the next eight λόγοι also. Before discussing the first virtue, self-control, Peter makes a general statement concerning his intentions. He writes,

> This is not the moment to speak systematically about every form of true piety or spiritual activity. Leaving to one side the ascetic practices pertaining to the body that precede the acquisition both of the higher kind of faith and of pure fear – for everyone knows what these practices are – I will speak of the trees of the spiritual paradise, that is, with the help of God's grace I will speak briefly about the virtues of the soul. (219; 119.21–26)

In this statement there are several important items: (1) Peter does not see the *Spiritual Alphabet* as being his systematic treatment of the spiritual life since he likely viewed the *Admonition* as his full treatment; (2) as stated in chapter 3, the seven forms of bodily discipline assist in the acquisition of the virtues; (3) the acquisition of the virtues is only accomplished with God's grace; and (4) Peter states that he will now discuss the virtues, and this is what he does.

For Peter, self-control is the most all-embracing of the virtues. He defines it as "abstinence from all the passions" (219; 119.26–27).[22] He distinguishes this

---

22 Such a simple definition stands in contrast to Evagrius of Pontus who writes that self-control "is a bridge for the stomach, a scourge of immoderation, a balance of

"higher" form of self-control from the "more partial form of self-control, that applies to bodily actions and teaches us the proper use of food and drink" (219; 119.27–29). This higher form of self-control "applies ... to the passions and that [which] restrains every thought and every movement of the limbs that is not in harmony with God's will" (219; 119.29–30).[23] Those who possess self-control do not tolerate any thought or word that is not essential to the life of the body or leads to the soul's salvation. Peter writes that once one has attained this virtue then the trials and temptations, incited by the demons, begin to multiply. This happens because the demons "see before them an embodied angel [ἐν σώματι Ἀγγελον], wholeheartedly committed to doing what is right and good" (219; 119.34–35).

Next, Peter returns to a theme that he considered in the *Admonition*: that one cannot learn about or, much less, acquire the virtues simply by hearing about them. One gains them through experience and then only through God's help. He writes,

> But the experience and acquisition of the virtues require God's help; and they are achieved only through much effort and over a long period of time. This is especially true of the virtues of the soul, for these are the more inward and essential virtues. The virtues that pertain to the body – which are better described as the tools of the virtues – are easier to acquire, even though they do demand bodily effort. But the virtues of the soul, although they demand the control of thought alone, are much more difficult to achieve. (220; 120.10–16)[24]

Unfortunately, says Peter, most people are like the Pharisees because they fast and hold vigils, yet are ignorant of why they do these things. This is the result

---

due proportion, a muzzle for gourmandise, renunciation of rest, the undertaking of austerity, a place of chastisement for thoughts, an eye for vigilance, deliverance from lustful burning, pedagogue of the body, a tower of ascetic works and a wall for our ways, reserve in morals and repression of the passions, mortification of one's (bodily) members, revivification of souls, imitation of the resurrection, a life of sanctification." Evagrius of Pontus, "On the Vices Opposed to the Virtues 2," in *Eva-grius of Pontus*, 60.

23   See also 219; 120.2–5.

24   As argued in chapter 3 we again see that the bodily disciplines assist in the acquisition of the virtues.

of a lack of discrimination so that we "do not know what it is that is being asked of us" (220; 120.21). As well, impatience prohibits a person from gaining the experience that they need from trials and temptations. Because of this state of affairs, Peter suggests that each person should rebuke themselves. Peter is so determined that his message be heard that he forgets his "limitations and [is] no longer troubled about the condemnation that awaits" him if he does not speak and act (220; 120.35–36).

To conclude this Λόγος, Peter returns to his discussion of the virtue of self-control, claiming that he wants to say something further about the virtue. For Peter, he who "enjoys great faith of contemplation together with pure and divine fear," if he wishes to retain possession of self-control "should first master himself both outwardly and inwardly" (221; 120.38–121.2). More pointedly,

> For these reasons every man should make it his whole concern to guard his senses and his thoughts, so as not to devise or do anything that does not seem to be in accordance with God's will. Let him prepare himself to accept patiently the things that befall him at the hands of men and demons, whether these things are pleasant or unpleasant. Neither the one nor the other should excite him or make him give way either to senseless joy and presumption, or to dejection and despair. (221; 121.11–17)

Λόγος Ε΄

Peter dedicates this chapter to the theme of patient endurance (ὑπομονὴ). As demonstrated in chapter 3, patient endurance plays a vital role in Peter's spiritual theology. Here, Peter again intimately connects it to trials and sufferings. He explains that "[p]atient endurance is the consolation of all the virtues, because without it not one of them can subsist" (221; 121.26–28). It is only after having "first endured to the end and escaped from the snares of the devil" (221; 121.30–31) that they can then be confident that they are in possession of all the virtues. This implies that Peter believes that the virtues, once obtained, are not lost again. Yet, it is only after the believer's salvation, during the kingdom of God, that one will possess all the virtues. This present life offers only "a foretaste of the kingdom" (222; 121.32). Thus, in the present context, Peter views patient endurance as that virtue that must be present throughout one's life in order to retain a hold on the other virtues. For, "patient endurance is required before anything can come about; and, once something has come about, it can be sustained and brought to perfection only through such endurance" (222; 122.3–5). If the believer acquires a virtue, then patient endurance "assists and guards it," but if the believer acquires something evil, patient endurance "confers relief and strength of soul" and keeps the person from growing "faint-hearted" (222; 122.5–7). According to Peter, Judas lacked patient endurance, the apostle Peter possessed it and the unchaste monk acquired it.[25]

Using Basil of Caesarea, Peter writes that believers should acquire the virtue of patient endurance before anything else. In this way, they fight the passions one at a time, starting "by patiently enduring whatever befalls [them]" (222; 122.25–26). This is necessary because the enemies of the virtues, the demons, are everywhere whether "in places of solitude and stillness [ἐν ἡσυχίᾳ ... καὶ πειρασμούς]" or in "human company [ἐν μέσῳ τῶν ἀνθρώπων]" (223; 122.35–36).[26] In Peter's thought, endurance is "born of fear and faith" (223; 122.38–39).[27] Susanna serves as the example of one who acquires patient endurance through her fear and faith. Peter believes that "[t]hrough Susanna God has shown how close He is to those who are willing to endure trials for His sake, and who will not abandon virtue out of cowardice because of the suffering involved, but cleave to the law of God by patiently enduring what befalls them" (223; 123.12–16). Peter writes that all believers should be like Susanna and all the saints and rejoice during times of trial; however, if one is unable to do this they should do so "simply out of constraint" (224; 123.23–24). For there are only two choices in this life, "to run bodily risks in this present life, thereby attaining the state of dispassion ... or else ... to fall away through fear of trials" (224; 123.24–26). In closing, Peter uses a vivid metaphor to show the power of patient endurance. Endurance is like "an unshakeable rock" that keeps the believer from falling away and being carried about "in the winds and waves of life" (224; 123.28–29). Therefore, Peter prays, "May God save us from punishment by giving us the strength patiently to endure whatever terrible things befall us" (224; 123.27–28).

25 As identified by the editors of the English translation, the account of the unchaste monk comes from John Cassian's *Conferences*. See Latin text in John Cassian, *Jean Cassien: Conférences I–VII*, ed. E. Pichery (Paris, 1955), 125–127; and English translation in John Cassian, *The Conferences*, trans. Boniface Ramsey (New York, 1997), 95.

26 These references to "solitude and stillness" and "human company" may subtly show that Peter's spiritual program is for all people. If monks live in solitude and stillness, the rest of humankind lives amidst human company. See my discussion in chapter 5 below.

27 By mentioning fear and faith, Peter is connecting this chapter to Λόγοι Β´ and Γ´.

Λόγος Z΄

In Λόγος E΄, Peter talked about patient endurance. Now he discusses the related virtue of hope (ἐλπίδος). Not only are believers to endure patiently, but they are to do so with hope. Hope is what causes farmers to work laboriously, sailors to endure dangers, and children to learn reading and writing. In Peter's thought, "[t]hey do this because they know from experience that they stand to gain something, while in the realm of the spiritual no one has risen from the dead so that we can know what rewards to expect" (225; 124.15). Yet, just as farmers, sailors, and children do these things because they, or someone else, has experienced the benefits of these activities, so those advancing spiritually too should wait patiently "and then, when the time is ripe, we like them will come to know the value of what is happening to us and so will work tirelessly and with joy and gladness" (225; 124.24–28). Again, Peter now turns to one of his favorite subjects: that the virtues come through experience and practice.

Using a comparison, Peter declares that no person in business has ever made a profit from faith alone. Likewise, no one has attained spiritual knowledge without laboring to acquire the virtues. Further, just as a businessperson always fears about loss or gain, so the spiritual person should also have fear. Finally, just as a person in business does not only exert himself or herself to make a profit but also when suffering loss, so should the spiritual person do the same when struggling to attain the virtues. This persistence is the result of hope, says Peter. If someone wants to learn hope through experience Peter recommends the seven forms of bodily discipline and "attention to the moral virtues as well, that is, to the virtues that pertain to the soul" (225; 125.9–10). He teaches that once a person has begun these practices, God begins to grant the virtues, but, like an "inexperienced student" or a "child," people do not realize this, so they view subsequent difficult experiences as trials. Yet, for Peter, "[h]e who wishes to inherit the kingdom of heaven, yet does not patiently endure what befalls him, shows himself even more ungrateful than such a child" (226; 125.24–25). Peter believes that it should be obvious that virtue is something to be desired and that even unbelievers respect "virtue in his opponent" (227; 126.6). In conclusion, Peter insists that God is good and righteous. Therefore, everything that he does is from his goodness, even if it does not appear so. This is why the believer should have hope, because all things come from God and God gives all things for the believer's benefit. The reward in this life for having hope and attaining the virtues, writes Peter, is the contemplation of God's nature as revealed in creation and the Scriptures (227; 126.13–16).

Λόγος Η΄

Peter now considers detachment (ἀπροσπάθεια) since "[d]etachment has its origin in hope, for he who hopes to acquire elsewhere eternal wealth readily despises that which is material and transient, even if it offers him every kind of comfort" (227; 126.28–30). For who, asks Peter, would value material wealth above the love of God? Only a person who lacked faith, for "[h]ad he possessed faith, he would have been enlightened; and had he through his firm faith received but a small measure of the enlightenment that comes from spiritual knowledge, he would have struggled to destroy those evil habits" (228; 127.1–4). Then, with the help of grace, God would have struggled with him. Yet, "few are saved" (228; 127.6). That is, few struggle with God's assistance, but for those who do "the kingdom is within and close to them, because they wish for it, and desire to attain here and now the state of dispassion" (228; 127.17–18). This attainment of dispassion, or salvation, is helped by the "will, and nothing else. If you want to do something good, do it" (228; 127.18–20).[28] In the *Admonition*, Peter also says that the will co-operates with God in attaining the virtues; here he elaborates by saying that the will assists when it overcomes both good and bad habits. In Peter's spiritual theology, the will is an active co-worker with God's grace in attaining the virtues.

Having said this, Peter now returns to the topic of detachment. He believes that detachment from material possessions is difficult for even the naturally poor. Though they renounced what did not belong to them at their baptism, they still "afterwards try to acquire possessions" (229; 127.37). Yet, even monks are prone to want those things that do not belong to their state. Just as salvation is for all people, in Peter's thought, so is the "obligation to keep the other commandments, because they pertain to our nature; that is to say, we are all required to love God and our neighbour, to endure patiently what befalls us, to make use of things according to their true nature, and to refrain from committing evil" (229; 128.10–13). A believer is to do this even if he/she does not want to because these actions are proper to nature, but a monk must do that which is beyond nature. Peter says that there is a reward for obeying God in these matters: "The more we suffer with Christ and imitate His poverty, tasting His sufferings and the ill-treatment to which He was subjected before He was crucified for our

---

28 In this Λόγος, Peter connects dispassion to salvation. This is consistent with his teaching in the *Admonition* where I demonstrated that dispassion results from or is the fruit of salvation.

sake and buried, the more we become with Him and the more we share in His glory" (230; 27–30). In conclusion, Peter, in moving words, invokes the example of those who live in the world, that is, non-monastics. He writes,

> Why, as we know, soldiers and thieves suffer simply trying to get food, travellers and sailors are absent from home for long periods, and people endure great trials quite apart from any hope of the kingdom of heaven, often indeed failing to achieve whatever it is they struggle for. But we are unwilling to endure even slight hardship for the sake of the kingdom of heaven and eternal blessings. Yet these might not prove so difficult to attain if our resolution abetted us and if we regarded the acquisition of the virtues not as a laborious and intolerable task, but rather as a joy and a relaxation, because of the hope, freedom from anxiety and unsolicited honour that come through virtue; for even its enemy respects it and admires it. Finally, virtue brings us happiness and exultation. Indeed, detachment is full of joy, just as material existence and its shameful passions are full of sorrow. May we be redeemed from this material existence, and may we attain eternal, immaterial life through the detachment that leads to the mortification of the body, in Jesus Christ our Lord, to whom belong all glory, honour and worship throughout the ages. Amen. (230; 128.31–129.9)

In short, the acquisition of the virtues is a joyful process whether one suffers little or greatly in the process. In either case, a person is to strive towards attaining all of the virtues and the virtue of detachment assists in obtaining the others.

Λόγος Θ´

Peter shifts to the next λόγος by continuing his discussion of detachment in the first part of Λόγος Θ´ and by connecting it to his next topic, mortification of the passions. He writes, "He who has achieved detachment has his attention fixed always on God through contemplation. For detachment from material things gives rise to the contemplation of spiritual realities ... For the detached person is taught about these things by grace, so that through inward grief he may mortify the passions [νέκρωσιν παθῶν]" (231; 129.16–20). Further, Peter connects this chapter to the preceding λόγοι of the *Spiritual Alphabet* by again discussing faith and fear, true piety, self-control and patient endurance (231; 129.20–32). He then further elaborates on detachment in order to move logically into a discussion about mortifying the passions. According to Peter, "From detachment comes mortification of the body ... For no one still attracted by any sensible object can overcome the passions" (231; 129.23–24, 32–33). Though it appears that saints in the past have, in fact, possessed material things, Peter insists that "they never used any of these objects under the influence of the passions" (231; 130.1–2). Peter writes that this detachment from things is by God's grace and is possible for those who have "a certain degree of spiritual knowledge and can understand the awesome things that occur before and after death as a result of man's primal disobedience" (232; 130.14–16). This then makes mortification of the passions possible since "[d]etachment is mortification, not of the intellect, but of the body's initial impulses towards pleasure and comfort" (232; 130.22–24). Once a person perceives his/her wretchedness and "God's great forbearance," he/she becomes motivated "from doing anything beyond what is unavoidably necessary" (232;130.30–38). Nonetheless, the temptation to pride is always real, therefore, the believer who mortifies the passions must always be on guard not to fall again. For Peter, the Israelite king and prophet David is the example of a person who fell after attaining "such heights," but who restored himself again through repentance (233; 130.39–131.3). Ultimately, such spiritual regression is attributed to the work of the devil,

> [f]or the devil is in the habit of promoting in the soul whatever he sees is in accordance with the soul's own disposition, whether this be joy or self-conceit, distress or despair, excessive toil or utter indolence, or thoughts and actions that are ultimately profitless, or blindness and unreflecting hatred of all that exists. Quite simply, he inflames in the soul whatever material he finds there already, so as to do it as much harm as he can. (233; 131.15–2)

Because of the activity of the devil, Peter argues that each person should be under someone's spiritual direction. Yet, not just anyone's direction is sufficient, but only the guidance of someone with the gift of discrimination, "[f]or without discrimination nothing good is ever done" (234; 131.29). Such discrimination comes through humility, therefore, one's spiritual director should be humble (234; 131.32–33). In conclusion, Peter again connects this λόγος on the mortification of the passions with what he discussed in the previous λόγοι: "From inward grief, then, and patient endurance come hope and detachment; and through hope and detachment we die to the world" (234; 131.34–35). He also includes in his conclusion a transition to the next λόγος on the remembrance of Christ's sufferings. He writes, "Shedding many tears of distress, we begin to see clearly before us the holy sufferings of the Lord, and we are greatly solaced by them" (234; 132.1–3).

Λόγος I´

Knowledge of the sufferings of Christ and the saints is given "[s]o that we will not think that we are doing something great through our ascetic efforts and our many sighs and tears" (234; 132.15–16). The purpose of meditating on the sufferings of the saints and of Jesus Christ is to "become aware of our own feebleness" (234; 132.20). As well, believers become "illumined by the knowledge of what the Lord said and did. And by understanding what is stated in the Gospel, [they] begin sometimes to mourn bitterly in sorrow, sometimes to rejoice spiritually in thanksgiving" (234; 132.21–24). This is not because they have done anything good themselves but because God grants them "the contemplation of these things" (235; 132.25–26). This knowledge of Christ's sufferings leads to humility and results in one practicing the seven forms of bodily discipline and the virtues of the soul and in keeping the Lord's commandments. Believers do not perform these forms of ascesis attempting to receive an award, but because they recognize the debt owed to God and the enormity of the gift of knowledge that God gave to them (235; 132.28–31).

In light of this knowledge given by God, believers progressing spiritually move forward with the assistance of a spiritual director, and pure prayer proper to their spiritual maturity, "while at the same time … [withdrawing their] intellect from all that it has known or heard, and … [concentrating] it on the remembrance of God" (235; 133.5–6). In other words, remembrance of Christ's sufferings is an essential virtue for progressing spiritually. Yet, Peter writes that one should move beyond mere remembrance of Christ's sufferings and instead emulate "Christ's life in this world, and becoming sinless in body and soul, as Christ was" (235; 133.10–11). True imitation (μίμησις) characterizes the spiritual life in Peter's spirituality.[29] Nonetheless, this imitation of the life of Christ should not lead a person to pray with any form, colour or thought in their

---

29 Μίμησις is most often understood by Byzantine scholars as a literary technique. For example, see Herbert Hunger, "On the Imitation (μίμησις) of Antiquity in Byzantine Literature," *Dumbarton Oaks Papers* 23–24 (1969–1970): 16–38. It could also be a reference to Ephesians 5:1: Γίνεσθε οὖν μιμηταὶ τοῦ θεοῦ. *The Greek New Testament*, 4th rev. ed., edited by Barbara Aland, Kurt Aland and Barclay Moon Newman (Stuttgart, 1994), 511.

mind, "in fact it may be extremely dangerous" to do this (235;133.13–14).[30] Peter teaches that since God is "undetermined and indeterminable [ἀπερίγραπτον γὰρ τὸ θεῖον καὶ ἀόριστον], without form or colour" (236; 133.18–19), then the mind is able to be free from forming an image of God in prayer. Images of God that arise in prayer may be the result of demonic activity, since the demons can take whatever shape they want, so one should always be careful and seek the assistance of a spiritual director (236; 133.20–28). Since this is the goal of the demons,

> one ought to constrain the intellect as much as possible within the bounds of some meditation acceptable to God. For as there are seven forms of bodily discipline, so there are eight types of contemplation, or types of spiritual knowledge, that pertain to the intellect. Three of these, which have already been mentioned, are connected with the holy sufferings of the Lord and we should always of our own accord meditate on them, so as to grieve over our own soul and over those of our fellow men. But in addition to these, we should also think about the terrible things that happened at the very beginning because of man's transgression; about how our nature succumbed to so many passions; about our own faults and the trials that occur for the sake of our correction and recovery. Finally we should think both of death and of the fearful punishments that await sinners after death. In this way the soul may be strengthened and devote itself to grief. At the same time it will be solaced and humbled. (236; 133.28–38)

Furthermore, as a result of these actions, the mind gains spiritual knowledge and discrimination that is necessary to make any spiritual discipline effective. All of these activities, says Peter, "have as their goal the preparation and planting of the trees of paradise" (237; 134.12–13) and they receive help from "divine providence, that acts like sun, rain, wind and growth ... For nothing good can come about without help from above" (237; 134.16–19). In Peter's thought, all things come in pairs and the "second does not come until the first has been actualized" (237; 134.22–23). So, without ascetic practice there is no spiritual knowledge, without free will no grace, without fear no hope and without struggle no reward. Oftentimes, however, believers think that they achieve the second

---

30 See also 241; 137.17–19; and chapter 3 of this thesis for a discussion of Peter's concept of "imageless prayer" as acquired from Evagrius.

without possessing the first. Since this is the case, Peter suggests that the believer "ought to cleave to God and to do all things with discrimination. Discrimination comes from seeking advice with humility and from criticizing oneself and what one thinks and does" (237; 134.27–30). To illustrate this truth, Peter gives a series of examples from the literature of the church fathers. This serves as his link to the next two λόγοι where he elaborates on the virtues of humility and discrimination.

Λόγος Κ´

Peter provides the textual link with the previous λόγος by stressing that a humble person undergoes self-reproach "in order to press forward actively and deliberately to embrace the sufferings of Christ" (239; 135.31–32). As in the *Admonition*, Peter reiterates that humility is "the greatest of all the virtues" (239; 135.32) and that it is "the gateway to the kingdom of heaven, that is to say, to dispassion. He who passes through this gateway comes to God" (239; 135.33–136.1). According to Peter, there are two fruits of humility: complete repose and perpetual grace, but humility itself is the "offspring of many different virtues: of obedience, patient endurance, shedding of possessions, poverty, fear of God, spiritual knowledge and others as well. But above all it is the offspring of discrimination" (239; 136.5–7). This makes humility difficult to acquire and beyond a person's natural powers. To gain humility, the spiritual person must acquire the other virtues. For example, since spiritual knowledge "is born of trials and temptations," then one must submit to them, "[f]or it is precisely through undergoing many trials and temptations, and through patiently enduring them, that a man acquires experience" and ultimately, humility (239–240; 136.13–17).

Peter now moves into a discussion of free will, since knowledge is the result of both divine impartation and free will. He writes, "Whatever is good in [humankind] comes from its Creator, and He is also the cause of its being made; but its fall or deviation will depend upon how it exercises its own free will" (240; 136.29–31). Thus when one progresses spiritually, it is the result of God's grace and not one's own ability, and for this reason, God deserves gratitude. For "no one, I trust, is so shameless as to claim that the gift was not freely bestowed on him and to pretend in his iniquity that he deserves praise, calmly puffing himself up and condemning those who are apparently not like him, on the grounds that he himself has conferred on himself the wealth he thinks he possesses, and has not received it by God's grace" (240; 136.37–40). Though each person possesses free will, right choices are the result of God's grace and this remains true throughout one's life, since "no one in this world is perfect ... [because] sin pursues him and will not disappear completely before his death" (242; 137.32–35). "Humility, then," says Peter, "is born from spiritual knowledge, and itself gives birth to discrimination; while from discrimination comes the spiritual insight which the prophet calls 'counsel' (Isa. 11:2). By means of such insight we see things according to their true nature, and the intellect dies to the world because it now contemplates the creation of God" (242; 138.10–14). In this way, Peter moves forward into the next two λόγοι – on discrimination, and on contemplation of the sensible world.

Λόγος Λ´

In Peter's spiritual theology, "[i]t is excellent to seek advice about everything, but only from those with experience. It is dangerous to ask questions of the inexperienced, because they do not possess discrimination" (242; 138.20–21). This is true because "[d]iscrimination knows when the time is ripe, what means to employ, the inner state of the questioner, what level he has reached, his strength, his degree of spiritual knowledge and his intention, as well as God's purpose and the meaning of each verse of Holy Scripture, and much else besides" (242–243; 138.21–24). Having referred everything to a person with discrimination, one must now accept whatever he/she says, even if its importance is unclear. In fact, one of the characteristics of someone with discrimination is that he "is able to communicate the sense of what he says even to those who do not want to know it" (243; 138.28–30). Yet, believes Peter, if there is "in this present generation no one [who] possesses discrimination, it is because no one has the humility that engenders it" (243; 139.1–2). The only remedy for this lack of people with discrimination is to pray, so that God will send down the Holy Spirit upon someone who has overcome the passions and gained humility. God "does not send down his Holy Spirit to someone who has not purified himself from the passions through the practice of the virtues that pertain both to body and to soul [ἠθικῶν]" (243; 139.15–16). Thus a person must first spend time in ascetic practice so that "through his devotion to God he will achieve spiritual insight and will begin to anticipate the snares prepared by the devil and his secret and stealthy attacks" (244; 139.32–35). This spiritual insight, or purified intellect,

emerges from the tyranny of the passions ... Then through humility, comes grace and opens the soul's eye, blinded by the devil, and immediately man begins to see things according to their true nature. He is no longer seduced by the outward appearance of things as he was before. He looks dispassionately on gold, silver and precious stones and is not led astray, nor does he assess them falsely because of his passions ... But the fact that we have served the passions from our youth up, and have practised virtually every form of malice and fraud with complete willingness and zeal, means that it is impossible for us to be freed from such evils and to see things as they truly are without effort, time, and God's help. It is indeed impossible, unless we devote ourselves to the acquisition of the virtues as once we devoted ourselves to the passions, and unless we cultivate these virtues diligently in thought and action. (244–245; 139.37–140.24)

Though this capacity to progress spiritually may come more easily to those whose minds are free from the business of life and under the direction of a spiritual father, it also comes through a "special dispensation of God's grace" (245; 140.18). Peter then reminds his readers that because the passions continually return to a person, this sequence is continual. Despite the difficulty of the process, Peter assures his readers that the end result is humility and, consequently, discrimination.

In the *Admonition*, Peter equated the "counsel" of Isaiah 11:2 with the fifth stage of contemplation (133; 52.17). Then, at the end of Λόγος Κ΄, Peter used this same reference from Isaiah to allude to what was coming in Λόγος Μ΄. In light of this, Peter now, at the end of the λόγος on discrimination, begins to talk about the fifth stage of contemplation, though this chapter has been largely dedicated to the process of acquiring discrimination. This, nevertheless, is logical to Peter, since in the fifth stage of contemplation "we are enabled to look with discrimination at sensible creation and at our own thoughts, not blinded by any delusion, or doing anything contrary to God's purpose because of our subjection to the passions, or submitting to any of our evil thoughts" (246; 141.7–10). In Peter's thought, contemplation of the sensible world, the fifth stage of contemplation, is possible because one has discrimination. With this Peter builds his bridge to the next λόγος.

Λόγος Μ΄

At the start, Peter warns that "[u]ntil our intellect has died to the passions, it should not attempt to embark on the contemplation of sensible realities [κτησάμενος ... τῶν αἰσθητῶν]" (247; 141.33–34). The reason is that

if [the intellect] is still subject to distraction and is unable to devote itself to meditation on the divine Scriptures in stillness and spiritual knowledge, then by turning prematurely to such contemplation we tend to sink more deeply into forgetfulness and gradually to approach a state of ignorance, even though our intellect may have already attained some degree of spiritual knowledge. (247; 141.34–142.2)

This warning applies, in particular, to those whose knowledge has not come through God's grace, but has come through reading and from others who have experience with the mysteries of God. To illustrate this further, Peter uses an agricultural metaphor. He writes, "Just as the earth – and especially good earth – becomes cloddish if the farmer does not work it, so our intellect becomes coarse and obtuse if we do not devote ourselves to prayer and reading, making this our chief task" (247; 142.4–7). Further, "just as the earth, even when moistened by rain and warmed by the sun, yields nothing unless the farmer sows and cultivates it, so our intellect cannot keep possession of spiritual knowledge, even if this knowledge has been bestowed on it by grace, unless we practice the moral virtues, those, that is to say, of the soul" (247; 142.7–10). This, explains Peter, is why the fathers, due to age or lack of physical strength, reduced their practice of the bodily disciplines but they never relaxed the practice of the moral virtues. This is absolutely necessary because "we cannot keep the soul sinless so that the intellect may be illumined unless we practise the virtues of the soul" (248; 142.16–17). Returning to his agricultural metaphor, Peter writes that the "farmer frequently changes his implements, and may even reduce their number, but he never leaves the ground unworked, unsown or unplanted, nor does he ever leave the fruit unprotected if he wishes to gather it" (248; 142.17–20). So, as farmers cultivate the land to grow fruit, so believers are to cultivate the virtues of the soul, even if they are forced to abandon the bodily virtues due to physical limitations. Thus for Peter it is the spiritual development of the mind that is of greater importance than the ascesis of the body.[31] Again, this fits well into Peter's spiritual theology if it is intended for all people and not just monastics.

Shifting his metaphor, Peter now turns to the question of how to maintain the contemplation of sensible realities. Peter warns that there are thieves who attempt to enter into our minds stealthily to distract us, but that the person filled with divine thoughts pays no attention to this intruder. This thief has only one purpose, to "deceive by hearsay, and kill the Scriptures by turning

---

31   See the conclusion to this chapter.

them into allegory, since he is unable to interpret them spiritually" (248; 142.23–25). Yet, the spiritual person, like a shepherd, has compassion for these divine thoughts and, by keeping the divine commandments, "enters in through the narrow gate (cf. Matt. 7:13), the gate of humility and dispassion" (248; 142.28–29). Assistance comes through studying and learning, listening to others and divine grace. Peter writes that

> by grace their intellect may be liberated and may thereby become unforgettingly mindful of God. In this way it comes to know the divine thoughts to which the Holy Scriptures and those with experience in spiritual knowledge bear witness; or else in its perplexity it realizes that in spite of its great knowledge it is still ignorant of them. Then it understands that its former thoughts were trials intended to test its free will. (249; 143.6–10)

In light of this, Peter believes that the humble person will turn away from his/her own thoughts and seek the advice of others but the prideful person will insist that he/she understands his/her own thoughts. Thus, "we should not attempt to embark on contemplation when it is not yet time for contemplation. Let us first acquire in ourselves the mother of the virtues, and then spiritual knowledge will come spontaneously through the grace of Christ" (249; 143.21–24).

Λόγος Ν΄

Having dedicated eight λόγοι to a discussion of the virtues, Peter then in Λόγος Μ΄ inserts into his progression a discussion of the fifth stage of contemplation. In Λόγος Ν΄ he remains within the stages of contemplation, turning now to the seventh stage of contemplation.[32] Though Peter does not provide a link at the conclusion of Λόγος Μ΄ to this chapter, he does so at the beginning of the current λόγος when he writes that "knowledge becomes spiritual after we are firmly established in the contemplation of sensible realities" (250; 143.32). However, not even a gnostic (ὁ γνωστικός) is able, by his own power, to see an angel that is immaterial. Yet, "[f]or the common good ... angels by God's providence often appeared to our fathers in visible form" (250; 144.1–2). Peter insists that this does not happen often because presumption makes

---

32 Compare with his discussion of the seventh stage of contemplation in the *Admonition* (141–142; 58.9–59.7).

seeing an angel an issue of pride instead of for the common good of all persons. According to Peter, angels usually appear when believers do "not think about such things at all, and perhaps do not even believe that they occur" (250; 144.7). So that believers can determine if they desire to see an angel for the right motives, Peter first suggests that they ask themselves whether they secretly wish to experience such a vision. Secondly, Peter also says that they should decide whether they would attach much importance to the vision if it did, in fact, happen. Finally, Peter writes that if believers behaved as though they did not know anything of the state they were in when the vision occurred, then they were worthy of the vision. Peter teaches that angels have the power to appear in one's intellect but the demons must receive this permission from God. A Christian's guardian angel given at baptism, however, chases these demons away in order to protect an individual's free will.[33] To conclude this λόγος, Peter briefly lays out an angelology that is largely derived from Pseudo-Dionysius and various Scriptural passages.

Λόγος Ξ´

For the first time in the *Spiritual Alphabet*, Peter moves to a new λόγος without providing a smooth textual transition. After giving his brief angelology, Peter abruptly moves back into his discussion of the passions that he will continue for the next eight λόγοι. He begins anew with dispassion (ἀπάθεια). In Peter's thought, "[d]ispassion is a strange and paradoxical thing" (251; 145.7). This is true because "once someone has consolidated his victory over the passions, it is able to make him an imitator of God, so far as is possible for man. For though the person who has attained the state of dispassion continues to suffer attacks ... he experiences them as if it were happening to someone else, as was the case with the holy apostles and martyrs" (251–252; 145.7–11). This equilibrium is because dispassionate persons are neither self-elated nor insulted when they suffer. They see that which is pleasant as the result of God's grace while the unpleasant is the result of trials. The ability to know the difference between the two is the result of discrimination.

---

33   See also 76; 7.14–15. In the Byzantine liturgy the priest prays over the baptizand, "Yoke unto his *(her)* life a radiant Angel, who shall deliver him *(her)* from every snare of the adversary, from encounter with evil, from the demon of the noonday, and from evil visions." See Isabel Florence Hapgood, *Service Book of the Holy Ortho-dox-Catholic Apostolic Church*, 3rd ed. (New York, 1956), 273.

As he fleshes out the concept of dispassion, Peter writes that it "is not a single virtue, but is a name for all the virtues ... Similarly, dispassion is the union of many virtues" (252; 145.16–20). Furthermore, dispassion is the result of the ministry of the Holy Spirit in the life of a believer for "unless the Holy Spirit is present can one properly speak of the all-embracing virtue of dispassion" (252; 145.24–25). For without the Holy Spirit what appears as dispassion is, in fact, insensitivity (ἀναισθησία). Peter insists this is true of the "pagan Greeks ["Ελληνες]" who thought that they taught about dispassion but, in Peter's view, could not have an understanding about dispassion since they lacked "the knowledge bestowed by the Holy Spirit" (252; 145.28–29).[34] Peter, having dismissed the "pagan Greeks," now returns again to the teaching of the Christian fathers on dispassion, to show that his teaching on dispassion is Christian. He says that "what we write about the acquisition of the virtues we have learnt from the fathers who were enabled by grace to attain the state of dispassion. For they say that because of his amity with the passions the highly impassioned person becomes like a prisoner and as one who is insensate" (252; 145.32–35). Contrarily, the "man who has attained dispassion becomes impassible out of his perfect love for God. At times he meditates on God, at times on the spectacle of some of God's marvellous works or on a passage from the divine Scriptures" (253; 145.38–146.3). Finally, what characterizes the dispassionate person is that "[e]ven if he is in the market place among crowds of people, his intellect acts as if it were alone" (253; 146.3–5).[35]

Λόγος Ο΄

In this λόγος Peter turns his attention to love and, in his mind, to God since "[t]o speak of love is to dare to speak of God" (253; 146.17). In Peter's thinking love is the "chief [κυριωτέρα] of all the virtues" and it is a natural virtue (253; 146.19–20). This is why it is given pride of place in the Deuteuronomic law where Christians are told they must love the Lord their God with all their heart

---

34 The Greek word ἀπάθεια originated in the philosophical vocabulary of Plato, and the Stoics subsequently elaborated upon this Platonic understanding. It is likely that this is whom Peter is referring to as "pagan Greeks." See Gustave Bardy, "Apatheia," in *Dictionnaire de spiritualité ascétique et mystique: Doctrine et histoire*, ed. Marcel Viller, F. Cavallera and A. Solinac (Paris, 1937), 1: cols. 727–728. This allusion to Greek philosophy indicates that Peter himself had a philosophical education.

35 This reference to "the market place" may, again, demonstrate Peter's desire to make his spiritual program available and applicable to non-monastics.

and "with all their soul, and with all [their] might." Having quoted this verse from Deuteronomy, Peter moves into a brief discussion of the soul. He writes,

> For 'with all your soul' means with the intelligent [λογιστικόν], incensive [θυμικόν] and desiring [ἐπιθυμητικόν] powers of the soul, because it is of these three powers that the soul is composed. Thus the intellect should think at all times about divine matters, while desire should long constantly and entirely, as the Law says, for God alone and never for anything else; and the incensive power should actively oppose only what obstructs this longing, and nothing else. (253; 146.22–27)[36]

In Peter's thought, God sees these three powers of the soul longing for him alone and responds by sending the Holy Spirit to "dwell and move within" the soul (253; 146.30–31). This, in turn, keeps the flesh from working against the Holy Spirit for "[j]ust as the sun and moon, at the command of God, travel through the heavens in order to light the world, even though they are soul-less, so the body, at the behest of the soul, will perform works of light" (253; 147.3–5). Peter warns, though, that just as the sun sets, it is possible for a virtue to disappear so that "passion and darkness come until he again acquires the virtue" (254; 147.8–9). Similarly, "[a]s the sun rises in the furthest east and slowly shifts its rays until it reaches the other extreme … so a man slowly grows from the moment he first begins to practise the virtues until he attains the state of dispassion" (254; 147.10–12). Peter also sees the phases of the moon as an image of the spiritual life. Just as the moon waxes and wanes every month, so does a man wax and wane each day with respect to the virtues.[37] In summary, "[a]t times, in accordance with God's will, he is afflicted, at times he rejoices and gives thanks to God, unworthy as he is to acquire the virtues; and sometimes he is illumined, sometimes filled with darkness, until his course is finished" (254; 147.15–18).

---

36 Peter also discusses these three "powers of the soul" in the *Admonition* (100; 26.26–30).

37 Though Peter never quotes directly from Symeon the New Theologian, this image is found in Symeon's "Fourth Ethical Discourse." See Greek text in Symeon the New Theologian, *Traités théologiques et éthiques*, ed. Jean Darrouzès (Paris, 1967), 2: 62–64. English translation in Symeon the New Theologian, *On the Mystical Life*, 36. Yet, as Golitzin (ibid., 37, n. 4) points out, this image may ultimately go back to Gregory of Nazianzus' "Fifth Theological Oration" which Peter quotes from elsewhere (170–171; 81.18–19).

To bring the discussion back to the love of God, Peter says that all of this happens as a result of God's providence. In a marvelous conclusion to the λόγος, Peter summarizes beautifully the spiritual life and its relationship to love. According to Peter,

> Just as in this present age the sun creates the solstices and the moon waxes and wanes, whereas in the age to come there will always be light for the righteous and darkness for those who, like me, alas, are sinners, so, before the attainment of perfect love and of vision in God, the soul in the present world has its solstices, and the intellect experiences darkness as well as virtue and spiritual knowledge; and this continues until, through the acquisition of that perfect love to which all our effort is directed, we are found worthy of performing the works that pertain to the world to be. For it is for love's sake that he who is in a state of obedience obeys what is commanded; and it is for love's sake that he who is rich and free sheds his possessions and becomes a servant, surrendering both what he has and himself to whoever wishes to possess them. He who fasts likewise does so for love's sake, so that others may eat what he would otherwise have eaten. In short, every work rightly done is done out of love for God or for one's neighbour. (254; 147.19–31)

For Peter, love provides the greatest motivation in the spiritual life. Whether one does something out of love for one's neighbor or for God, the only proper motivation is love.

Λόγος Π´

In this λόγος, Peter talks about knowing God. First, Peter establishes that all things have their origin in and were brought into existence by God. Moreover, all things were brought into existence from non-existence. Yet, God has neither origin nor end, says Peter, nor do his virtues have an origin or end. Second, Peter offers a list of God's virtues and this list is apophatic in nature, saying what God is not, as opposed to what God is.[38] This list is Pseudo-Dionysian in nature and, in fact, Peter quotes Pseudo-Dionysius immediately after he lists God's virtues. According to Pseudo-Dionysius, "the fact that God possesses these virtues does not mean that He is compelled to exercise each of them, as holy

---

38 This apophatic nature is clearly seen in the prefix ἀ used with most of the virtues.

men are" (255; 148.15–17). Holy persons must exercise the virtues because "[i]t is from God … [that] angels and holy [persons] have by grace received the virtues, and it is through emulating Him that they become righteous, good and wise" (255; 148.18–20). This is necessary because both holy persons and angels are creatures and are in need of God's assistance and inspiration. God is able to provide this assistance because he is not a creature, rather he is "bodiless, simple, unoriginate, one God" (255; 148.23–24). Fortunately, humankind can become like God, with one mind that is always focused on the divine, but this does not solve the problem of the sinful body. For although God is bodiless, humankind is not. On account of this the "soul does not reject the body, but uses it for every good work" (255; 148.33–34). A person "does not allow the four constituent elements of the body,[39] or its many members, to do what they wish, nor does he allow the three faculties of the soul to act, or impel the body to act, thoughtlessly and licentiously; but, guided by spiritual wisdom, he makes the will of the three faculties one and indivisible" (256; 148.37–149.3). Controlling all of this activity is the intellect endowed with spiritual wisdom, and spiritual wisdom is constituted by the four virtues of the soul: moral judgment, self-restraint, courage and justice.[40] The next four λόγοι investigate each of these in turn.

Λόγος Ρ΄

According to Peter, "Every other virtue has need of [the four principal virtues], and every undertaking has need of the first – moral judgment [φρονήσεως] – for without it nothing can be brought to a successful conclusion" (256; 149.15–17). For Peter, moral judgment "is born of the intelligence [του λογικου] and constitutes the mean between craftiness – that is, excessive astuteness – and thoughtlessness" (256; 149.18–19). Craftiness pulls moral judgment toward the passions of cunning and guile, while thoughtlessness makes a person obtuse and trivial, says

---

39 According to Byzantine philosophers and theologians, the body consisted of four elements (στοιχεια): earth (dry and cold), water (cold and wet), air (wet and warm) and fire (warm and dry). See Peter Brown, *The Body and Society: Men, Women and Sexual Renunciation in Early Christianity* (New York, 1988), 9–11; and Teresa M. Shaw, *The Burden of the Flesh: Fasting and Sexuality in Early Christianity* (Minneapolis, 1998).

40 In the *Admonition* Peter discusses these four virtues at 100–101; 26.21–26. As well, these are the first four virtues given in Peter's list of virtues near the end of the *Admonition* (203; 106.2).

Peter. Furthermore, thoughtlessness "does not allow the intellect to concentrate on divine matters or on something of profit to one's soul or to one's neighbour" (256; 149.21–23). For Peter, a person of moral judgment walks between the extremes of craftiness and thoughtlessness. This "middle way" is the "royal road of virtue" and one "keeps to this with the help of Christ our Lord" (257; 149.30–33).

Λόγος Σ´

"Self-restraint [σωφροσύνη] is a sure and unfailing sense of discretion ... [that] does not permit its possessor to lapse into either licentiousness or obduracy, but safely preserves the blessings reaped through moral judgments while rejecting all that is bad," writes Peter (257; 150.5–8). It unites intelligence to itself and leads this intelligence up to God. More importantly, "Like a good shepherd it folds the sheep – the divine thoughts – and through refraining from what is harmful it slays licentiousness as if it were a mad dog. It expels stupidity as though it were a fierce wolf, and prevents it from devouring the sheep one by one" (257; 150.9–12). Unlike moral judgment that is born of the intelligent part of the soul, self-restraint "is born of the desiring power of the soul" (257; 150.14–15). One cannot maintain anything good without self-restraint, for without it "the soul's three powers are carried either upward towards licentiousness or downwards towards stupidity" (257; 150.16–17). Using Peter's analogy, self-restraint is the shepherd of the soul, keeping it within its God-established boundaries but also keeping out that which affects the soul and body. In Peter's words, "self-restraint disciplines all things and bridles the mindless impulses of soul and body, directing them towards God" (257; 150.20–23).

Λόγος Τ´

Moving to the third virtue of the soul, courage (ἀνδρείας), Peter once again defines the virtue through the passions that he views as being opposed to it. For courage, those are overbearingness and cowardice.[41] He writes that

[c]ourage does not consist in defeating and oppressing one's neighbour; for this is overbearingness, which oversteps the bounds of courage. Nor

---

41 Peter provides a list of these eight "unnatural passions" that oppose each of the four virtues of the soul in the *Admonition* (101; 26.30–34).

again does it consist in fleeing terrified from the trials that come as a result of practising the virtues; for this is cowardice and falls short of courage. Courage itself consists in persisting in every good work and in overcoming the passions of soul and body. (258; 150.30–151.3)

Peter believes that overbearingness and cowardice are both caused by weakness "though they appear to be opposites" (258; 151.8). For "[o]verbearingness pulls one upwards and is outwardly something startling and frightening, like some powerless bear, while cowardice flees like a chased dog" (258; 151.9–11). No one, says Peter, who struggles with these two passions places proper trust in God, therefore they cannot withstand a battle. Those with courage, on the other hand, are "as bold as a lion," so they are victorious in battle (258; 150.13–14).[42]

Λόγος Υ´

To conclude his λόγοι on the four virtues of the soul, Peter now discusses justice (δικαιοσύνη). Peter thinks that "without justice all things are unjust and cannot endure" (258; 151.23–24). Further, "[j]ustice is sometimes called discrimination: it establishes the just mean in every undertaking, so that there will be no falling short due to over-frugality, or excess on account of greed" (258; 151.24–26). As Peter states, both over-frugality and greed push one towards injustice. If a line is convex or concave, it deviates in one direction or the other, giving a benefit to the side to which it curves. The same is true of the passions and the virtues. If one does not walk between two passions then one is not in possession of the virtue that characterizes the middle way. Justice is that virtue which keeps the other virtues from deviating from this straight line, or middle way. A spiritual person "is neither dragged down through thoughtlessness, licentiousness, cowardice or greed ... nor does [he/she] fall victim to craftiness and overbearingness, to stupidity and over-frugality, to excessive astuteness and cunning" if he/she possesses the virtue of justice given by the grace of God (259; 151.33–152.2). If one ascribes the possession of justice to one's own ability, one, in reality, commits an injustice. Likewise, he who "thinks that any good thing he possesses is due to himself, then what he thinks that he has will be taken

---

42   At this point it is observable that Peter often draws his imagery from either agricultural or zoological contexts. This suggests, perhaps, that Peter's monastic cell was located away from a metropolitan environment and was likely located in a rural area of the Byzantine Empire, like that at Areia.

away from him" (259; 152.4–6). Thus by devoting these last four λόγοι to the four virtues of the soul; Peter fleshes out in more detail the characteristics of these virtues that were only briefly mentioned in the *Admonition*.

Λόγος Φ´

In the *Admonition*, Peter's seventh commandment was peace (97; 24.10). He now returns to this commandment by trying to define the true meaning and depth of peace as a virtue. In the *Admonition*, Peter based his comments regarding peace on the words of Jesus Christ in the fifth chapter of the Gospel of Matthew. Significantly, Peter begins this discussion of peace by also quoting Jesus Christ, though this time he uses John 14:27 as the basis. Peter insists that the true peace of Christ is not the peace that is given "in a simple, conventional manner, as people do when they greet one another with the words 'Peace to you'" (259; 152.16–17). According to Peter, "Christ's peace is the peace which transcends every intellect ... and which God gives to those who love Him with all their soul, because of the dangers and battles they have been through" (259; 152.19–21). In Peter's spiritual theology, the afflictions and the dangers that a person experiences at the hands of the demons and other people are as nothing if one possesses the Lord's peace. In addition to afflictions and dangers, "each of us faithful is attacked and led astray by the passions; but if he is at peace with God and with his neighbour he overcomes them all" (260; 152.28–30). In short, Peter teaches that peace makes the patient endurance of trials and tribulations possible, but this is only when the soul is at peace. Peter writes that the "soul is at peace with God when it is at peace with itself and has become wholly deiform [κατὰ θεόν]. It is also at peace with God when it is at peace with all men, even if it suffers terrible things at their hands" (260; 152.31–153.3). The soul at peace is able to live "in a state of noetic contemplation and pure prayer to God," believes Peter (260; 153.8–9). Thus Peter sees the presence of peace in one's soul as a foundational virtue in the spiritual life. In light of this, it is imperative that each believer strive to attain this true and Christ-like peace.

Λόγος Χ´

Spiritual joy occurs near the end of Peter's list of virtues in the *Admonition* (204; 106.35) and now he devotes all of Λόγος Χ´ to the topic. Using the apostle Paul's admonition to "Rejoice in the Lord" (Phil. 3:1), Peter says that "he was right to say, 'in the Lord'. For if our joy is not in the Lord, not only do we not rejoice, but in all probability we never shall" (260; 153.17–19). Acknowledging Job, Basil of Caesarea and Gregory of Nyssa as his inspirations, Peter argues that nature teaches humankind to grieve because life is full of pain and effort, "like a state of exile dominated by sin" (260–261; 153.25). The animal world rejoices because of its lack of awareness but humankind is not endowed with such innocence. Yet, a person does not have to remain in this state of grief. Rather, "if a person is constantly mindful of God, he will rejoice ... For when the intellect is gladdened by the remembrance of God, then it forgets the afflictions of this world, places its hope in Him, and is no longer troubled or anxious" (261; 153.25–29). This loss of anxiety makes one joyful and thankful, and as God grants additional blessings one continues to be more joyful and thankful.

This process, writes Peter, is slow and follows a particular pattern. Peter states that "[t]hrough the things that bring him pleasure, he is made humble and grateful; through trials and temptations his hope in the world to come is consolidated; in both he rejoices, and naturally and spontaneously he loves God and all men as his benefactors" (261; 154.1–3). As a result, believers find nothing in the whole of creation that can harm them, so they rejoice in the Lord on account of the creation, amazed by God's care for it. Furthermore, the person who attains spiritual knowledge moves beyond perception of the visible creation to the perception of God's invisible creation. In Peter's words,

> he looks with wonder not only on the light of day, but also at the night. For the night is a benediction to all: to those practising the virtues that pertain to the body it offers stillness and leisure; it encourages the remembrance of death and hell in those who grieve; those engaged in practising the moral virtues it spurs to study and examine more closely the blessings they have received and the moral state of their souls ... For the practice of the moral virtues is effectuated by meditating on what has happened during the day, so that during the stillness of the night we can become aware of the sins we have committed and can grieve over them. (261; 154.9–21)

In essence, Peter believes that once one acquires spiritual joy, one is able to advance spiritually because one no longer meditates exclusively on the grief that comes through knowledge of nature. Spiritual joy helps believers to contemplate God's creation properly because the condemnatory aspects of creation resulting in grief do not distract them.

Having shifted into a discussion about the bodily and moral virtues, Peter continues with this topic throughout the remainder of the λόγος. As spiritual persons make progress both bodily and morally through God's grace, they give thanks with fear and humility to God. The next step, says Peter, is to "struggle to preserve that moral virtue by means of prayer and many tears offered to God ... For it takes much time to make a moral virtue effective in ourselves, while what has been achieved with so much time and effort can be lost in a single instant" (262; 154.25–29). Peter's spiritual theology consistently emphasizes that for "those practising the virtues [πρακτικῶν]" (262; 154.29) the spiritual life progresses through much effort and any progress that is made can be lost in an instant.[43] Yet, the same is not true for those in the stages of contemplation. For them, they contemplate God's creation, causing them to feel "alone in the world like Adam and, united with the angels, in full knowledge [they] praise the Maker and Creator of the universe" (262; 155.2–4). Peter sums up his own thought when he writes, "In short, the man of spiritual knowledge finds that everything contributes to his soul's salvation and to God's glory ... [so his goal] is to suffer with the Lord through dispassion and spiritual knowledge, and to boast because of Him, in that, unworthy though he is, he has been enabled by God's grace to be a servant of such a master and imitator of His humility" (263; 155.14–16, 24–27).

Λόγος Ψ´

As discussed in chapter 3, Peter had much to say concerning the Holy Scriptures in the *Admonition*. In the *Spiritual Alphabet*, he dedicates Λόγος Ψ´ to the topic. Just as he did in the previous λόγος on joy, Peter begins this λόγος with scriptural quotations. First, he quotes the psalmist who writes, "Sing the psalms with understanding" (Ps. 47:7). Second, he quotes Jesus Christ who said, "Search the Scriptures" (John 5:39). Immediately, Peter explains why singing and reading the Scriptures is necessary: "He who pays attention to them is illumined [φοτίζεται], while he who pays no attention is filled with darkness. For unless a person attends to what is said in divine Scripture, he will gather but little fruit, even though he sings or reads them frequently" (263–264; 156.8–10). This is especially true of those who have "made some progress in the practice of the moral virtues" (264; 156.12–13) and know only in part since the intellect is still affected by the passions, says Peter. Yet, the believer who has made little progress "does not know all the mysteries hidden by God in each verse in Scripture, but

---

43 On the early Christian teaching regarding spiritual progress, see Jeremy Driscoll and Mark Sheridan, eds., *Spiritual Progress: Studies in the Spirituality of Late Antiquity and Early Monasticism* (Rome, 1994); and Jeremy Driscoll, *Steps to Spiritual Perfection: Studies on Spiritual Progress in Evagrius Ponticus* (New York, 2005).

only as much as the purity of his intellect is able to comprehend through God's grace" (264; 156.14–16). This is proven by "the fact that we often understand a certain passage in the course of our contemplation, grasping one or two of the senses in which it was written; then after a while our intellect may increase in purity and be allowed to perceive other meanings, superior to the first" (264; 156.16–20). In Peter's thought, then, an understanding of the Scriptures is aided by progress in the spiritual life. The more advanced one is spiritually, the more one is able to understand the mysteries hidden in the Scriptures.

As in the *Admonition* (144–145; 60.7–61.15), Peter insists that there are no contradictions in the Scriptures. For those who are advanced spiritually distrust their understanding of the Scriptures enough to find either another scriptural passage or a comment from one of the "saints" that confirms their understanding of a scriptural passage. This can result in multiple meanings of the same passage, but one "should not lose faith and think that there is a contradiction. For one text or object can signify many things" (264; 156.29–30). This principle, acknowledges Peter, "applies to everything, whether visible or invisible, and to every word of the divine Scriptures. For the saints neither know the whole of God's purpose with regard to every object or scriptural text, nor on the other hand do they write down once and for all everything that they do know" (264–265; 157.2–5). Since God is incomprehensible and his wisdom is not limited in such a way as to be understood by humankind, and because the mental capacity of each believer varies, then there will always be multiple understandings of the Scriptures. The principle of non-contradiction, for Peter, applies to the writings of the fathers also, since they are not saying something contrary to the truth of the Scriptures. Peter writes,

For this reason the same saint may say one thing about a certain matter today, and another tomorrow; and yet there is no contradiction, provided the hearer has knowledge and experience of the matter under discussion. Again, one saint may say one thing and another say something different about the same passage of the Holy Scriptures, since divine grace often gives varying interpretations suited to the particular person or moment in question. The only thing required is that everything said or done should be said or done in accordance with God's intention, and that it should be attested by the words of Scripture. (265; 157.13–20)

As an example, Peter uses the book of Hebrews and Pseudo-Dionysius as examples. He says that some claim that the apostle Paul did not write the book of

Hebrews, whereas others say that Pseudo-Dionysius did not write one of the treatises ascribed to him. Peter believes that these are the mistakes of someone without experience,

> [b]ut if a man will pay attention to these same works, he will discover the truth. If the matter pertains to nature, the saints gain their knowledge of it from spiritual insight, that is, from the spiritual knowledge of nature and from the contemplation of created beings that is attained through the intellect's purity; and so they expound God's purpose in these things with complete accuracy, searching the Scriptures. (266; 157.33–37)

In short, a mistake in understanding the Scriptures or the fathers is the result of spiritual immaturity. The spiritually advanced believer avoids these mistakes.

Having discussed those things "that pertain to nature" (266; 158.1), Peter now moves on to a discussion of those things that are beyond nature. When the saints know something that is beyond nature, they "know about it through the gift of prophecy and through revelation, provided that such knowledge is given them by the Holy Spirit" (266; 158.4–6). A true saint, writes Peter, is one who will admit when he/she does not know something, just as Paul the apostle, Solomon and John Chrysostom confessed that they also had limited knowledge (266; 158.8–11). "In short," writes Peter, "the saints possessed both spiritual and secular knowledge but preferred the first; they made use, however, of their worldly education wisely and for a limited purpose ... [For] the fathers themselves often deliberately write in a very simple manner, depending on the particular circumstances and the people for whom they were writing" (266–267; 158.11–13, 20–21). Such simplicity is the result of humility because "[w]hoever is experienced in the spiritual interpretation of Scripture knows that the simplest passage is of a significance equal to that of the most abstruse passage, and that both are directed to the salvation of man" (267; 159.4–6). In Peter's thought, the Holy Spirit and one's secular education work together. A person's secular education acts as a "vehicle for the higher wisdom of the Spirit. For the wisdom of the Spirit bestows inspired thoughts, while secular learning provides power of expression, so long as it is accompanied by moral judgment and ... humility" (268; 159.8–10).[44] According to Peter, one

---

44 This section on secular education and spiritual wisdom may be autobiographical. Perhaps Peter is explaining how he is combining both the secular education that

understands the Scriptures better the farther one advances spiritually. Further, God gives the highest knowledge to the saints who then, using their secular education, write down this spiritual knowledge and holy wisdom for others to benefit from also. In this light, all knowledge of the Scriptures is a gift of God's grace.

Λόγος Ω´

Peter concludes the *Spiritual Alphabet* with a discussion about what he calls "insight into the heart" (αἴσθησιν τῇ καρδίᾳ); however, this λόγος serves, in many ways, as a treatise on patient endurance and as a summary of Peter's spiritual program. Peter begins with a discussion of sin and the battle between the passions and virtues within each person. Yet, he finds hope when he realizes that "many, because they had a firm faith, received crowns of victory after going through battles and trials like these. It was because of their faith that they were granted fear of God; and through this fear they were enabled to practise the other virtues" (269; 160.7–10). Peter insists that one who has this kind of faith is granted the virtues because "[t]hese are the gifts conferred on those who, free from anxiety, wait on God and devote themselves to the Holy Scriptures with the patience that makes it possible to view all things, whether from above or from below, with an equal mind" (269; 160.13–15). Time and experience, says Peter, make it clear when a virtue replaces a passion. When a virtue veers back toward a passion the believer is to endure it patiently "[f]or if such endurance is not born in the soul out of faith, the soul cannot possess any virtue at all" (269; 160.17–18). Throughout this process we need a spiritual guide, but if a visible guide is unavailable then we are to have Christ as our guide or else Satan will guide us. Those who have Satan as guide lack patient endurance so they impetuously hurry to seize those things that are not properly their own. Yet, "he who by enduring patiently has gained experience of the devil's machinations will fight and strive forward with patience so as to reach the goal" (270; 160.33–34). Since Satan is so active, and those without experience are prone to his temptations, it is good for an inexperienced believer to say, when tempted, "I do not know" (270; 160.39). Thus "In this way we reach the haven of active spiritual knowledge" (270; 161.5).

---

he received before becoming a monk and his spiritual knowledge together to write this book. It was suggested above that Peter received a philosophical education. If this is true, it is more likely that Peter is, in fact, writing autobiographically.

Peter continues this discussion by writing that patient endurance is the result of fear, therefore, "we should never abandon fear until we have reached the haven of perfect love and are no longer in the world or the body. Even the person who has reached that haven will not abandon such fear of his own accord ... It is through fear in the face of such blessings that God leads the soul towards love, so that ... it may become worthy of the good things that have been and will be bestowed on it" (271; 161.18–21, 26–29). Moreover, they who receive these blessings from God must never think for a moment that it is due to their own actions. Rather, God gives all things through grace. Peter writes that discrimination gives a person some spiritual knowledge but ultimately he is thrown back on the grace of God because "he sees how many men, beginning with Adam, have fallen in spite of their efforts and their knowledge ... Thus the man who acknowledges that he is stupid and witless, ignorant and weak, weeps and laments because he thought he had received what he now realizes that he does not have" (271–272; 162.34, 8–11). In short, he gains humility.

Returning again to the chief of all the virtues, Peter reminds his readers that humility is also "born of many virtues, and in its turn gives birth to things more perfect still" (272; 162.11–12).[45] He describes how this works in great detail (272–275; 162.13–164.30).[46] In summary, Peter teaches that:

1. Believers realize they are sinners, which causes them to practice self-control and patient endurance in the face of voluntary and involuntary trials.

2. When their patient endurance of trials proves their worthiness, they receive great faith through which they gain victory over their enemies.

---

45 In Λόγος Ο´ Peter writes that love is the "chief [κυριωτέρα] of all the virtues" (253; 146.19–20) whereas in Λόγος Κ´ humility is said to be the "greatest [μείζονα] of all the virtues" (239; 135.32). Peter makes a distinction between being "chief" and "greatest" and is I think, therefore, not contradicting himself.

46 Peter indicates the termination point of this extended summary of the spiritual life by writing, "This, then, is the position of those who have acquired the virtues [Καὶ οὕτω μὲν γίνεται πρὸς τοὺς ἐναρέτους]" (275; 164.29–30).

3. Once they achieve this victory over their enemies, they become aware of their own weaknesses and ignorance.

4. As a result of this weakness and ignorance, they give thanks with humble souls and tremble in fear that they may relapse into disobedience.

5. Due to this fear, they begin to have hope that by God's grace they will obtain mercy.

6. In his mercy, God gives greater humility and more intense prayer from the heart and the more these increase the greater knowledge the humble person receives.

7. After receiving increased knowledge, a humble person contemplates both the particular and universal blessings of God.

8. By not being able to adequately give thanks for these blessings, the humble person grieves and weeps "when he regards himself as lower than all other men and does not even think that he is anybody at all, but holds himself indebted to God and to all men as much as to God" (273; 163.1–3).

9. While experiencing these tears the humble person's intellect begins to attain purity, returning to its prelapsarian state, that is, to the state of natural spiritual knowledge. According to Peter, this natural spiritual knowledge comes from discrimination and allows one to contemplate God's visible creation. Yet, this knowledge is darkened by the passions, therefore one practices the virtues to regain this natural spiritual knowledge.

10. Those who acquire and maintain this natural spiritual knowledge may be granted by God, through grace, the "gift of prophecy" (274; 163.23).

Having reached the end, Peter summarizes his thought by writing, "For from faith is born fear, and from fear comes inward grief. This in turn produces humility, which gives rise to discrimination. Discrimination, finally, gives birth to spiritual insight and, by God's grace, to the gift of prophecy" (275; 164.11–13). Before concluding this excursus on the stages of the spiritual life, Peter takes a moment to admonish the gnostic, that is, the person who has the gift of prophecy. For Peter, "The gnostic ought not to rely in any way on his own thoughts, but should always seek to confirm them in the light of divine Scripture or of the nature of things themselves" (275; 164.13–15). This is true, writes Peter, because the Scriptures speak of those things that can save the soul; as well, it intends to reveal the mysteries that it contains including "the inner principles of created things, that is, the purpose for which each thing was created" (275; 164.20–21). The Scriptures illumine the intellect enabling it to perceive the true nature of God that in turn makes us afraid of breaking his commandments. In a sense, Peter is saying that the gnostic is the one who knows the true meaning and the purpose of the Scriptures. In addition, the gnostic also knows the true nature of God both through a full understanding of the Scriptures and through the gift of prophecy.

Concluding his admonition of the gnostics, Peter now writes to those "who lack knowledge" (275; 164.30). For these persons, God sends trials and temptations so that they will refrain from sin, while at the same time bestowing on them bodily blessings to keep them from despondency. God does this in his goodness so that everyone can come to salvation. In the same way, "in accordance with the propensity of each reader and with what is to his profit, God either conceals the meaning of Holy Scripture or allows it to be known" (275–276; 164.36–38). Unlike the "teachers of secular wisdom" (276; 164.38) who tried to discover God through their own efforts, Peter says that such knowledge comes only through "the humility and the simplicity that come through faith, that is, through the contemplation of the Scriptures and of created beings" (276; 165.1–3). For Peter, the saints serve as the role models for those struggling to progress spiritually. In short, God does all things for the salvation of humankind. This is why "we ought to abandon other things and as intelligent beings cleave to the intelligence, offering with the intelligence intelligible worship to the divine Intelligence [ὀφείλομεν καταλιπεῖν πάντα καὶ τὸν λόγον ὡς λογικοὶ προτιμῆσαι καὶ λόγους λόγῳ προσφέρειν τῷ τοῦ Θεοῦ Λόγῳ]" (277; 165.26–28). Peter stresses again, however, that any progress is only possible through humility. For "self-satisfied haughtiness [ἡ ὑψηλοφροσύνη τῇ αὐταρεσκείᾳ]" (278; 166.15) reduces one's ability to progress spiritually.

To conclude the *Spiritual Alphabet*, Peter returns to a consistent theme throughout his entire corpus. He again insists that what he is teaching did not originate with him. Rather, he learned these things from his spiritual father. He writes, "I am not here recording something that I discovered with my own understanding and discrimination, but I write what I have learnt from the saint who was my spiritual father" (278; 166.23–25).[47] This claim is then supported with several insights that Peter apparently learned from his spiritual father about how past saints have modeled the spiritual life as understood by Peter. In conclusion Peter writes,

> For the prophets, apostles and martyrs did not gain their knowledge of God and their wisdom at second hand, as we have gained ours. On the contrary, they poured out their blood and received the Spirit ... Thus the fathers suffered martyrdom, not in an outward sense, but in their conscience: instead of undergoing physical death they showed themselves willing to die, and in this way their intellect proved victorious over all earthly desires and reigns in Christ Jesus our Lord. (280–281; 168.15–21)

Concluding Remarks

As stated in the introduction to this chapter, I conclude that although the organization of the *Spiritual Alphabet* is in twenty-four Λόγοι, its purpose is to summarize Peter's spiritual theology as given in the *Admonition*. Peter's own words reveal his understanding of the spiritual life as explained in the *Spiritual Alphabet*. Apart from Λόγος Ω′, there are two other places in the *Spiritual Alphabet* where Peter summarizes his spiritual theology. The first occurs at the end of Λόγος Ι′, where Peter writes, "Ascetic practice is a good thing, but only when done with the right goal in mind. We ought to think of it not as the real task, but as a preparation for the real task; not as the fruit, but as the earth that can – with time, labour and the help of God – bear trees from which the fruit will

---

47 As illustrated repeatedly throughout the *Spiritual Alphabet*, Peter lays great stress on the role of experience as a prerequisite of knowledge. For example, he writes, "I know from experience that this can happen" (211; 113.13) and "those with experience in spiritual knowledge bear witness" (249; 143.7–8). Peter's confession that what he knows he learned from his spiritual father may be the result of his not having experienced all that he discusses in the *Spiritual Alphabet*. For instance, in Λόγος Μ′ Peter talks about contemplation of the sensible world. Yet, if Peter never reached this level of contemplation then he would not be able to speak about it since experience is vital to the attainment of knowledge. For Peter, however, he could gain knowledge from someone else (in this case his spiritual father) who had the requisite first-hand experience. On the role of experience in another Byzantine spiritual writer, see H.J.M. Turner, *St. Symeon the New Theologian and Spiritual Fatherhood* (Leiden, 1990), 113–117.

come: the fruit that is purity of intellect and union with God [ἕνωσις τῷ Θεῷ]" (238–239; 135.15–20). In this short statement, we see Peter's understanding that the spiritual life is not simply how one lives, whether monastic or non-monastic. Nor does Peter view the spiritual life as composed of a series of rules and regulations that must be followed to the letter. Rather, for Peter the spiritual life has one purpose, union with God. This is why Peter dedicates more space in his corpus to discussing the virtues and the results of acquiring the virtues than he does to giving explicit details about how to perform ascetic practices. For Peter, the goal is one's salvation, not a strict ascetic life.

The second summary of Peter's spiritual theology appears at the end of Λόγος Λ΄. He writes,

> For if we endure with patience, and do not grow presumptuous or lapse from virtue, we will be raised from the deathlike state of the body and of material things to the spiritual knowledge of created realities. Indeed, according to St. Paul [κατὰ τὸν Ἀπόστολον] (cf. Rom.6:4–6), we are crucified with Christ bodily through the practice of bodily discipline, and in soul through the practice of the virtues that pertain to the soul. We are then buried through the mortification of the senses and of natural knowledge. Finally, through attaining the state of dispassion we are resurrected spiritually in Christ Jesus our Lord. (246–247; 141.19–26)

Again, Peter displays that his spiritual theology is not a "how to" book of the spiritual disciplines. Rather, his spiritual theology concerns itself with the salvation of humankind. Beginning with humankind's sinfulness ("the deathlike state of the body"), Peter summarizes the stages of his spiritual program, culminating in a spiritual resurrection in Christ Jesus. For Peter, true spirituality is the perfect contemplation of God, not the means by which one attains this state of contemplation. Though Peter speaks at length on these means, he always keeps the ultimate goal of pure contemplation in view.

CHAPTER FIVE

Monk and Laity in the Thought of Peter of Damascus

It is evident that Peter is, without doubt, a monk and without question his spiritual program is envisioned by Peter himself to be largely applicable to his fellow monastics. Peter makes this abundantly clear early in the *Admonition to his own soul* when he writes,

> The person enabled by grace to devote himself utterly and always to God [καταξιωθεὶς ὁλοκλήρως καὶ ἀείποτε σχολάζων] has achieved the highest good; he who has not reached this point should take care not to grow negligent in any way. Blessed are they who are completely devoted to God [ὁλοκλήρως σχολάζοντες],[1] either through obedience to someone experienced in the practice of the virtues and living an ordered life in stillness [ἡσυχάζοντι κατὰ τὸν λόγον], or else through themselves living in stillness and total detachment [ἡσυχία καὶ ἀμεριμνία ἐκ πάντων], scrupulously obedient to God's will, and seeking the advice of experienced men [ἐμπείρων] in everything they say or think. Blessed above all are those who seek to attain dispassion and spiritual knowledge unlaboriously through their total devotion to God [ὁλοκλήρου καὶ κατὰ Θεὸν σχολῆς]: as God Himself has said through His prophet, 'Devote yourself to stillness and know that I am God' (Ps. 46:10). (103–104; 29.3–11)

That is, those who are monks have achieved the "highest good [ἀκροτάτου ἀγαθοῦ]" and are the "blessed." Peter reiterates this sentiment again in the *Spiritual Alphabet* when he writes,

---

1   On the use of σχολάζοντες as a description for a monk, see John Climacus, *The Ladder of Divine Ascent*, Step 29; trans. Colm Luibheid and Norman Russell (New York, 1982); PG 88: 1152B: Σχολάσωμεν, ἀδελφοί, καὶ γὰρ σχολασταὶ ἀπεγράφημεν.

If by Christ's grace someone is religious, or a monk [εὐλαβής, ἢ καὶ Μοναχός], what prevents him from achieving sanctity, as criminals have achieved it? They were far from sanctity, he is near it; he has already completed the greater part of the journey, helped by grace, or by nature, or by the devotion and reverence he has inherited from his parents. Is it not strange, then, that when brigands and grave-robbers become saints, monks are condemned? ... In what way is the monk exceptional if he does not persevere in virginity and a state of total dispossession? All men are under an obligation to keep the other commandments, because they pertain to our nature; that is to say, we are all required to love God and our neighbour, to endure patiently what befalls us, to make use of things according to their true nature, and to refrain from committing evil. We should keep these commandments even if we do not want to ... Everyone does and wants to do these things because they accord with nature – indeed, we insist that they should be done. But the lot of the monk as a soldier of Christ is to do that which is beyond nature. (228–230; 127.25–128.20)

For monks, says Peter, the average or natural Christian life is not wholly sufficient. Rather, monastics must strive to move "beyond nature [ὑπὲρ φύσιν]," though this does not necessarily mean that he believes that *only* monks and nuns can achieve this supernatural level of spiritual commitment and maturity. Peter's expectation appears to be that monastics will move beyond the merely natural, achieving more quickly an advanced (though not necessarily superior) level of holiness, for even criminals can achieve sanctity, he says. With certainty Peter's teachings disclose that they were applicable to non-monastic readers even if they were more fully applicable to monastics. This reveals an understanding of the spiritual life that extends beyond the walls of the cloister.[2]

As already touched upon at times in chapters 3 and 4 of this book, Peter's spiritual program was clearly open to all persons – both monastics and non-monastics.[3] Kallistos Ware affirms this when he writes, "Although writing for

---

2 See *ODB*, s.v. "Damaskenos, Peter," by A.P. Kazhdan, 580: "... he argues that the way of salvation is open to lay persons."

3 As will be seen in this chapter, in the middle Byzantine era Peter was not unique with this emphasis. In the earlier Byzantine period Maximus the Confessor also postulated a spirituality that was applicable to non-monastics. As Andrew Louth summarizes, "Maximus' ascetical theology in principle applies to all Christians. Although most of the writings that developed this ascetical theology in the Byzan-

monks, he insists that salvation and spiritual knowledge are within the reach of everyone; continual prayer is possible in all situations without exception."4 This openness to non-monastics is seen in the introduction to the *Admonition*, where Peter writes that "there is no object ... that can prevent us from becoming what God from the beginning has wished us to be ... whether we are rich or poor, married or unmarried, in authority and free or under obedience and in bondage – in short, whatever our time, place or activity" (76; 7.21–27). As well, "marriage is natural" (83; 12.31)5 and "if someone wants to be saved, no person or no time, place or occupation can prevent him" (83; 13.2–5). Elsewhere in the *Admonition* Peter writes, "For we should all, as Christians, keep the command-ments" (195; 100.7–8). Again, though monastics may be more readily able to advance in spiritual growth, Peter believed that there were not necessarily aspects to the spiritual life that were beyond the reach of all Christian people. In this regard, Peter would have found company with many earlier Christian authors, especially John Chrysostom:

'But it is not the same,' you will say, 'when a person in the world [βιωτικòν] sins and when someone does so who has dedicated himself once and for all to God. They do not fall from the same height; therefore, their wounds are not equal.' You certainly deceive yourself and are greatly mistaken if you think that there is one set of requirements for the person in the world and another for the monk. The difference between them is that one is married and the other is not; in all other respects they will have to render the same account. For the person who becomes angry with his brother without cause, whether he is a person in the world or a monk, will offend God in the same manner. The person who looks lustfully at a woman, no matter what his state of life, will be punished in the same way for that fornication

---

tine world were for monks and by monks (and Maximus himself was a monk), what is being discussed is something that takes place in the life of any Christian who strives to be faithful to his baptism." Andrew Louth, "Introduction," in his *Maximus the Confessor* (London; New York, 1996), 3–70, at 35.

4 *Phil.*, 3: 72.

5 For Peter, marriage is natural because it belongs to the realm of matter and it is provided for man by God. It is not something created by man but rather given by God to man.

... Nor do the scriptures know anything like this, but they want everyone to live the life of monks, even if they should happen to have wives.[6]

Chrysostom, of course, is not saying that the institution of monasticism is unimportant. Rather, Chrysostom is elevating the institution of marriage in importance by comparing it to monasticism. In this quotation, Chrysostom is writing to those who are opposed to the monastic life, giving his comments particular force that both monastic and married persons are able to live holy lives. As well, as Peter Brown reminds us, Chrysostom "feared ... that excessive admiration for the life of the monks might provide the Christian householders of the city with an alibi for abandoning their own quest for Christian perfection."[7] Elsewhere Chrysostom says that "the Beatitudes [pronounced] by Christ, were not addressed to solitaries only: since in that case the whole world would have perished, and we should be accusing God of cruelty. And if these beatitudes were spoken to solitaries only, and the secular person cannot fulfill them, yet He permitted marriage, then He has destroyed all men. For if it be not possible, with marriage, to perform the duties of solitaries, all things have perished and are destroyed, and the [functions] of virtue are shut up in a strait."[8] Again, Chrysostom makes a comparison between monastics and those who are married, insisting that both institutions are conducive to godly living, as long as the two are not confused.[9] When commenting on Matthew 2:4–5 he writes,

6 John Chrysostom, *Adversus oppugnatores vitae monasticae* 3.14; *A Comparison between a King and a Monk; Against the Opponents of the Monastic Life: Two Treatises of John Chrysostom*, trans. David G. Hunter (Lewiston, NY, 1988), 156-157. Greek text in PG 47: 372–373, and *Sancti Joannis Chrysostomi Opera selecta*, ed. Friedrich Dübner (Paris, 1861), 1: 59. The text is also cited in Irénée Hausherr, *Spiritual Direction in the Early Christian East*, trans. Anthony P. Gythiel (Kalamazoo, 1990), 308. Original French edition Irénée Hausherr, *Direction spirituelle en orient autrefois* (Rome, 1955). See also J.N.D. Kelly, *Golden Mouth: The Story of John Chrysostom – Ascetic, Preacher, Bishop* (Grand Rapids, MI, 1995), 34–35.

7 Peter Brown, *The Body and Society: Men, Women and Sexual Renunciation in Early Christianity* (New York, 1988), 311. See also Jean-Marie Leroux, "Saint Jean Chrysostome et le monachisme," in Charles Kannengiesser, ed., *Jean Chrysostome et Augustin: Actes du colloque de Chantilly, 22–24 septembre 1974* (Paris, 1975), 125–144.

8 John Chrysostom, *Homily 7 on Hebrews* 11; trans. Frederic Gardiner in *Nicene and Post-Nicene Fathers*, ed. Philip Schaff (1886–89; repr. Peabody, MA, 2004), 14: 402.

9 Chrysostom was strongly opposed to the practice of "spiritual marriage" where the institutions of monasticism and marriage were, in one sense, combined into a unique ascetic practice. See Greg Peters, "Spiritual Marriage in Early Christianity:

"Well," says one, "and what do you require us to do? To occupy the mountains, and become monks?' Why it is this which makes me sigh, that you think them alone to be properly concerned with decency and chastity; and yet assuredly Christ made His laws common to all. Thus when He says, "if any one look on a woman to lust after her," He speaks not to the solitary, but to him also that has a wife; since in fact that mount was at that time filled with all kinds of persons of that description.[10]

Finally, just as chastity does not only pertain to monastics but to those married also, so does the reading of Scripture:

But what is the answer to these charges? "I am not," you will say, "one of the monks, but I have both a wife and children, and the care of a household." Why, this is what has ruined all, your supposing that the reading of the divine Scriptures appertains to those only, when you need it much more than they. For they that dwell in the world, and each day receive wounds, these have most need of medicines.[11]

It is clear that for Chrysostom there were not too different sets of expectations regarding the spiritual life. Rather, both monastics and those married were expected to grow holy. In the end, Chrysostom did not believe that there was much difference between a hermit's mountain and a married woman's home.

Scholars agree that a Byzantine monastic's contacts with his/her non-monastic world "were often close and frequent."[12] In fact, this contact was most frequent when monastics functioned as spiritual guides for non-monastics, since it was deemed that both groups needed spiritual guidance.[13] As stated by

---

1 Corinthians 7:25–38 in Modern Exegesis and the Earliest Church," *Trinity Journal*, n.s., 23 (Fall 2002): 211–224; and Elizabeth Clark, *Jerome, Chrysostom, and Friends: Essays and Translations* (New York, 1979).

10 John Chrysostom, *In Matt.* 7.8; trans. George Prevost in *Nicene and Post-Nicene Fathers* (1886–89; repr. Peabody, MA, 2004), 10: 49.

11 John Chrysostom, *In Matt.* 2.10; trans. Prevost in *Nicene and Post-Nicene Fathers*, 10: 13.

12 Rosemary Morris, *Monks and Laymen in Byzantium, 843–1118* (Cambridge, 1995), 90.

13 On spiritual guidance in the Christian East in general, see Kallistos Ware, "The Spiritual Father in Orthodox Christianity," *Cross Currents* (1974): 296–313.

Morris, "Central to the relationship between monks and laity was the rôle of the monk as spiritual guide."[14] Elsewhere she similarly writes, "Like the monastic life itself, spiritual fatherhood did not exist in isolation from secular society and was, indeed, closely intertwined with it."[15] Perhaps the greatest proponents of this need for non-monastic persons to have spiritual guides were Symeon (Eulabes) the Stoudite[16] and his spiritual son, Symeon the New Theologian.[17] According to H.J.M. Turner, "[Symeon the] Stoudite had numerous [non-monastic] disciples living in the city whom he visited from time to time."[18] Symeon the New Theologian confirms this when he writes that "one day ... we were going into the city in which he [Symeon the Stoudite] had his dwelling [κατοίκησιν], in order that we might visit his spiritual children. We spent the whole day among them, for there were many whom he helped even by his mere presence."[19] It is possible that Symeon the New Theologian took over the direc-

---

14 Morris, *Monks and Laymen in Byzantium*, 90.

15 Morris, *Monks and Laymen in Byzantium*, 93. The following discussion is greatly indebted to Morris.

16 See Symeon the New Theologian, *The Epistles of St. Symeon the New Theologian*, trans. H.J.M. Turner (Oxford, 2009), 3; and Symeon the New Theologian, *Syméon le Nouveau Théologien: Catéchèses 1–5*, ed. Basile Krivochéine (Paris, 1963), 313–315, n. 4. For the only extant work of Symeon the Stoudite, *The Ascetical Discourse*, see Symeon the Stoudite, *Discours ascétique*, ed. Hilarion Alfeyev (Paris, 2001), 72–130.

17 On Symeon the New Theologian, see his *The Epistles of St. Symeon the New Theologian*, ed. and trans. H.J.M. Turner (Oxford, 2009); and Karl Holl, *Enthusiasmus und Bussgewalt beim griechischen Monchtum: Eine Studie zu Symeon dem Neuen Theologen* (Leipzig, 1898). On the relationship of the elder Symeon to his younger disciple and on Symeon the New Theologian's view of spiritual fatherhood and direction, see H.J.M. Turner, *St. Symeon the New Theologian and Spiritual Fatherhood* (Leiden, 1990); Hilda Graef, "The Spiritual Director in the Thought of Symeon the New Theologian," in *Kyriakon: Festschrift Johannes Quasten*, ed. Patrick Granfield and Josef A. Jungmann (Münster, 1970), 2: 608–614; and Basil Krivocheine, *In the Light of Christ: St. Symeon the New Theologian – Life, Spirituality, Doctrine*, trans. Anthony P. Gythiel (Crestwood, NY, 1986), 91–101.

18 Turner, *St. Symeon the New Theologian and Spiritual Fatherhood*, 24.

19 Symeon the New Theologian, *Catechesis* 26.1; *Symeon the New Theologian: The Discourses*, trans. Carmino J. de Catanzaro (New York, 1980), 199. Greek text in Symeon the New Theologian, *Syméon le Nouveau Théologien, Catéchèses*, vol. 2, ed. Basile Krivochéine and Joseph Paramelle (Paris, 1964). As de Catanzaro notes, the two Symeons would have been going towards the center of Constantinople since the Stoudite monastery was on the western outskirts of the city. See Symeon the New Theologian, *Symeon the New Theologian: The Discourses*, 199, n. 2.

tion of these non-monastic individuals upon the death of the elder Symeon.[20] Possibly Symeon the New Theologian's very reason for doing this would have been his strong emphasis on one's need for a spiritual director.[21] For example,

> He who has despised all things visible and even his own soul in order to exhibit genuine penitence in accordance with the Lord's commandment and begin this enterprise does not imagine that he can learn this on his own. He goes to a man who is an experienced craftsman [τεχνίτη] and submits himself to him with great fear and trembling. He learns from him as he teaches him the spiritual work of virtuous actions and what one who is penitent must do.[22]

Similarly, "constantly call on God, that He may show you a man who is able to direct you well, one whom you ought to obey as though he were God Himself, whose instruction you must carry out without hesitation."[23] He also wrote "that without a spiritual father or a teacher it is impossible for a man to keep God's commandments, and live rightly and irreproachably, and rise superior to the snares of the Devil."[24] Basil Krivocheine has argued that "Symeon's main moral

---

20 When Symeon was sent into exile in 1009, he settled in a ruined oratory that belonged to his spiritual son Christopher Phagura, a layman of high standing. Other lay persons under Symeon's direction also brought their influence to bear on the patriarch of Constantinople on behalf of Symeon. See epistles 5 and 8 in Symeon the New Theologian, *The Epistles of St. Symeon the New Theologian*; and Nicetas Stethatos, *Life of Our Holy Father Symeon the New Theologian* 54.6, 100.2 and 102.1–13. Greek text of the *Life* in Irénée Hausherr, ed., *Un grand mystique byzantin: Vie de Siméon le Nouveau Théologien (949–1022) par Nicetas Stethatos* (Rome, 1928).
21 See Turner, *St. Symeon the New Theologian and Spiritual Fatherhood*, 70–73.
22 Symeon the New Theologian, *Catechesis* 14.1; *Symeon the New Theologian: The Discourses*, 186.
23 Symeon the New Theologian, *Catechesis* 20.2; *Symeon the New Theologian: The Discourses*, 232.
24 Symeon the New Theologian, *Letter 3*; *The Epistles of St. Symeon the New Theologian*, 114–115. English translation also available in Krivocheine, *In the Light of Christ*, 96. Krivocheine's translation is based on the unedited text of three of Symeon's letters in Paris, Bibliotheque Nationale, Coislin gr. 292, fol. 262v–273v. These letters are now numbered as *Letters 2–4*. Turner's translation is based on the previously unpublished Greek edition of the letters by Joseph Paramelle. For a discussion of Symeon's writings, see Basil Krivocheine, "The Writings of St. Symeon the New Theologian," *Orientalia Christiana Periodica* 20 (1954): 298–328.

and spiritual concerns, despite his monastic 'isolationism' and his radical renouncement of the world, were not limited to matters monastic but were extended to the life of lay people and to society in general."[25] For, as has been noted, "[s]piritual direction in the Christian East was always more personal, significantly less institutional." That is, "in the East, one sought out an elder, an Old Man (*geron* in the Greek; or *abba*, the Coptic word). Indeed, the chief social role of monastic centers in the East through the centuries was to provide spiritual directors."[26] In early Christian history, this acquisition of spiritual directors was not limited to monastics alone. In the early Syrian monastic context, as Arthur Vööbus has noted:

> Having noticed that the official church could not offer what they needed, the people came with their religious needs to the huts of anchorites and to the monasteries of the monks and nuns making their peace of heart dependent upon the blessings and intercessory prayers available in these places. Here they laid down their problems of the inner life and their restless thoughts before men to whom they supposed all the secrets of heart and thought were known.[27]

In fact, two of the greatest givers of spiritual counsel in the early church, the Palestinian monks Barsanuphius and John, were often approached by non-monastic persons.[28] This frequent communication is evidence that the wall separating the monastery from the outside world were neither necessarily high nor very thick, "rather the instructions of Barsanuphius and John to lay Christians reveal the many ways in which the monastery was intimately connected to the population outside the monastery."[29] At the core of this practice was the

---

25　Krivocheine, *In the Light of Christ*, 154.

26　Barsanuphius and John, *Letters From the Desert: A Selection of Questions and Responses*, trans. with an introduction by John Chryssavgis (Crestwood, NY, 2003), 13–14.

27　Arthur Vööbus, *History of Asceticism in the Syrian Orient, A Contribution to the History of Culture in the Near East*, vol. 2: *Early Monasticism in Mesopotamia and Syria* (Louvain, 1960), 318.

28　Approximately two hundred of the extant letters of Barsanuphius and John are addressed to non-monastic, lay persons. See Jennifer L. Hevelone-Harper, *Disciples of the Desert: Monks, Laity, and Spiritual Authority in Sixth-Century Gaza* (Baltimore; London, 2005), 79.

29　Ibid., 80.

urge to find the assurance of eternal salvation, "[f]or the question 'How may I be saved?' lay at the root of the relationship of both monks and laymen and their spiritual guides."[30] Peter adopted this practice and appears to have taken it one step further by making the means of attaining salvation the same for both monastics and non-monastics. Irénée Hausherr believes that "if there were differences between spiritual direction for monks and that given to Christians in the world, they lie not in the doctrine or in the goal professed, but in the means to be used to reach it."[31] For Peter, the means of attaining salvation is the same for both those living in monasteries and those living outside of monasteries. He appears to share this view in common with Symeon the New Theologian who wrote that

> [m]any people hold the eremitical life in high esteem, others the common or the cenobitic life, and others the governance of the people, or education and teaching, or the administration of churches. Different persons earn their bodily and spiritual sustenance in all these ways. For myself, I cannot judge in favor of any one of these states. I would not exalt one kind and deprecate another. In any case, whatever our works or activities, the most blessed life of all is one that is [lived] for God and according to God in each single act and deed we do.[32]

Elsewhere Symeon writes that both monks and laypersons are foreknown and predestined by God to become conformed to the image of his Son.[33] Symeon's letters further demonstrate his belief that the means of salvation for both monks and lay persons is the same. Symeon's *Letter* 2, says Turner, "is a letter of

30 Morris, *Monks and Laymen in Byzantium*, 96.
31 Hausherr, *Spiritual Direction in the Early Christian East*, 308.
32 Symeon the New Theologian, *Theological and Practical Chapters* 3.65; in *Symeon the New Theologian: The Practical and Theological Chapters and the Three Theological Discourses* trans. Paul McGuckin (Kalamazoo, 1982), 91. Cited also in Krivocheine, *In the Light of Christ*, 149. Greek text in Symeon the New Theologian, *Syméon le Nouveau Théologién: Chapitres théologiques, gnostiques et pratiques*, ed. Jean Darrouzès (Paris, 1957).
33 Symeon the New Theologian, *Ethical Discourses*, 2; *Symeon the New Theologian, On the Mystical Life: The Ethical Discourses*, vol. 1: *The Church and the Last Things*, trans. Alexander Golitzin (Crestwood, 1995), 89. Greek text in Symeon the New Theologian, *Syméon le Nouveau Théologién: Traités théologiques et éthiques*, ed. Jean Darrouzès (Paris, 1966).

direction written to one of Symeon's spiritual children living in the world." Turner's proof for this is that Symeon has to give the recipient directions on how to fast, something that would not have been necessary should the receiver have been a monk given that "this would all have been prescribed for him in the *typikon* (rule)."[34] That Symeon uses King David of Israel as an example of one with a proper "disposition of the soul" may also be evidence that the letter was originally intended for a layperson, especially since Symeon says that David accomplished this despite being "encompassed ... by the world and the cares of this life" and "even though he was a king and responsible for taking thought for his people, while caring for his wife and his children and his house."[35] The letter is concerned with repentance and how one is to repent and how one is to behave after repentance. Though repentance for monks would involve some form of asceticism,[36] Symeon does not recommend this for his non-monastic, lay recipient. Symeon states that those in the Bible who repented did not do so by fasting, keeping vigils, "sleeping on the floor," embracing poverty or through some other bodily asceticism. Rather, the apostle Peter – as for the tax collector, thief, prostitute and prodigal son – gained pardon "simply by repentance, and heart-felt tears, and by being condemned by their conscience."[37] Furthermore, Turner goes so far as to suggest that the letter may be an example of a kind of form letter that Symeon used with those non-monastics who he directed, making use of a standard pattern but adapting the contents to the needs of the individual.[38] This view is lent credibility due to the letter's inclusion of "a brief memorandum" where Symeon lists "[those] things you ought to do and observe"[39] that form a kind of non-monastic *typikon*. First, non-monastic Christians, in this case a catechumen who exits the liturgy at the words "[a]s

---

34   Symeon the New Theologian, *The Epistles of St. Symeon the New Theologian*, 17–18.
35   Symeon the New Theologian, *Letter* 2.15–17, 26–28; in *The Epistles of St. Symeon the New Theologian*, 71.
36   Samuel Rubenson, "Asceticism: Christian Perspectives," in *Encyclopedia of Monasticism*, vol. 1: *A–L*, ed. William M. Johnston (Chicago; London, 2000), 92: "In the *Sayings of the Fathers* (*Apophthegmata Patrum*), thousands of stories and sayings of fourth-century monks are recorded, giving a wide variety of ascetic practice and instruction. Two main features stand out. First, asceticism is closely linked to repentance. Ascetic practice is seen as a sign of remorse, the road that makes it possible to stand in front of God, asking for and receiving forgiveness of one's sins."
37   Symeon the New Theologian, *Letter* 2.38–39; in *The Epistles of St. Symeon the New Theologian*, 73.
38   Ibid., 18.
39   Ibid., 2.84–85, at 75.

many as are catechumens, depart," are not to go away immediately from the church nor engage is useless conversation with other catechumens but are to "stand in the narthex in front of the doors and recollect [their] faults and bewail them."[40] Later that evening they are to recite the *Trisagion*, Psalm 51 and Psalm 6, the "Lord, have mercy" (fifty times), the "Lord, pardon me a sinner" (fifty times), "Lord, pardon me for whatever I have sinned by word and deed and in thought (fifty times) and perform twenty-five prostrations.[41] Second, the non-monastic disciple is to fast from meat, cheese, eggs, wine and fish on Wednesday and Friday unless this is too much, in which case they may eat fish and drink wine in moderation. During Lent and Christmas these fasts are made more severe yet they are always to be done "by being sparing and practising restraint to the extent that [their] natural constitution allows."[42] Third, Symeon admonishes non-monastic Christians to avoid partaking of the Eucharist until their will is in "an unchangeable state vis-à-vis the ugly deeds of sin, and until [they] acquire a disposition which will not be turned away from good and is perfectly possessed of a hatred for sin."[43] The purpose of these actions and disciplines, writes Symeon, is to assist the non-monastic disciple achieve salvation.[44]

Like Symeon, it is this comprehensive understanding of salvation and the spiritual life that causes Peter of Damascus to remind his readers that "God desires the salvation of everyone" (214; 115.39). This is in continuity with earlier practice where both monastics and non-monastics were held to the same standard of spiritual ascent.[45] As Hevelone-Harper comments concerning the

40   Ibid., 2.90–91, at 75.

41   Ibid., 2.92–98, at 77. Compare with Peter's instructions on how to read the Psalms: "[R]eciting the *Trisagion* after each subsection of the Psalter ... After the *Trisagion* say 'Lord, have mercy' forty times; and then make a prostration and say once within yourself, 'I have sinned, Lord, forgive me.' On standing, you should stretch out your arms and say once, 'God, be merciful to me a sinner.' After praying in this way, you should say once more, 'O come, let us worship ...' three times, and then another subsection of the Psalter in the same way" (118–119; 41.25–32).

42   Ibid., 2.99–110, at 77.

43   Ibid., 2.114–117, at 79.

44   See ibid., 2.108–109; and ibid., 2.121–125.

45   Hausherr, *Spiritual Direction in the Early Christian East*, 306: "First all were invited to perfection, according to the very teaching of the Lord which is applicable to all Christians. No orthodox thinker ever thought of dividing Christians into two categories according to the degree of charity toward God and neighbor to which they were called."

relationship of sixth-century Palestinian monks to their non-monastic followers, "The same sins afflicted both monks and laity, and although sometimes
monks were required to maintain a somewhat higher standard of piety, both
groups were measured against the same scale."[46] Similarly, another Byzantine
monk who argued most persuasively for a kind of spiritual equivalence of
monks and lay persons was the ninth-century reformer of the monastic life at
the Stoudios monastery in Constantinople – Theodore the Stoudite.[47]

Like many, if not most, Byzantine spiritual theologians, Theodore believed
that the attainment of ἀπάθεια was the goal of the spiritual life: "He who is
in control of his passions is truly blessed, above every nobility, more glorious
than kings, above every power and authority, worth more than the whole
world."[48] According to Theodore, ἀπάθεια is "not only the goal of the monk,
but being the very reason for the Lord's incarnation it is therefore the goal of
every Christian."[49] He writes that God the Son took on human flesh "so that we
might no longer be slaves, but free; that we might no longer be exposed to the
passions, but be free from them; that we might no longer be friends of the world,
but friends of God; that we might no longer live according to the flesh, but
according to the Spirit."[50] Baptism was the sacramental act that initiated and
illuminated all Christians – monks and laity alike – into the beginning progress
of spiritual ascent. As Cholij writes concerning Theodore, "But God had called
individuals to different vocations, which were different ways of 'pleasing the
Lord' and living according to his commandments, including belonging to the
'lay order' [ἐν τῷ λαικῷ τάγματι]. The laity ... were bound essentially to the
same obligations of Christian living as monks were."[51] Like Peter, Theodore
believes that the "sole difference between lay people and monks was in the way

---

46 Hevelone-Harper, *Disciples of the Desert*, 81.

47 On Theodore in general, see Irénée Hausherr, *Saint Théodore Studite: L'homme et
l'ascète (d'après ses Catéchèses)* (Rome, 1926).

48 Cited in Roman Cholij, *Theodore the Stoudite: The Ordering of Holiness* (Oxford,
2002), 220. The original is an unedited Catechesis available in a Russian translation from the monastery of St Panteleimon on Mt Athos. See ibid., 70–73.

49 Ibid., 220.

50 Theodore the Stoudite, *Parva Catechesis* 64.169. English translation in Cholij,
Theodore the Stoudite, 220, n. 117. Greek text in Theodore the Stoudite Τοῦ ὁσίου
πατρὸς ἡμῶν καὶ ὁμολογητοῦ Θεοδώρου ἡγουμένου τῶν Στουδίου μικρὰ
κατήχησις: *Sancti patris nostri confessoris Theodori Studitis praepositi parva catechesis*,
ed. Emmanuel Auvray (1891; repr. Thessaloniki, 1984).

51 Cholij, *Theodore the Stoudite*, 224.

or circumstances in which Christian life was lived, especially with regard to marriage."[52] In one letter, after listing those things that define a spiritually mature Christian, Theodore writes, "Do not think ... that what I have said only concerns the monk. Although it affects the monk more intensely all these things equally [τὰ πάντα ἐφίσης] affect the lay person, with the exception of celibacy and poverty, for which a secular [ὁ κοσμικὸς] is not to be condemned."[53]

Peter too, like Theodore, does not see the monastic life as superior in kind to the non-monastic life, especially for Peter in regard to a person's eternal salvation. Rather, they both acknowledge that for monks and nuns there is a difference of emphasis or form of life, albeit all Christians are working towards the same end – holiness and/or salvation.[54] This is true even if monks are more predisposed, because of their rejection of the world, towards a quicker spiritual progression. For as Peter writes, "For concern with this life prevents that concern with one's own soul and its state which is the purpose of the man who devotes himself to God and is attentive to himself" (104; 29.26–39).[55] Renunciation of the world is an interior disposition for non-monastics but an exterior reality for monks and nuns and it is this that distinguishes the lifestyles of monastics and non-monastics.[56] Yet, even Peter realizes that there often is not much of a difference between a "bad" monk and a non-monastic: "Those who live in the word – or rather who live after the fashion to the world, for this includes many so-called monks [δῆθεν Μοναχοί] – should try to attain a measure of devo-

52 Cholij, *Theodore the Stoudite*, 226.
53 Theodore the Stoudite, *Epistles*, 464; cited in Cholij, *Theodore the Stoudite*, 227, but omitting some Greek insertions.
54 Though theologically some modern Christian churches and groups would treat salvation as separate from holiness, this distinction was not a concern to Byzantine theologians who often viewed holiness or sanctification as a category of salvation. An early Christian example comes from Athanasius of Alexandria who wrote, "He [the Word of God], indeed, assumed humanity that we might become God." Athanasius of Alexandria, *On the Incarnation* 54; in *Athanasius on the Incarnation: The Treatise De incarnatione Verbi Dei*, new rev. ed., trans. and ed. a Religious of CSMV, with an introduction by C.S. Lewis (1953; repr. Crestwood, NY, 1998), 93. It would appear that Athanasius has both salvation and sanctification in mind, in that we will be restored to our prelapsarian state of sinlessness and holiness.
55 Compare with Cholij, *Theodore the Stoudite*, 233: "The 'superiority' of the monastic vocation, therefore, with regard to the lay vocation, was that the one was a sure way that led to being a zealous or true Christian, the other was fraught with dangers."
56 See Cholij, *Theodore the Stoudite*, 232–233.

tion" (104; 29.12–13). Symeon the New Theologian recognizes this too and addresses it most straightforwardly in his *Hymn* 27, entitled "What sort of a person a monk should be, what is his activity and what is his progress and ascension."[57] In this hymn, Symeon defines a monk not as one who lives alone but one whose "soul is united in God and God is in the soul ... [For] they are considered as solitaries since they are separated from others [καὶ μοναχηοὶ καθίστανται τῶν ἄλλων ὄντες δίχα]."[58] Thus a monastic living a life of sin is not, in fact, living a monastic life at all. He or she may be living "alone" but they are not living as a solitary, that is, a true monk: "And this is what makes them suffer that they do not completely contemplate Christ, even if they do see Him entirely, for they are incapable of throwing off the shackles of flesh even if they have been freed from the passions and every attachment, yet they are still held by one, in spite of being freed from all the other many bonds [εἰ καὶ παθῶν ἀνέθησαν καὶ πάσης προσπαθείας]."[59] In this regard, Theodore the Stoudite, Symeon the New Theologian and Peter of Damascus all agree that monastics and non-monastics are all striving towards the same end, albeit monastics will likely arrive there more quickly.

As a result, unlike much extant Byzantine monastic literature of the twelfth to the fourteenth century, Peter's contribution to Byzantine monasticism is not institutional or legislative. Rather, his contribution is spiritual. For a reading of surviving Byzantine monastic foundation documents reveals a belief which assumes that individuals wishing to be saved will join a monastery. Patriarch Athanasius I says as much in his typikon, dated to 1303–1305, when he writes,

> If you wish to enroll anyone [as a member of the] community, [do not do so] for some human reason of gain and not for reasons of salvation, nor because of a gift or personal influence or family connection, because the condemnation of the canons lies against these motives, but consider [that person] worthy if he passionately desires salvation and [is motivated] by piety.[60]

---

57 Symeon the New Theologian, *Hymns of Divine Love by St. Symeon the New Theologian*, trans. George Maloney (Denville, NJ, 1976), 142. Greek text in Symeon the New Theologian, *Hymnen*, ed. Athanasios Kambylis (Berlin; New York, 1976).
58 Symeon the New Theologian, *Hymns of Divine Love*, 143.
59 Ibid., 144.
60 *BMFD*, 1502.

There were primarily two kinds of monastic houses in the twelfth century, those founded by imperial and royal persons and the independent foundations of other individuals. For Peter, then, whether living as a monastic or not, the relationship between those inside the monastery and those outside the monastery was built upon the same premise – the need for salvation. Yet, Peter himself suggests that the monastic life is a surer guarantee of salvation. For example, he writes that "bodily asceticism does help in the acquisition of the virtues, especially in the case of those who lead a life of stillness and are completely undistracted and detached. For a man cannot see his own habits and correct them unless he is free from worry about worldly things. Hence we ought first to acquire dispassion by withdrawing from worldly affairs and human society" (195; 100.11–16). Also, "if one does not first flee from distraction and acquire complete quietude, one will never be dispassionate with regard to anything, or be able to say what is right and good. In short, this total flight from distraction is of prime importance in all things" (147; 62.21–25). Elsewhere, he states that "nothing so quickly fosters the acquisition of virtue as the solitary life [μόνωσις] and meditation" (162; 74.27–28) and "the world ... [is] a hindrance to perfection" (87; 16.2–3). For Peter, then, as for Theodore the Stoudite especially, a Byzantine person has a greater assurance of eternal salvation by becoming a monastic, though this does not negate his teaching that his spiritual program is open to all persons. This being the case, how could a non-monastic gain a greater assurance of his/her salvation vis-à-vis the institution of monasticism? The answer, according to many Byzantine authors, is by partaking in the life of a monastery in well-defined and legislated ways: foundation and commemoration.

Catia Galatariotou identifies eternal salvation as one of the reasons why aristocratic persons founded monasteries.[61] She writes that the founding of a monastery "was a manifestation to God of the piety and love of the founder towards God, so that the latter in his turn would be better disposed towards the [founder] on the Day of Judgment."[62] For example, Gregory Pakourianos, in his late-eleventh-century typikon for the monastery of the Θεοτόκου τῆς Πετριτζιωτίσσης in Bačkovo, writes,

61 Catia Galatariotou, "Byzantine *ktetorika typika*: A Comparative Study," *Revue des Études Byzantines* 45 (1987): 91–95.

62 Ibid., 91.

Since it is profitable and the duty of every faithful orthodox Christian who has been baptized ... always to expect the end that is common to all, to take thought for the day of his death, to expect the resurrection of everyone and himself from the dead, and to meditate on that fearful and awful examination in the just judgment of Christ our God and Savior and the just requital for each of his deeds ... to gain salvation from that fearful and "eternal punishment" and the threat of "hell fire" (Matt. 25:46; 5:22) ... for by doing this we will be reckoned worthy to become joint heirs with those who have gained their everlasting inheritances, to Christ, and to gain release from our sins – for all these reasons, I the often-mentioned *sebastos* Gregory ... longed to build a very beautiful church and round it a dwelling for monks.[63]

Concerning commemoration, once a non-monastic individual made the proper liturgical and financial arrangements for commemoration, the monks would then memorialize and intercede for them on the appropriate day(s).[64] The result of this commemoration, it was concluded, was the hope of deliverance from condemnation at the last judgment. In fact, the entire structure of monastic foundation and commemoration is built upon the premise that monastics have a greater audience with God.[65] Further, Galatariotou points out that "[a]ll the writers of aristocratic *typika* without exception lay down precise and detailed directions for prayers [of commemoration] for the salvation of their souls, and for the soul of their beloved relatives or friends."[66] For example, concerning his own commemoration, Isaac Comnenos, in his twelfth-century typikon for the monastery of the Mother of God Savior of the World, writes,

I have made the services to commemorate me, and their form, dependent upon the virtuous conduct and the good conscience of the superior, not wishing to burden his freedom of choice by any perverse or compulsory [requirements]. Hark to my words, O my father and superior, and by no

---

63 *BMFD*, 522–523. Greek text in Paul Gautier, "Le typikon du sébaste Grégoire Pakourianos," *Revue des études byzantines* 42 (1984): 19–133.

64 On the many aspects of commemoration in Byzantine monasticism, see *BMFD*, 1882–1883.

65 See Morris, *Monks and Laymen in Byzantium*, 90. In Byzantine terminology this access to God was known as παρρησία. On παρρησία. See *ODB*, s.v. "Parrhesia," by Elizabeth M. Jeffreys, 1591; and Giuseppe Scarpat, *Parresia: Storia del termine e delle tradizioni in latino* (Brescia, 1964).

66 Galatariotou, "Byzantine *ktetorika typika*: A Comparative Study," 93.

means disdain my wretched soul's prayer for mercy. Expect payment for this from the Ruler of All, who is sure to grant better things to good men. For I, the unfortunate and unhappy, who am [but] earth and ashes, dare not because of my series of failures raise my eyes to the heavenly height and the very light source of the divine dispensation. I am blinded in the eyes of the soul. For this reason, I, a thorough wretch, am naturally in need of prayer for salvation of those blessed men like you, for the confidence [achieved] from some good deed is not for me [to enjoy]. Therefore, do not overlook, O Mother of God, [the monastery of] *Kosmosoteira*, my wretched appeal for salvation. For what else [can] I say and what speak, from the multitude of my sins?[67]

In short, either founding a monastery or being remembered in the commemorative prayers of a monastery helped to give a non-monastic person hope that they would receive deliverance from God's condemnatory judgment.

Peter of Damascus, however, goes some distance in countering this understanding with a spiritual theology that is directed toward all persons regardless of station in life.[68] Granted, though Peter may suggest that the monastic life is preferable, in no place does he insist that one *must* be a monastic to attain salvation. Peter is explicitly providing the framework for an all-encompassing spiritual theology. In a sense, Peter is interiorizing the monastic/spiritual vocation, making it applicable to each individual person despite his or her station or position in life. This is Peter's significant contribution to Byzantine monasticism and it is spiritual in nature.

---

67 *BMFD*, 839–840. Greek text in Georgios Papazoglou, Τυπικὸν Ἰσαακίου Ἀλεξίου Κομνηνοῦ τῆς μονῆς Θεοτόκου τῆς Κοσμοσωτείρας (Komotini, Greece, 1994), 33–154.

68 The inclusion of a request for commemoration is common in *typika* and it must be kept in mind that Peter is not writing a *typikon*. Though literary forms can sometimes dictate what is and what is not included in a text, individual authors often do not adhere strictly to imposed genre guidelines. In other words, in theory, one expects to find in Isaac Comnenos' *typikon* a request for commemoration whereas such a request would appear out of place in the Petrine corpus. Yet, in the extant *typikon* for the monastery of Christ Savior (dated ca. 1131–1132), Luke of Messina makes no mention of commemoration, suggesting that a request for commemoration is not an absolutely necessary element of a *typikon*. See the Greek text in J. Cozza-Luzi, ed., *Novum patrum bibliotheca* (Rome, 1905), 10.2:121–130; English translation in *BMFD*, 643–647. At their core, both *typika* and works of spiritual theology, like the Petrine corpus, are concerned about the spiritual life of individuals and Peter's texts are more inclusive in this regard than the *typika*.

A Treasury of Divine Knowledge and Wisdom

When writing his introduction to Peter of Damascus' *Admonition to His Own Soul* and *Spiritual Alphabet*, Nicodemus of the Holy Mountain referred to Peter as a "treasury of divine knowledge and wisdom."[1] It has been the assertion of this book that Nicodemus is correct in this assessment. Though Jean Gouillard, Kallistos Ware, Jacques Touraille, and Artioli and Locato each gave a more negative assessment of Peter, it appears that this assessment is often the result of some set of biases that are never fully articulated nor revealed. As I suggested above, there is a kind of "likely story" or historiography that most Byzantinists and historians of spirituality like to tell when it comes to Byzantine spirituality. Evagrius of Pontus developed a robust and innovative spiritual theology that was standardized and/or made orthodox and acceptable by Maximus the Confessor. The Evagrian/Maximian spirituality then pervades and dominates all subsequent Byzantine spiritual writers, at least until the fourteenth century. At that time, Gregory of Sinai and Gregory Palamas, themselves Evagrian/Maximian in the details of their spiritual theologies, give full and definitive shape to the spirituality of hesychasm, which is then said to be the crowning achievement of all the Evagrian/Maximian writers of the earlier centuries. It is commonly but erroneously believed that most Byzantine spiritual writers of the previous centuries were hesychastic; therefore, Gregory of Sinai and Gregory Palamas were not developing anything new (for, as the Preacher in Ecclesiastes writes, "there is nothing new under the sun") but were simply systematizing what had been said from the time of the earliest Greek fathers.[2] This would also account for Ware's assessment that Peter "is concerned throughout [his

---

1   See, Φιλοκαλία τῶν ἱερῶν νηπτικῶν, Τόμος Γ, ed. Nicodemus of the Holy Mountain and Macarius of Corinth (Athens, 1991), 4: τῆς θείας γνώσεως καὶ σοφίας τὸ ταμεῖον.

2   An example of this "likely story" is found in George A. Maloney, *A Theology of "Uncreated Energies"* (Milwaukee, 1978).

works] with the personal ascesis and prayer of the individual hesychast; and yet he does not envisage the situation of one who is entirely solitary, for he often mentions 'the brethren.'[3] As this book has shown, at best Peter infrequently discusses the concept and/or practice of ἡσυχία, rather, he expands his spiritual program to the point of encompassing all baptized Christians. Again, monks and nuns may achieve holiness in a timelier manner, but all Christians are capable of becoming holy.[4] Why is it, then, that Peter has consistently received such a negative judgment regarding his originality?

Throughout my exposition of the Petrine corpus, I worked with the assumption that Peter employed a literary technique now known as intertextuality. M.M. Bakhtin says that, ultimately, a writing "cannot fail to be oriented toward the 'already uttered', the 'already known' ... Only the mythical Adam, who approached a virginal and as yet verbally unqualified world with the first word, could really have escaped from start to finish this dialogic inter-orientation with the alien world ... Concrete historical human discourse does not have this privilege."[5] In light of this, readers of Peter today should expect to find him quoting from, and anonymously drawing from, his predecessors. Peter does this in at least two ways. Again, following Elizabeth Clark, "[i]n its simplest form, a form that barely merits the label of 'intertextuality', texts are placed next to each other to reinforce a point."[6] Peter does this throughout his treatises, as is well attested by the extensive list of his identified sources. Another way that Peter employs intertexts is by pushing a "suggestive" text in a more definitive direction. For example, Peter quotes Anthony the Great from the *Apophthegmata patrum* five times in the *Admonition* and *Spiritual Alphabet*. In one use, while commenting on discernment, Peter uses Anthony to say that a believer who attains bodily virtues but neglects his intellect accomplishes nothing (153; 67.16–18). Yet, Anthony actually says that he who lacks discernment is "far from God."[7] Peter alters the original meaning and intent of Anthony's words to say

3 *Phil.*, 3: 71.
4 See chapter 5.
5 Mikhail M. Bakhtin, *The Dialogic Imagination: Four Essays*, ed. Michael Holquist, trans. Caryl Emerson and Michael Holquist (Austin, TX, 1981), 279. Cited in Elizabeth A. Clark, *Reading Renunciation: Asceticism and Scripture in Early Christianity* (Princeton, NJ, 1999), 122–123.
6 Ibid., 125.
7 Benedicta Ward, trans., *The Sayings of the Desert Fathers: The Alphabetical Collection* (Kalamazoo, 1975), 3. Greek text in PG 65: 77.

something much more absolute than Anthony intended. Similarly, Peter also alters a saying of Sisoes from the *Apophthegmata patrum* regarding how often ascetics eat. Peter states that "those who have attained a state of dispassion, they often do not eat for days on end" and continues by saying "St Sisois was such a person" (151; 66.7–9). If Peter had stopped here, then his use of Sisoes as a dispassionate person who did not eat regularly would be accurate. Yet, Peter pushes the discussion a step further by saying that "in the ecstasy of his love for God he [Sisoes] asked to take communion after he had eaten" (151; 66.9–11). However, nowhere is this detail recorded in the *Apophthegmata patrum* which reads, "Abba Sisoes' disciple often said to him, 'Abba, get up, and let us eat.' And he would say to him, 'Have we not eaten, my child?' He would reply, 'No, Father.' Then the old man would say, 'If we have not eaten, bring the food, and we will eat.'"[8] From these examples, one concludes that Peter pushed texts to say something more definitive than they originally said. In essence, he constructed an intertextual interpretation. For, as Clark remarks, "Intertexts, whether overt or hidden, have the ability to reinforce or to constrain the text in ways that produce new textual meaning."[9] Again, a reader of the Petrine corpus should expect to hear reminiscences of the Byzantine spiritual authors who wrote before Peter. On account of this, this book did not devote space to examining each occurrence of an intertext. Instead, it focused on those parts of Peter's works where he appears to be saying something unique, as explained above. There is at least one manuscript of the *Spiritual Alphabet* (i.e., Paris, Bibliothèque Nationale, Ancien gr. 1135) that identifies the sources for many of Peter's quotations and allusions. Until this and other manuscripts, if any, that also provide attributions are fully examined, it is impossible to do an exhaustive study of intertextuality in Peter since it is imperative to know whom Peter believed that he was quoting. Similarly, once Peter's sources have been exhaustively identified, it is then necessary to determine where Peter found his quotation; that is, was a quotation taken directly from an author's works or from another intermediate work. If the quotation came from a currently unknown *florilegium*, for example, then it is necessary to determine if Peter altered the original text or if he simply restated an already altered quotation. In other words, did Peter provide the intertext or did he simply quote an existing intertext? Regardless, in light of the literary

---

8 Ward, trans., *The Sayings of the Desert Fathers*, 213.
9 Clark, *Reading Renunciation*, 125.

technique of intertextuality, one is able to conclude, against Gouillard's remarks in particular, that Peter was not simply an organizer of his predecessors nor simply unoriginal. It is incorrect to place Peter in the mainstream of the Byzantine monastic and spiritual tradition and then to fail to fully recognize Peter's distinctive use of that tradition. I suggest that if Gouillard had had access to the theory of intertextuality,[10] then his conclusion regarding Peter and the quality of his literary output would be more positive. In short, Peter was not "putting into clear formulas the teachings of the greatest contemplatives of the east,"[11] rather he was giving to his successors a distinctive and particular spiritual theology. He was giving to the church a "treasury of divine knowledge and wisdom."

As I have argued, given that the *Admonition to His Own Soul* and the *Spiritual Alphabet* of Peter of Damascus form the second-largest component of writings in the *Philokalia*, it is important that Peter's works be studied in more detail. Studying the Petrine corpus brings into sharp relief the fact that not all Byzantine spiritual writers operated within the Evagrian/Maximian understanding of spiritual theology. Was Peter aware of the writings of Evagrius of Pontus (known to him as Nilus) and Maximus the Confessor? Of course. Yet, reading Byzantine spiritual texts through this lens has skewed the historical reality that not all Byzantine spiritual theologies fit into this schema. Now that Peter's writings have received the attention that they are due, the writers that come after him need to be evaluated, at least in part, against Peter's spiritual theology. For example, what happened to the Petrine conviction (shared in part by Symeon the New Theologian and Theodore the Studite) that a robust spiritual life was possible not only for monastics but for non-monastics as well? Why was this emphasis lost in later Byzantine spiritual writers such as Gregory of Sinai and Gregory Palamas? Further, Peter's emphasis on grace and discrimination is unique, why were these emphases lost in the essence and energy distinctions and controversies of the fourteenth century?[12] It would seem that modern scholars engaged in

---

10   The origin of the theory of intertextuality dates to 1969 with the publication of Julia Kristeva's *Séméotikè: Recherches pour une sémanalyse* (Paris, 1969).

11   Jean Gouillard, "Un auteur spirituel byzantin du XIIe siècle, Pierre Damascène," *Échos d'Orient* 38 (1939), 278.

12   See John Meyendorff, "Introduction," in *Gregory Palamas: The Triads*, ed. John Mayendorff, trans. Nicholas Gendle, (Mahwah, NJ, 1983), 20–22.

the study of Byzantine spirituality now need to give due consideration to the spiritual theology of Peter of Damascus. To fail to do so will only result in a partial picture of the range of spiritual practices and spiritual theologies that characterize the Byzantine era. Peter of Damascus is too important of a figure to be neglected any longer.

APPENDIX I

Chart of Topical Comparisons

In order to provide a point of comparison of the contents of both the *Admonition to His Own Soul* and the *Spiritual Alphabet*, the titles of the sections of the *Admonition* are placed alongside the λόγος or λόγοι from the *Spiritual Alphabet* that has similar subject matter. The English translation of the *Philokalia* has, in several instances, shortened the originally longer title of the section offered by the editors of the Greek edition of the *Philokalia*.[1] These titles of the *Admonition* are not in the oldest manuscripts. For example, Vatican City, Bibliotheca Apostolica Vaticana, Palat. gr. 210 and Paris, Bibliothèque Nationale, Ancien gr. 1134 and 1137 lack section titles though they all indicate section breaks with stylistic initials.[2]

---

1 For these editions, see *Phil.*, vol. 3; and Φιλοκαλία των ίερων νηπτικων, Τόμος Γ´, ed. Nicodemus of the Holy Mountain and Macarius of Corinth (Athens, 1991).
2 In all three of the manuscripts the initials lack both colour and ornamentation. They are simply a more stylistic first letter of the first word of each section.

Admonition to His Own Soul	*Spiritual Alphabet*
Introduction	Λόγος Β΄, Λόγος Ω΄
The Seven Forms of Bodily Discipline (Greek: Declaration, necessary and extremely beautiful, on the seven forms of bodily discipline)	
The Seven Commandments (Greek: That the one who wants to observe the commandments must start with the fear of God, not to fall into chaos)	Λόγος Γ΄
The Four Virtues of the Soul	Λόγος Ρ΄, Λόγος Σ΄, Λόγος Τ΄, Λόγος Υ΄
Active Spiritual Knowledge	
The Bodily Virtues as Tools for the Acquisition of the Virtues of the Soul	
The Guarding of the Intellect (Greek: That it is impossible to be saved other than by rigorous attentiveness and the guarding of the intellect)	
Obedience and Stillness (Greek: That those who wish to see where they are have nothing else to do but to flee their own will, by submission and stillness, and especially those who are held by the passions)	
The Eight Stages of Contemplation	
The First Stage of Contemplation	
The Second Stage of Contemplation	
The Third Stage of Contemplation	
The Fourth Stage of Contemplation	Λόγος Γ΄
The Fifth Stage of Contemplation	Λόγος Μ΄
The Sixth Stage of Contemplation	Λόγος Α΄
The Seventh Stage of Contemplation	Λόγος Ν΄
The Eighth Stage of Contemplation	Λόγος Π΄
That There are No Contradictions in Holy Scripture	Λόγος Ψ΄

The Classification of Prayer According to the Eight Stages of Contemplation (Greek: The classification of prayer according to whole spiritual knowledge)

Humility	Λόγος Κ´
Dispassion	Λόγος Η´, Λόγος Ξ´
A Further Analysis of the Seven Forms of Bodily Discipline	
Discrimination	Λόγος Λ´
Spiritual Reading	
True Discrimination	
That We Should Not Despair Even If We May Sin Many Times	Λόγος Ζ´
Short Discourse on the Acquisition of the Virtues and on Abstinence from the Passions	Λόγος Θ´
How to Acquire True Faith	
That Stillness is of Great Benefit to Those Subject to Passion	
The Great Benefit of True Repentance	
God's Universal and Particular Gifts	
How God Has Done All Things for Our Benefit	
How God's Speech is Not Loose Chatter	
How it is Impossible to Be Saved Without Humility	
On Building Up the Soul Through the Virtues	Λόγος Δ´, Λόγος Ε´, Λόγος Χ´, Λόγος Φ´
The Great Value of Love and of Advice Given with Humility	Λόγος Ο´
That the Frequent Repetition Found in Divine Scripture is Not Verbosity	
Spurious Knowledge	
A List of the Virtues	
A List of the Passions	
The Difference between Thoughts and Provocations	

The Introductory Verses of Peter of Damascus's *Alphabetum asceticum*

In the English translation of the *Philokalia*, the editors state that "Each of the *Twenty-Four Discourses* [i.e., the *Spiritual Alphabet*] begins with four or more lines of verse. Since these add nothing to the substance of the text that follows … they have been omitted from our translation; but we have assigned short titles to each *Discourse*."[1] As argued in this book, however, there are no definitive indications that these texts are not original Peter. Therefore, they are given here in English translation for the first time.

Discourse 1[2]
Here is the prologue, the letter Alpha,
it concerns spiritual wisdom.
For just as it happens to be the beginning of all letters in every language,
so too is spiritual wisdom the starting-point of every virtue and the end of all things.
But just as the alphabet is an elementary lesson,
without which it is impossible to understand even basic lessons,
in the same manner is this the beginning of knowledge,
even if it is very small, and apart from it
no virtue is to be found at all.
Now, bless the beginning, O Father.

---

1 *Phil.*, 3: 211, n. 1.
2 Greek text in *Φιλοκαλία τῶν ἱερῶν νηπτικῶν, Τόμος Γ΄*, ed. Nicodemus of the Holy Mountain and Macarius of Corinth (Athens, 1991), 112–159. As I have discussed elsewhere, there is uncertainty as to which manuscript of the *Spiritual Alphabet* the editors used in the compilation of the *Philokalia*. For the purposes of this book, I have consulted both the printed Greek text of the introductory verses and Paris, Bibliothèque Nationale, Ancien gr. 1135. As well, I would like to acknowledge the assistance of T. Allan Smith, CSB, with an earlier translation of these verses.

Discourse 2
The prologue has now been written with all hope.
And here is the second letter, that is Beta, the second discourse,
in which it will be said in summary that
one faith gives birth to another, and it is great faith,
as the holy fathers say.
[Great faith is] the foundation of the virtues, as the Apostle of the Lord says,
who lays the same foundation.[3]
For one arises apart from the workings of the law,
the other is made perfect by works.
One is found in stillness,
one is brought to perfection through many battles.
Now, bless the beginning, O Father.

Discourse 3
Gamma is the third among letters,
And here is the third discourse, it is on fear.
For the fears of the Lord are two,
an initial fear, which keeps evil away,
and perfect fear, which works fervently.[4]
Now, bless the beginning, O Father.

Discourse 4
Behold, the present discourse is the fourth and concerns piety,
and the letter is Delta, for the essential part[5] is there,
since it concerns self-control,
which is the beginning of the eight virtues opposed to the eight passions,

---

3   See Colossians 1:23.
4   See Dorotheus of Gaza, *Didaskalia* 4: "there are two kinds of fear: one preliminary, the other perfect." English translation in Dorothy of Gaza, *Dorotheus of Gaza: Discourses and Sayings*, trans. Eric P. Wheeler (Kalamazoo, 1977), 109. Greek text in Dorothy of Gaza, , *Dorothée de Gaza: Oeuvres spirituelles*, ed. Lucien Regnault and Jacques de Préville (Paris, 1963).
5   The Greek word ψῆφος could also be translated as kernel or seed, which is the sense in the text of Ecclesiasticus 18:10: "Like a drop of water from the sea and a grain of sand, so are a few years among the days of eternity," in *The New Oxford Annotated Apocrypha: The Apocryphal/Deuterocanonical Books of the Old Testament*, new rev. stan. ver., ed. Bruce M. Metzger and Roland E. Murphy (Crestwood, NY, 1991), 109. Peter's use of the term seems to imply both that which is the seed of all subsequent spiritual growth as well as that which is essential to true spiritual growth. Thus my choice of "essential part."

together with self-restraint.[6]
For these are the works of piety.
Now, bless the beginning, O Father.

Discourse 5
This is the fifth discourse, and the letter is Epsilon,
concerning patience.
For this is the first and greatest among the virtues,
with respect to all knowledge.
Now, bless the beginning, O Father.

Discourse 6
Here again is written an evangelical discourse,
but now about the hope of things to come.
Because Zeta is the sixth among letters,
and the mind seeks to become free from anxiety.
Now, bless the beginning, O Father.

Discourse 7
Seventh among the letters is Eta.
The present discourse is about dispassion [ἀπροσπαθείας].
This one is born out of hope
and it is complete flight from the world.
Now, bless the beginning, O Father.

Discourse 8
Eighth is the discourse and it is Theta.
Dispassion gives birth to the death of the passions.
For unless he possesses it by toil,
he will not be delivered from the passions.
Now, bless the beginning, O Father.

---

6 The word used here is σωφροσύνη, which is commonly translated as "chastity."
However, Peter himself provides the meaning when he writes in Λόγος Δ᾽, "Καὶ
οὐχ ὁμοίως ἔχουσιν αἱ δύο ἐγκράτειαι καὶ αἱ σωφροσύναι. ἀλλ᾽ ἡ μὲν τὴν
πορνείαν κατέχει καὶ τὰ αἴσχιστα πάθη. ἡ δὲ καὶ τὸν λεπτότατον λογισμὸν
καὶ ἀναμάρτητον συνάγει πρὸς ἑαυτήν, καὶ δι᾽ ἑαυτῆς ἀνάγει πρὸς τὸν
Θεόν" (120.2–5). That is, "As I have said, the two forms of self-control and self-
restraint are not identical, for while the first curbs unchastity and the other shameful passions, the second controls even the slightest thought, bringing it under sur-
veillance before it can lead to sin, and then conducting it to God" (219). Peter's use
as "self-restraint" is consistent with the three New Testament passages that use the
term (see Acts 26:25; and 1 Tim. 2:9, 15).

Discourse 9

Here is Iota and the ninth discourse,
concerning the holy sufferings of Christ.
From the memory of death and sin
are born many tears for the one who labours.
And from these [tears] one is able to bear in the mind
the sufferings of Christ and of his saints.
Now, bless the beginning, O Father.

Discourse 10

Here is the tenth [letter], Kappa, and the discourse
concerning the humiliation of Christ.
To take no thought whatsoever about anything,
but to work completely on herself,
this the soul must do forever with all her effort.
Now, bless the beginning, O Father.

Discourse 11

Eleven are the discourses and it is Lambda.
For humility gives birth to discernment
according to the nature of the sensible creation [αἰσθητῶν κτισμάτων].
Now, bless the beginning, O Father.

Discourse 12

The letter is Mu, and twelfth is the present discourse.
It discloses therefore the temptation to contemplate the sensible creation
so that no one may ask for it when it is not yet time.
Now, bless the beginning, O Father.

Discourse 13

The letter is Nu, the thirteenth discourse
concerning herein knowledge of spiritual beings [νοητῶν],
that is to say, of the hosts of bodiless intelligences [νοερῶν].
From the sensible signs the one who looks infers [the existence of spiritual beings].
Now, bless the beginning, O Father.

Discourse 14

The present discourse designated by the letter Xi
is in general about true apatheia.
By the grace of Christ there are already fourteen chapters in brief.
Now, bless the beginning, O Father.

Discourse 15
Keeping the divine commandments
Is a sign of love of God and neighbor.
The present discourse therefore is about love.
It has Omicron as its letter,
which is the fifteenth [letter of the alphabet].
For love is the beginning and the end of the law.
Now, bless the beginning, O Father.

Discourse 16
The letter is Pi and the sixteenth discourse
concerning the knowledge of God, briefly.
Because many have spoken of theology
in many canons and discourses.
Now, bless the beginning, O Father.

Discourse 17
Here now is the seventeenth discourse
Concerning one of the principal virtues.
We have arrived already at the letter Rho.
Moral judgment [φρόνησίς] is the first of the four [virtues].
Now, bless the beginning, O Father.

Discourse 18
Sigma is the eighteenth letter.
The present discourse concerns self-restraint [σωφροσύνης].
Now, bless the beginning, O Father.

Discourse 19
The letter is Tau. The discourse concerns courage.
It is therefore the nineteenth.
[Courage] is born from the incensive power [θυμικοῦ]
and is midway between over-boldness [θράσους] and cowardice [δειλίας].
Now, bless the beginning, O Father.

Discourse 20
The twentieth discourse, which is the letter Upsilon,
concerns the justice of all the virtues.
For this one dispenses equal measure
and is reborn out of the mind.
Now, bless the beginning, O Father.

Discourse 21
The letter is Phi and the twenty-first discourse
concerning perfect peace of thoughts,
as the disciples received from the Lord.
For it has been given by God.
Now, bless the beginning, O Father.

Discourse 22
The twenty-second discourse and the letter is Chi.
It tells how joy is born of peace.
About it little will be said,
since there is spiritual joy, and another kind [of joy].
Now, bless the beginning, O Father.

Discourse 23
The twenty-third discourse concerns the Scriptures
in order that those who want to search them may have no disagreement at all,
so that they may understand all that is written, as is proper.
Now, bless the beginning, O Father.

Discourse 24
Omega, the twenty-fourth, is now.
The present discourse gives perception to the heart,
so that anyone may know that which is profitable.
Now, bless the beginning, O Father.

APPENDIX 3

Paris, Bibliothèque Nationale, Ancien gr. 1134 Variant

Joseph and Aseneth is a pseudepigraphal work that is first attested toward the end of the fourth century CE According to Genesis 41:45, Aseneth, the daughter of Potiphera, a priest of On, was given to Joseph as a wife by Pharaoh. The intent of the work is to demonstrate that Aseneth, as the daughter of an idolatrous priest, became a Yahweh-fearing convert before she was betrothed to Joseph. *Joseph and Aseneth* also includes the details of Pharaoh's firstborn son's infatuation with Aseneth and his attempt, in collusion with Joseph's brothers Dan and Gad, to kidnap Aseneth and kill Joseph and Pharaoh. The passage below is absent from the extant manuscripts of *Joseph and Aseneth*.[1]

Greek text from Paris, Bibliothèque Nationale, Ancien gr. 1134, folios 88v–89r

ὡς φᾶσί περὶ τοῦ Λευί τοῦτά τῶν δώδεκα πατριάρχῶν, ὅτι περ ἐν οὐρανῷ γράμματα ἀνεγίνωσκε· καὶ ἀπεκάλυψε ταῦτά τῇ θαυμαστῇ ἐκείνῃ γυναικί τοῦ σώφρονος Ἰωσήφ τοῦ ἀδελφοῦ αὐτοῦ, τῇ λεγομένῃ Ἀσενέθ· καὶ γενομένη ἀξία τῆς ἀποκαλύψεως δι ἁγίου ἀγγέλου ἐπί τοῦ ἀχράντου πάθους καὶ τῆς ἁγίας ἀναστάσεως τοῦ Κυρίου· πρὸς ἥν ἔφη ὁ ἄγγελος ὅτι ἡ μετάνοια, θυγάτηρ ἐστί τοῦ βασιλέως τοῦ θεοῦ. καὶ πολλήν παρρησίαν ἔχει πρὸς τόν θεόν. ὡςτε δυνηθῆ[ναι]² καὶ τοῖς ἄγαν ἀμαρτωλοῖς σῶσαι· διά γάρ τῆς θέρμης αὐτῆς μετανοίας καὶ ἀρνήσεως τῶν εἰδώλων ἡ παρθένος αὐτη, ἐγένετο σύζυγος τοῦ δικαίου Ἰωσήφ·

---

1   For the critical edition, see Christoph Burchard, "Ein vorläufiger griechischer Text von Joseph und Aseneth," *Dielheimer Blätter zum Alten Testament* 14 (1979): 2–53; and for an English translation, see Christoph Burchard, trans., "Joseph and Aseneth" in *The Old Testament Pseudepigrapha*, ed. James H. Charlesworth (Garden City, NY, 1985), 2: 239–242.

2   This emendation supplied by Paris, Bibliothèque Nationale, Ancien gr. 1135, fol. 175r.

ἐκείνου φημί, περὶ οὗ εἴρηται που, δευτέραν εὖ αὐτήν Αἰγυπτίαν εὑρών
ὁ δράκων, διά ῥήματι³ ἔσπευδε κολακείαις ὑποσκελίσαι τόν Ἰωσήφ· ἀλλ
αὐτός καταλιπών τόν χιτῶνα, ἔφυγε τήν ἁμαρτίαν· καὶ γυμνός οὐκ
ἠσχύνετο ὡς ὁ πρωτόπλαστος πρὸ τῆς παρακοῆς· αὐτόυ ταῖς ἱκεσίαις
Χριστέ.

As they say about Levi of the twelve Patriarchs, that he was reading heavenly letters; and he revealed these [things about heaven] to that wonderful wife of the
prudent Joseph, his brother, whose name was Aseneth. And she became[4] worthy of this revelation through a holy angel about the immaculate suffering and
the holy resurrection of the Lord. To whom (i.e., Aseneth) the angel said that
repentance is the daughter of God the King. And it has much familiarity
towards God, so that she is able to save even the very sinners. For through her
own fervor of repentance and rejection of the idols, this virgin became the wife
of the righteous Joseph. I say about him, about whom has been said somewhere,
the dragon[5] having found that Egyptian woman second, and with words of flat-
tery he hurried to trip up Joseph. But he (i.e., Joseph), leaving his tunic behind,
escaped the sin. And naked, he was not ashamed as the first created man before
the disobedience. By his entreaties O Christ, [hear].

---

3 This use of διά with the dative is anomalous in Byzantine literature and is likely the
   result of a textual error.
4 Lit. "becoming."
5 This is a reference to Pharaoh's firstborn son.

Bibliography

The Works of Peter of Damascus

Εὐεργετινός ἤτοι Συναγωγὴ τῶν θεοφθόγγων ῥημάτων καὶ διδασκαλιῶν τῶν θεοφόρων καὶ ἁγίων πατέρων. Ed. Macarius of Corinth and Nicodemus of the Holy Mountain. Venice, 1783.

Dobrotoliubie. Trans. Paisius Velichkovsky. Moscow, 1793.

Dobrotoliubie. Trans. Theophan the Recluse. 5 vols. Moscow, 1877–1889.

Dobrotoliubie: La Philocalie slavonne de Paissy Velitchkovsky: Reproduction anastatique intégrale de l'édition princeps, Moscou, 1793. Bucharest: Editions Roza Vinturilor, 1990.

Φιλοκαλία τῶν ἱερῶν νηπτικῶν, Τόμος Γ. Ed. Nicodemus of the Holy Mountain and Macarius of Corinth. Athens: Εκδότικος οἶκος "Asthr," 1991.

La Filocalia. Ed. Saint Nicodemos the Hagiorite and Saint Makarios, Metropolitan of Corinth. Trans. M. Benedetta Artioli and M. Francesca Lovato. Vol. 3. Turin: P. Gribaudi, 1985.

Philocalie des Pères Neptiques. Fasc. 2: *Pierre Damascène*. Ed. Jacques Touraille. Bégrolles-en-maugés: Abbage de Bellefontaine, 1980.

The Philokalia: The Complete Text Compiled by St. Nicodemus of the Holy Mountain and St. Makarios of Corinth. Ed. and trans. G.E.H. Palmer, Philip Sherrard and Kallistos Ware. Vols. 2 and 3. London: Faber and Faber, 1981, 1984.

Other Works

Alfeyev, Hilarion. *St. Symeon the New Theologian and Orthodox Tradition*. Oxford: Oxford University Press, 2000.

Allen, Graham. *Intertextuality*. London: Routledge, 2000.

Andreevskii, I.E., F.F. Pretushevskii, Vladimir Timofeevich Sheviakov and K.K. Arsenev, eds. *Entsiklopedicheskii Slovar*. Vol. 10. St Petersburg: I.A. Efron, 1893.

Andreopoulos, Andreas. *The Sign of the Cross: The Gesture, the Mystery, the History*. Brewster, MA: Paraclete Press, 2006.

Angold, Michael. *Church and Society in Byzantium Under the Comneni, 1081–1261*. Cambridge: Cambridge University Press, 1995.

Anna Comnena. *Alexiadis*. Ed. and trans. Ludovicus Schopenus. Bonn: E. Weber, 1839.

Anselm of Havelberg. *Anticimenon: On the Unity of the Faith and the Controversies with the Greeks.* Trans. Ambrose Criste and Carol Neel. Trappist, KY: Cistercian Publications; Collegeville, MN: Liturgical Press, 2010.

Antoniadis-Bibicou, Hélène. "Quelques notes sur l'enfant de la moyenne époque byzantine." *Annales de Démographie Historique* (1973): 77–84.

Archetti, G. "Grosolano (Grossolano)." In *Dizionario Biografico degli Italiani LIX: Grosso – Guglielmo da Forlì,* ed. Alberto M Ghisalberti and Mario Caravale, 792–796. (Rome: Istituto della Enciclopedia italiana, 2003).

Atchley, E.G. Cuthbert F. *On the Epiclesis of the Eucharistic Liturgy and in the Consecration of the Font.* Oxford: Oxford University Press, 1935.

Athanasius of Alexandria. *Athanasius on the Incarnation: The treatise "De incarnatione Verbi Dei".* New rev. ed. Trans. and ed. a Religious of CSMV, with an introduction by C.S. Lewis. 1953. Reprint, Crestwood, NY: St Vladimir's Seminary Press, 1998.

Avvakum Petrovich. *The Life of Archpriest Avvakum, by Himself.* Trans. Jane Ellen Harrison and Hope Mirrlees. London: Hogarth Press, 1963.

Bakhtin, M.M. *The Dialogic Imagination: Four Essays.* Ed. Michael Holquist. Trans. Caryl Emerson and Michael Holquist. Austin: University of Texas Press, 1981.

Bakirtzis, C. "Byzantine Monasteries in Eastern Macedonia and Thrace (Synaxis, Mt. Papikion, St. John Prodromos Monastery)." In *Mount Athos and Byzantine Monasticism,* ed. Anthony Bryer and Mary Cunningham, 47–54. (Brookfield, VT: Variorum, 1996)

Baldick, Chris. *The Concise Oxford Dictionary of Literary Terms.* Oxford; Crestwood, NY: Oxford University Press, 1990.

Barsanuphius and John. *Letters from the Desert: A Selection of Questions and Responses.* Trans. and introduction by John Chryssavgis. Crestwood, NY: St. Vladimir's Seminary Press, 2003.

Barmann, Lawrence F. "Reform Ideology in the *Dialogi* of Anselm of Havelberg." *Church History* 30 (1961): 379–395.

Basil of Caesarea. *Exegetic Homilies.* Trans. Agnes Clare Way. Washington: Catholic University of America Press, 1963.

Bebis, George S. "Introduction." In *Nicodemus of the Holy Mountain: A Handbook of Spiritual Counsel,* by Nicodemus the Hagiorite. Crestwood, NY: Paulist Press, 1989.

Beck, Hans-Georg. *Kirche und Theologische Litteratur in Byzantinischen Reich.* Munich: C.H. Beck'sche Verlagsbuchhandlung, 1959.

Bible. Revised Standard Version. In *The Layman's Parallel New Testament.* Grand Rapids: Zondervan Publishing House, 1970.

Bibliotheca Casinensis seu codicum manuscriptorum. Montecassino: Ex typographia Casinensi, 1873–1894.

Bloomfield, Morton W. "The Origin of the Concept of the Seven Cardinal Sins." *Harvard Theological Review* 34 (1941): 121–128.

Bludau, Augustinus. *Die Pilgerreise der Aethena.* Studien zur Geschichte und Kultur des Altertums 15. Paderborn: Schöningh, 1927.

Bompaire, Jacques. *Actes de Xéropotamou.* Paris: P. Lethielleux, 1964.

Bréhier, Louis. *Le schisme oriental du XIe siècle.* Paris: Ernest Leroux, 1899.

Brown, Peter. *The Body and Society: Men, Women and Sexual Renunciation in Early Christianity.* Crestwood, NY: Columbia University Press, 1988.

Browning, Robert. "The Patriarchal School at Constantinople in the Twelfth Century." *Byzantion* 32 (1962): 167–202 and 33 (1963): 11–40. Reprinted in Robert Browning, *Studies on Byzantine History, Literature and Education.* London: Variorum Reprints, 1977.

Bryer, Anthony, and Mary Cunningham, eds. *Mount Athos and Byzantine Monasticism: Papers from the Twenty-eighth Spring Symposium of Byzantine Studies, Birmingham, March 1994.* Brookfield, VT: Variorum, 1996.

Burchard, Christoph. "Ein vorläufiger griechischer Text von Joseph und Aseneth." *Dielheimer Blätter zum Aeten Testament* 14 (1979): 2–53.

—, trans. "Joseph and Aseneth." In *The Old Testament Pseudepigrapha*, ed. James H. Charlesworth, 2: 177–247. Garden City, NY: Doubleday, 1985.

Casiday, Augustine. "Church Fathers and the Shaping of Orthodox Theology." In *The Cambridge Companion to Orthodox Christian Theology*, ed. Mary B. Cunningham and Elizabeth Theokritoff. Cambridge: Cambridge University Press, 2008.

Cavarnos, Constantine. *St. Macarios of Corinth.* Belmont, MA: Institute for Byzantine and Modern Greek Studies, 1972.

Cave, William. *Scriptorum ecclesiasticorum historia literaria.* Vol. 2. Oxford, 1743.

Charlesworth, James H., ed. *The Old Testament Pseudepigrapha.* Vol. 2. Garden City, NY: Doubleday, 1985.

Cheynet, Jean-Claude, Cécile Morrisson, and Werner Seibt. *Les sceaux byzantins de la collection Henri Seyrig.* Paris: Bibliotheque nationale, 1991.

Cholij, Roman. *Theodore the Stoudite: The Ordering of Holiness.* Oxford: Oxford University Press, 2002.

Choras, George A. Ἡ "ἁγία μονή" Ἀρείας ἐν τῇ ἐκκλησιαστικῇ καὶ πολιτικῇ ἱστορίᾳ τοῦ Ναυπλίου καὶ Ἀργους. Athens, 1975.

Chryssavgis, John. *John Climacus: From the Egyptian Desert to the Sinaite Mountain.* Aldershot, UK: Ashgate, 2004.

—, trans. *Barsanuphius and John: Letters.* Vol 1. Fathers of the Church 113. Washington: Catholic University of America Press, 2006.

Citterio, Elia. "Nicodemo Agiorita." In *La théologie byzantine et sa tradition II*, ed. Carmello Giuseppe Conticello and Vassa Conticello. Turnhout: Brepols, 2002.

Citterio, Elia, and Antonio Rigo, eds. *Nicodemo l'Aghiorita e la Filocalia: Atti dell'VIII Convegno Ecumenico intern: Di Spiritualità Ortodossa: Bose, 16–19 settembre 2000.* Magnano: Edizioni Qiqajon, Comunità di Bose, 2001.

Clark, Elizabeth. *Jerome, Chrysostom, and Friends: Essays and Translations.* Crestwood, NY: Edwin Mellen, 1979.

—. *Reading Renunciation: Asceticism and Scripture in Early Christianity.* Princeton, NJ: Princeton University Press, 1999.

—. *History, Theory, Text: Historians and the Linguistic Turn.* Cambridge: Harvard University Press, 2004.

Classen, P. "Das Konzil von Konstantinopel 1166 und die Lateiner." *Byzantinische Zeitschrift* 48 (1955): 339–368.

Constable, Giles. *Three Studies in Medieval Religious and Social Thought: The Interpretation of Mary and Martha, the Ideal of the Imitation of Christ, the Orders of Society.* Cambridge: Cambridge University Press, 1995.

—. "Preface." In *Byzantine Monastic Foundational Documents: A Complete Translation of the Surviving Founders' Typika and Testaments*, ed. John Thomas and Angela Constantinides Hero, xi–xxxviii. Washington: Dumbarton Oaks Research Library and Collection, 2000.

Conticello, Vassa, and Elia Citterio. "La Philocalie et ses versions." In *La théologie byzantine et sa tradition*, ed. Carmello Giuseppe Conticello and Vassa Conticello, 2: 999–1021. Turnhout: Brepols Publishing, 2002.

Cozza-Luzi, J., ed. *Novum patrum bibliotheca.* Vol. 10. Rome, 1905.

Cuddon, J.A. *A Dictionary of Literary Terms and Literary Theory.* 4th ed. Rev. C.E. Preston. Oxford: Blackwell, Publishers, 1998.

Cunningham, Lawrence S. "Theological Table Talk: On Reading Spiritual Texts." *Theology Today* 56, no. 1 (1999), 98–104.

Cunningham, Mary B., and Pauline Allen. "Introduction." In *Preacher and Audience: Studies in Early Christian and Byzantine Homiletics*, ed. Mary B. Cunningham and Pauline Allen. Leiden: Brill, 1998.

Dahl, George. *The Materials for the History of Dor.* Transactions of the Connecticut Academy of Arts and Sciences 20. New Haven: Yale University Press, 1915.

Darrouzès, Jean. *Georges et Dèmètrios Tornikès: Lettres et discours.* Paris: Éditions du Centre national de la recherche scientifique, 1970.

Delehaye, Hippolyte, ed. *Acta sanctorum novembris.* Vol. 3. Brussels: Société des Bollandistes, 1910.

Demacopoulos, George E., and Aristotle Papanikolaou. "Augustine and the Orthodox: 'The West' in the East." In their *Orthodox Readings of Augustine.* Crestwood, NY: St Vladimir's Seminary Press, 2008.

Demetrakopoulos, A.K. Ἐκκλησιαστικὴ Βιβλιοθήκη. Leipzig, 1866.

Devreesse, Robert. *Catalogue des manuscrits grecs*, 2: *Le fonds Coislin.* Paris: Imprimerie Nationale, 1945.

Dictionnaire de spiritualité ascétique et mystique: Doctrine et histoire. Vols. 1 and 12. Ed. Marcel Viller, F. Cavallera and A. Solinac. Paris: Beauchesne, 1984.

Dorothy of Gaza. *Dorothée de Gaza: Oeuvres spirituelles.* Ed. Lucien Regnault and Jacques de Préville. Paris: Éditions du Cerf, 1963.

—. *Dorothy of Gaza: Discourses and Sayings.* Ed. and trans. Eric P. Wheeler. Kalamazoo: Cistercian Publications, 1977.

Dositheos II of Jerusalem. Τόμος ἀγάπης, συλλεγεὶς καὶ τυπωθεὶς παρὰ Δοσιθέου, πατριάρχου Ἱεροσολύμων. Jassy, 1698.

Dräseke, Johannes. "Der Dialog des Soterichos Panteugénos." *Zeitschrift für wissenschaftliche Theologie* 29 (1886): 228–237.

Driscoll, Jeremy. *Steps to Spiritual Perfection: Studies on Spiritual Progress in Evagrius Ponticus.* Crestwood, NY: Newman Press, 2005.

Driscoll, Jeremy, and Mark Sheridan, eds. *Spiritual Progress: Studies in the Spirituality of Late Antiquity and Early Monasticism.* Rome: Pontifico Ateneos Anselmo, 1994.

Dvornik, Francis. *The Photian Schism.* Cambridge: Cambridge University Press, 1948.

Egeria. *Diary of a Pilgrimage.* Trans. George E. Gingras. Crestwood, NY; Ramsey, NJ: Newman Press, 1970.

Eustratiades, Sophronios. "Τυπικοιν τῆς μονῆς τοῦ ἁγίου μεγαλομάρτυρος Μάμαντος." *Hellenica* 1 (1928): 256–311.

—. *The Praktikos, Chapters on Prayer.* Trans. John Bamberger and John Eudes. Kalamazoo: Cistercian Publications, 1972.

—. *Evagrius of Pontus: The Greek Ascetic Corpus.* Trans. Robert E. Sinkewicz. Oxford: Oxford University Press, 2003.

Fabricius, Johann Albert, Gottlieb Harles, and Christopher Heumann. *Bibliotheca graeca sive notitia scriptorum veterum graecorum.* New ed. Vol. 9. 1804. Reprint, Hildensheim: George Olms Verlagsbuchhandlung, 1966.

Festa, Nicholas. "Niceta di Maronea e i suoi dialoghi sulla processione dello Spirito Santo." *Bessarione* 16 (1912): 80–107, 266–286; 17 (1913): 104–113, 295–315; 18 (1914): 55–75, 243–259; 19 (1915): 239–246.

Festugière, A.-J., and A. D. Nock, eds. *Corpus Hermeticum.* Vol 1. Paris: Les Belles Lettres, 1946.

Galatariotou, Catia. "Byzantine *ktetorika typika*: A Comparative Study." *Revue des études byzantines* 45 (1987): 77–138.

—. *The Making of a Saint: The Life, Times and Sanctification of Neophytos the Recluse.* Cambridge: Cambridge University Press, 1991.

Garzya, Antonio. "Precisazioni sul processo di Niceforo Basilace." *Byzantion* 40 (1970): 309–316.

Gautier, Paul. "Jean V l'Oxite, patriarche d'Antioche: Notice biographique." *Revue des études byzantines* 22 (1964): 128–157.

—. "Le typikon du Christ Saveur Pantocrator." *Revue des études byzantines* 32 (1974): 27–131.

—. "La diataxis de Michel Attaliate." *Revue des études byzantines* 39 (1981): 17–130.

—. "Le typikon de la Théotokos Évergétis." *Revue des études byzantines* 40 (1982): 15–95.

—. "Le typikon du Sébaste Grégoire Pakourianos." *Revue des études byzantines* 42 (1984): 19–133.

Gero, Stephen. *Byzantine Iconoclasm During the Reign of Leo II.* Louvain: Corpus Scriptorum Christianorum Orientalium, 1973.

Giorgetti, Corrado. *Nicetas de Maronée et ses dialogues V et VI sur la procession du Saint-Esprit.* Rome: Lateran University, Rome, 1965.

—. "Un teologo greco del XII sec. precursore della riunificazione fra Roma e Costantinopoli: Niceta di Maronea, arcivescovo di Tessalonica." *Annuario 1968*, ed. Biblioteca civica di Massa, 129–148. Lucca: Nuova grafica lucchese, 1969.

Gouillard, Jean. "Un auteur spirituel byzantin du XIIe siècle, Pierre Damascène." *Échos d'Orient* 38 (1939): 257–278.

—. "Le synodikon de l'Orthodoxie: Édition et commentaire." *Travaux et mémoires* 2 (1967): 1–316.

—. *La vie religieuse à Byzance.* London: Variorum, 1981.

Graef, Hilda. "The Spiritual Director in the Thought of Symeon the New Theologian." In *Kyriakon: Festschrift Johannes Quasten*, ed. Patrick Granfield and Josef A. Jungmann, 2: 608–614. Münster: Verlag Aschendorff, 1970.

Gregory Palamas. *The Triads.* Ed. with an introduction by John Meyendorff. Trans. Nicholas Gendle. Mahwah, NJ: Paulist Press, 1983.

The Greek New Testament. 4th rev. ed. Ed. Barbara Aland, Kurt Aland and Barclay Moon Newman. Stuttgart: Deutsche Bibelgesellschaft/United Bible Societies, 1994.

Griffiths, Paul J. "Reading as a Spiritual Discipline." In *The Scope of Our Art: The Vocation of the Theological Reader*, ed. L. Gregory Jones and Stephanie Paulsell, 32–47. Grand Rapids: Eerdmans Publishing Company, 2002.

Grumel, V. "Autour du voyage de Pierre Grossolanus archevêque de Milan, à Constantinople, en 1112." *Echos d'Orient* 32 (1933): 22–33.

Guibert, Joseph de. *Theologia spiritualis, ascetica et mystica: Quaestiones selectae in praelectionum usum.* Rome: Apud aedes Universitatis Gregorianae, 1926.

—. *Leçons de théologie spirituelle.* Toulouse: Éditions de la Revue d'ascétique et de mystique et de l'Apostolat de la prière, 1946.

Guilland, Rodolphe. *Recherches sur les institutions byzantines.* Vol. 2. Berlin: Akademie-Verlag, 1967.

Antoine Guillaumont. "Étude historique et doctrinale." In *Évagre le Pontique: Traité pratique ou le moine*, ed. Antoine Guillaumont and Claire Guillaumont, 1: 21–126. Paris: Éditions du Cerf, 1971.

Gummey, Henry Riley. *The Consecration of the Eucharist: A Study of the Prayer of Consecration in the Communion Office from the Point of View of the Alterations and Amendments Established Therein by the Revisers of 1789.* Philadelphia: Henry F. Anners Press; London: De La More Press, 1908.

Hagenmeyer, Heinrich. *Peter der Eremite: Ein kritischer Beitrag zer Geschichte des erstan Kreuzzuges.* Leipzig: Otto Harrassowitz, 1879.

Hajdú, Kerstin. *Die Sammlung griechischer Handschriften in der Münchener Hofbibliothek bis zum Jahr 1803: Eine Bestandsgeschichte der Codices graeci Monacenses 1–323 mit Signaturenkonkordanzen und Beschreibung des Stephanus-Katalogs (Cbm Cat. 48).* Katalog der griechischen Handschriften der Bayerischen Staatsbibliothek München 10.1. Wiesbaden: Harrassowitz, 2002.

Halkin, François. *Bibliotheca hagiographica graeca.* 3rd ed. Brussels: Société de Bollandistes, 1957.

Hapgood, Isabel Florence. *Service Book of the Holy Orthodox-Catholic Apostolic Church*, 3rd. ed. Crestwood, NY: Syrian Antiochian Orthodox Archdiocese of Crestwood, NY and all North America, 1956.

Hardt, Ignaz. *Catalogus codicum manuscriptorum Graecorum Bibliothecae Regiae Bavaricae.* Vol. 3. Munich: J.E. Scidel, 1806.

Harrison, Verna E.F. "Poverty in the Orthodox Tradition." *St. Vladimir's Theological Quarterly* 34 (1990): 15–47.

Hausherr, Irénée. *Penthos: La doctrine de la compunction dans l'orient chrétien.* Rome: Pontificale Institutum Orientalium Studiorum, 1944.

—. *Direction sprirituelle en Orient d'autrefois.* Rome: Pontificale Institutum Orientalium Studiorum, 1955.

—. "L'hésychasme: Étude de spiritualité." *Orientalia Christiana Periodica* 32 (1956): 5–40, 247–285.

—. *Penthos: The Doctrine of Compunction in the Christian East.* Trans. Anselm Hufstader. Kalamazoo: Cistercian Publications, 1982.

—. *Spiritual Direction in the Early Christian East.* Trans. Anthony P. Gythiel. Kalamazoo: Cistercian Publications, 1990.

—, ed.: see also Nicetas Stethatos *Un grand mystique byzantin: Vie de Siméon le Nouveau Théologien (949–1022) par Nicetas Stethatos.* Rome: Pontificale Institutum Orientalium Studorium, 1928.

Heiser, Lothar. *Die Engel im Glauben der Orthodoxie.* Trier: Paulinus-Verlag, 1976.

Hergenröther, Joseph. *Photius, Patriarch von Constantinopel: Sein Leben, seine Schriften und das griechische Schisma.* Vol. 3. Regensburg: Georg Joseph Manz, 1869.

Herman, Emil. "Die Regelung de Armut in den byzantinischen Klöstern." *Orientalia Christiana Periodica* 7 (1941): 406–460.

Hevelone-Harper, Jennifer L. *Disciples of the Desert: Monks, Laity, and Spiritual Authority in Sixth-Century Gaza.* Baltimore; London: The Johns Hopkins University Press, 2005.

Høgel, Christian. *Symeon Metaphrastes: Rewriting and Canonization.* Copenhagen: Museum Tusculanum Press, 2002.

Holl, Karl. *Enthusiasmus und Bussgewalt beim griechischen Monchtum: Eine Studie zu Symeon dem Neuen Theologen.* Leipzig: JC Hinrichs, 1898.

Hugh of St Victor. *Hugonis de Sancto Victore Didascalicon de studio legendi: A Critical Text.* Ed. Charles Buttimer. Washington: Catholic University of America Press, 1939.

—. *The* Didascalicon *of Hugh of St. Victor: A Medieval Guide to the Arts.* Trans. with an introduction and notes Jerome Taylor. Crestwood, NY: Columbia University Press, 1961.

Hunger, Herbert. "On the Imitation (μίμησις) of Antiquity in Byzantine Literature." *Dumbarton Oaks Papers* 23–24 (1969–1970): 16–38

Isaac of Ninevah. *Mystic Treatises.* Trans. from Bedjan's Syriac text with an introduction and registers by A.J. Wansinck. Amsterdam: Koninklijke Akademie van Wetenschappen, 1923.

Janin, R. *La géographie ecclésiastique de l'Empire Byzantine, Première partie, La siège de Constantinople et la Patriareat cecuménique.* Vol. 3: *Les églises et les monastères.* Paris: Institut français d'études byzantines, 1969.

—. *Les églises et les monastères des grands centres byzantins: Bithyrie, Hellespont, Latros, Galèsios, Trébizonde, Athènes, Thessalonique.* Paris: Institut français d'études byzantines, 1975.

Johannes Oxites. *Joannis Oxeitae oratio de monasteriis laicis non tradendis*. Ed. Tiziana Creazzo. Spoleto: Centro italiano di studi sill'alto medioevo, 2004.

John Cassian. *Jean Cassien: Conférences I-VII*. Ed. E. Pichery. Paris: Éditions du Cerf, 1955.

—. *The Conferences*. Trans. Boniface Ramsey. Crestwood, NY: Paulist Press, 1997.

John Chrysostom. *Jean Chrysostome: Huit catéchèses baptismales inédites*. Ed. Antoine Wenger. Paris: Éditions du Cerf, 1957.

—. *Sancti Joannis Chrysostomi opera selecta*. Ed. Friedrich Dübner. Vol. 1. Paris: Didot, 1861.

—. *St. John Chrysostom: Baptismal Instructions*. Trans. Paul W. Harkins. Westminster, MD: The Newman Press; London: Longmans, Green and Company, 1963.

—. *A Comparison between a King and a Monk; Against the Opponents of the Monastic Life: Two Treatises of John Chrysostom*. Trans. with an introduction by David G. Hunter. Lewiston, NY: Edwin Mellen Press, 1988.

John Climacus. *The Ladder of Divine Ascent*. Trans. Archimandrite Lazarus Moore. Boston: Holy Transfiguration Monastery, 1979.

—. *The Ladder of Divine Ascent*. Trans. Colm Luibheid and Norman Russell. Crestwood, NY: Paulist Press, 1982.

John of Damascus. *Opera Omni*. Ed. Michel Lequien. Paris, 1712.

—. *Die Schriften des Johannes con Damaskos*. Vol. 4: Liber de haeresibus: Opera polemica. Ed. P. Bonifatius Kotter. Berlin; Crestwood, NY: Walter de Gruyter, 1981.

Jugie, Martin. *Theologia dogmatica christianorum orientalium ab Ecclesia catholica dissidentium*. Vol. 2: *Theologiae dogmatical Graeco-Russorum expositio de theologia simplici, de oeconomia*. Paris, 1933.

Justin, Martyr. *The First and Second Apologies*. Trans. Leslie William Barnard. Crestwood, NY: Paulist Press, 1997.

Kazhdan, A.P. "Hermitic, Cenobitic and Secular Ideals in Byzantine Hagiography of the Ninth Centuries." *The Greek Orthodox Theological Review* 30 (1985): 473–487.

Kazhdan, A.P., and Giles Constable. *People and Power in Byzantium: An Introduction to Modern Byzantine Studies*. Washington: Dumbarton Oaks, 1982.

Kazhdan, A.P., and Simon Franklin. *Studies on Byzantine Literature of the Eleventh and Twelfth Centuries*. Cambridge; Crestwood, NY: Cambridge University Press; Paris: Editions de la Maison des Sciences de l'Homme, 1984.

Kelly, J.N.D. *Golden Mouth: The Story of John Chrysostom – Ascetic, Preacher, Bishop*. Grand Rapids, MI: Baker Books, 1995.

Kristeva, Julia. *Séméotikè: Recherches pour une sémanalyse*. Paris: Éditions du Seuil, 1969.

Krivocheine, Basil. *In the Light of Christ: St. Symeon the New Theologian – Life, Spirituality, Doctrine*. Trans. Anthony P. Gythiel. Crestwood, NY: St. Vladimir's Seminary Press, 1986.

Krumbacher, Karl, A. Ehrhard, and Heinrich Gelzer. *Geschichte der byzantinischen Literatur von Justinian bis zum Ende des Oströmischen Reiches (527–1453)*. 2nd. ed. Munich: CH Beck'sche Verlagsbuchhandlung, 1897.

Lampe, G.W.H., ed. *A Patristic Greek Lexicon*. Oxford: Clarendon Press, 1961.

Lamprinidou, Michael. Ἡ Ναυπλία ἀπὸ τῶν ἀρχαιοτάτων χρόνων μέχρι τῶν καθ᾽ ἡμᾶς, Ἔκδοσισ B v. Athens, 1950.

Lampros, Spyrindon. P. *Greek Manuscripts on Mount Athos*. Vol. 1. Cambridge: Cambridge University Press, 1895.

Langen, Joseph. *Johannes von Damaskus: Eine patristische Monographie*. Gotha: Friedrich Andreas Perthes, 1879.

Latte, Kurt. *Hesychii Alexandrini lexicon*. Copenhagen: Muuksgaard, 1953–1966.

Laurent, V. "Remarques critiques sur le texte du typikon du monastère de Saint-Mamas." *Echos d'Orient* 30 (1931): 233–242.

—. "Légendes sigillographiques et familles byzantines." *Echos d'Orient* 31 (1932): 331–335.

Lees, Jay T. *Anselm of Havelberg: Deeds into Words in the Twelfth Century*. Leiden; Crestwood, NY: Brill, 1998.

Lefort, Jacques, Nicolas Oikonomidès, and Denise Papachryssanthou, eds. *Actes d'Iviron*. Vol. 2: *Du milieu du XIe siècle à 1204*. Paris: P. Lethielleux, 1990.

Leib, Bernard. "Deux inédits byzantins sur les azymes au début du XIIe siècle." *Orientalia Christiana Periodica* 2 (1924): 177–239.

—. *Rome, Kiev et Byzance à la fin du XIe siècle: Rapports religieux des Latins et des Gréco-Russes sous le Pontificat d'Urban II (1088–1099)*. 1924. Reprint, Crestwood, NY: Burt Franklin, 1968.

Leroux, Jean-Marie. "Saint Jean Chrysostome et le monachisme." In *Jean Chrysostome et Augustin: Actes du colloque de Chantilly, 22–24 septembre 1974*, ed. Charles Kannengiesser, 125–144. Paris: Éditions Beauchesne, 1975.

Les Constitutions apostoliques. Vol. 3. Ed. Marcel Metzger. Paris: Éditions du Cerf, 1987.

Leithart, Peter J. *Deep Exegesis: The Mystery of Reading Scripture*. Waco, TX: Baylor University Press, 2009.

Ljubarskij, Jakov. "How Should a Byzantine Text be Read?" In *Rhetoric in Byzantium*, ed. Elizabeth Jeffreys, 117–126. Burlington, VT: Ashgate Publishing Company, 2003.

Loosen, Josef. *Logos und Penuma im begnadeten Menschen bei Maximus Confessor*. Münster: Aschendorff, 1940.

Louth, Andrew. "Introduction." In his *Maximus the Confessor*, 3–77. London; Crestwood, NY: Routledge, 1996.

—. "The Body in Western Catholic Christianity." In *Religion and the Body*, ed. Sarah Coakley, 111–128. Cambridge: Cambridge University Press, 2000.

—. *St John Damascene: Tradition and Originality in Byzantine Theology*. Oxford: Oxford University Press, 2002.

Maloney, George A. *A Theology of "Uncreated Energies."* The 1978 Pere Marquette Theology Lecture. Milwaukee: Marquette University Press, 1978.

Mansi, Giovan Domenico. *Sacrorum Conciliorum nova et amplissima collectio*. Vol. 21. Venice, 1776.

Mark the Monk. *Traités I*. Trans. Georges-Matthieu de Durand. Paris: Éditions du Cerf, 1999.

—. *Counsels on the Spiritual Life*. Trans. Tim Vivian and Augustine Casiday. Crestwood, NY: St. Vladimir's Seminary Press, 2009.

Martyrologium Romanum Gregorii XIII jussu editum. Rome, 1583.

Mayendorff, John. *A Study of Gregory Palamas*. Trans. George Lawrence. Crestwood, NY: St. Vladimir's Seminary Press, 1974.

—. "Introduction." In *Gregory Palamas: The Triads*. Ed. with an introduction by John Meyendorff. Trans. Nicholas Gendle. Mahwah, NJ: Paulist Press, 1983.

—. *Byzantine Theology: Historical Trends and Doctrinal Themes*. Crestwood, NY: Fordham University Press, 1979.

Michel, Anton. *Amalfi und Jerusalem im griechischen Kirchenstreti (1054–1090): Kardinal Humbert, Laycus von Amalfi, Nicetas Stethatos, Symeon II. Von Jerusalem, und Bruno von Segni über die Azymen*. Rome: Pontificium Institutum Orientalium Studiorum, 1939.

Miklosich, Franz, and Joseph Müller. *Acta et diplomata graeca medii aevi sacra et progana*. Vol. 6. Vienna: Carolus Gerold, 1890.

Morris, Rosemary. "Monasteries and their Patrons in the Tenth and Eleventh Centuries." *Byzantinische Forschungen* 10 (1985): 185–231.

—. *Monks and Laymen in Byzantium, 843–1118*. Cambridge: Cambridge University Press, 1995.

Mullett, Margaret, and Anthony Kirby, eds. *The Theotokos Evergetis and Eleventh-Century Monasticism*. Belfast: Belfast Byzantine Enterprises, School of Greek, Roman and Semitic Studies, the Queen's University of Belfast, 1994.

New Oxford Annotated Apocrypha: The Apocryphal/Deuterocanonical Books of the Old Testament, The. New rev. stan. ver. Ed. Bruce M. Metzger and Roland E. Murphy. Crestwood, NY: Oxford University Press, 1991.

Nicholas I of Constantinople. *Miscellaneous Writings*. Ed. and trans. L.G. Westerlink. Washington: Dumbarton Oaks Center for Byzantine Studies/Trustees for Harvard University, 1981.

Nicetas Stethatos. *Un grand mystique byzantin: Vie de Siméon le Nouveau Théologien (949–1022) par Nicetas Stethatos*. Rome: Pontificale Institutum Orientalium Studorium, 1928

—. *Opuscules et Lettres*. Ed. Jean Darrouzès. Paris: Éditions du Cerf, 1961.

Nilus of Ancyra. *Narratio*. Ed. Fabrizio Conca. Leipzig: Teubner, 1983.

Noret, Jacques. "Ménologes, Synaxaires, Menées: Essai de Clarification d'une terminologie." *Analecta Bollandiana* 86 (1968): 21–24.

Oikonomos, S.K., ed., Τοῦ ὁσίου πατρός ἡμῶν Ἰωάννου μητροπολίτου Ρωσίας ἐπιστολή πρός Κλήμεντα παπαν Ῥώμης. Athens, 1868.

Omont, Henri. *Inventaire sommaire des manuscrits grec de la Bibliothèque Nationale*. Vol. 1: *Ancien fonds grec, Théologie*. Paris: Alphonse Picard, 1886.

—. *Inventaire sommaire des manuscrits grecs de la Bibliothèque nationale*. Vol. 2: *Ancien fonds grec, Droit-Histoire-Sciences*. Paris: Alphonse Picard, 1888.

The Oxford Dictionary of Byzantium. 3 Vols. Ed. A.P. Kazhdan, Alice-Marie Talbot, Anthony Cutler, Timothy E. Gregory and Nancy P. Ševčenko. Crestwood, NY: Oxford University Press, 1991.

Pachali, Heinrich. "Soterichos Panteugenos und Nikolaos von Methone." *Zeitschrift für wissenschaftliche Theologie* 50 (1907): 347–374.

Pachomian Koinonia. Vol. 2: *Pachomian Chronicles and Rules.* Trans. Armand Veilleux. Kalamazoo: Cistercian Publications, 1981.

Pahlitzsch, Johannes. "Die Bedeutung der Azymenfrage für die Beziehungen zwischen griechisch-orthodoxer und lateinischer Kirche in den Kreuzfahrerstaaten." In *Die Folgen der Kreuzzüge für die orientalischen Religionsgemeinschaften*, ed. Walter Beltz. Halle/Wittenberg: Martin-Luther-Universität, 1996.

Palmer G.E.H., Philip Sherrard, and Kallistos Ware. "Introductory Note." In *The Philokalia: The Complete Text Compiled by St. Nicodemus of the Holy Mountain and St. Makarios of Corinth*, ed. and trans. G.E.H. Palmer, Philip Sherrard and Kallistos Ware, 1: 11–18. London: Faber and Faber, 1983.

—. "Introductory Note." In *The Philokalia: The Complete Text Compiled by St. Nicodemus of the Holy Mountain and St. Makarios of Corinth*, ed. and trans. G.E.H. Palmer, Philip Sherrard and Kallistos Ware, 3: 71–73. London: Faber and Faber, 1984.

—. "Glossary." In *The Philokalia: The Complete Text Compiled by St. Nicodemus of the Holy Mountain and St. Makarios of Corinth*, ed. and trans. G.E.H. Palmer, Philip Sherrard and Kallistos Ware, 3: 355–366. London: Faber and Faber, 1984.

Papachryssanthou, Denise. *Actes de Prôtaton.* Paris: P. Lithielleux, 1975.

Papadopoulos, Chrysostomos. Ζυμβολαί εἰς τὴν ἱστορίαν τοῦ μοναχικοῦ βίου ἐν Ἑλλάδι. Ὁ ὅσιος Μελέτιος ὁ Νέος (1035–1105). Athens, 1968.

Papadopoulos-Kerameus, Anastasios. Ἱεροσολυμιτκὴ Βιβλιοθήκη, Τομος Πρωτος. En Petroupodei: Tipogr. B. Kirschbaum, 1891.

—. *Noctes Petropolitanae: Sbornik vizantiĭskikh tekstov XII-XIII viêkov.* 1913. Reprint, Leipzig: Zentralantiquanat der deutschen demokratischen Republik, 1976.

—, ed *Varia graeca sacra.* St Petersburg, 1909.

Papazoglou, Georgios. Τυπικὸν Ἰσαακίου Ἀλεξίου Κομνηνοῦ τῆς μονῆς Θεοτόκου τῆς Κοσμοσωτείρας. Komotini, Greece: University of Thrace, 1994.

Patrich, Joseph. *The Sabaite Heritage in the Orthodox Church from the Fifth Century to the Present.* Leuven: Peeters, 2001.

Pavlov, Aleksěj Stepanovič, ed. *Kritičeskie opyty po istorii drevnejšej greko-russkoj polemiki protiv latinjan.* St Petersburg, 1878.

Peeters, Paul. "La Passion de S. Pierre de Capitolias (†13 janvier 715)." *Analecta Bollandiana* 57 (1939): 299–333; 58 (1940): 123–125.

Pelikan, Jaroslav. *The Growth of Medieval Theology (600–1300).* Chicago: The University of Chicago Press, 1978.

Peters, F.E. *Greek Philosophical Terms: A Historical Lexicon.* Crestwood, NY: Crestwood, NY University Press; London: University of London Press, 1967.

Peters, Greg. "Spiritual Marriage in Early Christianity: 1 Corinthians 7:25–38 in Modern Exegesis and the Earliest Church." *Trinity Journal*, n.s., 23. (Fall 2002): 211–224.

—. "Towards a Definition of 'Spiritual Theology': A Historiography of Recent Writings on Byzantine Spirituality." *Studia Monastica* 46 (2004): 25–41.

—. "Peter of Damascus and Early Christian Spiritual Theology." *Patristica et Medievalia* 26 (2005): 89–109.

—. "Recovering a Lost Spiritual Theologian: Peter of Damascus and the *Philokalia*." *St. Vladimir's Theological Quarterly* 49 (2005): 437–459.

—. "Monasteries." In *The Encyclopedia of Christian Civilization*. Vol. 3: *M–R*, ed. George Thomas Kurian. Malden, MA: Wiley; Oxford: Blackwell, 2011.

Philonenko, Marc. *Joseph et Aséneth: Introduction, texte critique, traduction et notes*. Leiden: E.J. Brill, 1968.

Photius I of Constantinople. *The Homilies of Photius Patriarch of Constantinople*. Trans. Cyril Mango. Cambridge, MA: Harvard University Press, 1958.

—. Φωτίου ὁμιλίαι. Ἔκδοσις κειμένου, εἰσαγωγὴ καὶ σχόλια. Ed. B. Laourdas. Thessaloniki: Hetaireia makedonikon spoudon, 1959.

Plato. *Republic*. Trans. G.M.A. Grube with revisions by C.D.C. Reeve. In *Plato: Complete Works*, ed. John M. Cooper. Indianapolis; Cambridge: Hackett, 1997.

Plottel, Jeanine Parisier. "Introduction." In *Intertextuality: New Perspectives in Criticism*, ed. Jeanine Parisier Plottel and Hanna Chamey. Crestwood, NY: Crestwood, NY Literary Forum, 1978.

Podskalsky, Gerhard. *Griechische Theologie in der Zeit der Turkenherrschaft (1453–1821)*. Munich: Beck, 1988.

Principe, Walter H. "Towards Defining Spirituality." *Studies in Religion/Sciences Religieuses* 12 (1983): 127–141.

Pseudo-Dionysis. *Pseudo-Dionysis: The Complete Works*. Trans. Colm Luibheid. Crestwood, NY: Paulist Press, 1987.

Renz, Franz. *Die Geschichte des Messopfer-Begriffs*. Vol. 1: *Altertum und Mittelalter*. Freising: Selbstverlag des Verfassers, 1901.

Richard, Marcel. *Répertoire des bibliothèque et des catalogues de manuscrits grecs*. 2nd ed. Paris: Centre national de la recherche scientifique, 1958.

Rigo, Antonio. "Gregorio il Sinaita." In *La théologie byzantine et sa tradition*, ed. Carmelo Giuseppe Conticello and Vassa Conticello, 2: 35–132. Turnhout: Brepols, 2002.

—, ed. *Nicodemo l'Aghiorita e la Filocalia: Atti dell'VIII Convegno Ecumenico intern. Di Spiritualità Ortodossa. Bose, 16–19 settembre 2000*. Magnano: Edizioni Qiqajon, 2001.

Roberts, Alexander, and James Donaldson, eds. *Ante-Nicene Fathers*. Rev. A. Cleveland Coxe. Vols. 2 and 7. 1885–96. Reprint, Peabody, MA: Hendrickson, 1995.

Rubenson, Samuel. "Asceticism: Christian Perspectives." In *Encyclopedia of Monasticism*. Vol. 1: *A–L*, ed. William M. Johnston. Chicago; London: Fitzroy Dearborn Publishers, 2000.

Russell, Norman. "Anselm of Havelberg and the Union of the Churches." *Sobornost* 1.1 (1979): 19–41; 2.1 (1980): 29–41

Sakkelion, John. Ἄργους καὶ Ναυπλίου παλαιοὶ Ἱεράρχαι." Δελτίον τῆς Ἱστορικῆς καὶ Ἐθνολογικῆς Ἑταιρείας τῆς Ἑλλάδος 2 (1885): 32–38.

—. Πατμιακὴ βιβλιοθήκη. Athens: Ἐκδόσεις Παπαγεωργίου Papageorgivou, 1890.

Scarpat, Giuseppe. *Parresia: Storia del termine e delle tradizione in latino*. Brescia: Paideia, 1964.

Schaff, Philip, ed. *Nicene and Post-Nicene Fathers*. Vol. 10. Peabody, MA: Hendrickson, 2004.

—, ed. *Nicene and Post-Nicene Fathers*. Vol. 14. Peabody, MA: Hendrickson, 2004.

Schaff, Philip, and Henry Wace, eds. *Nicene and Post-Nicene Fathers*. Vol. 8. Peabody, MA: Hendrickson, 2004.

Schema-monk Metrophanes. *Blessed Paisius Velichkovsky: The Man Behind the Philokalia: The Life and Ascetic Labors of Our Father, Elder Paisius, Archimandrite of the Holy Moldavian Monasteries of Niamets and Sekoul*. Trans. Seraphim Rose. Platina, CA: Saint Herman of Alaska Brotherhood, 1976.

Schopenus, Ludovicus, ed. *Alexiadis*. Bonn, 1839.

Setton, Kenneth M. "The Byzantine Background to the Italian Renaissance." *Proceedings of the American Philosophical Society* 100, no. 1 (1956): 1–76.

Ševčenko, Nancy P. *Illustrated Manuscripts of the Metaphrastian Menologion*. Chicago: University of Chicago Press, 1990.

Shaw, Teresa M. *The Burden of the Flesh: Fasting and Sexuality in Early Christianity* (Minneapolis: Fortress Press, 1998)

Simplex, F. *Theologia spiritualis fundamentalis*. Oliva, 1687.

Sinkewicz, Robert E. *Manuscript Listings for the Authors of the Patristic and Byzantine Periods*. Toronto: Pontifical Institute of Medieval Studies, 1992.

Smith, William. *A Dictionary of Greek and Roman Biography and Mythology by Various Writers*. Vol. 2: *Oarses–Zygia*. Crestwood, NY: AMS Press, 1967.

Smith, William, and Henry Wace, eds. *A Dictionary of Christian Biography, Literature, Sects and Doctrines: Being a Continuation of "The Dictionary of the Bible"*. Vol. 3: *Hermogenes–Myensis*. London: John Murray, 1882.

Sophocles, E.A. *Greek Lexicon of the Roman and Byzantine Periods (From BC 146 to 1100)*. Vol. 2. Crestwood, NY: Frederick Ungar, n.d.

Spink Auction 135: Byzantine Seals from the collection of George Zacos, Part III with Ancient and Islamic Coins. London: Spink, 1999.

Steitz, G.E. "Die Abendmahlehre der griechischen kirche in ihrer geschichtlichen Entwicklung." *Jahrbücher fur deutsche Theologie* 13 (1868): 23–31.

Stewart, Columba. *Cassian the Monk*. Crestwood, NY; Oxford: Oxford University Press, 1998.

—. "Imageless Prayer and the Theological Vision of Evagrius Ponticus." *Journal of Early Christian Studies* 9 (2001): 173–204.

Stylianopoulos, Theodore G. "The Philokalia: A Review Article." *The Greek Orthodox Theological Review* 26 (1981): 252–263.

Symeon the New Theologian. *Chapitres théologiques, gnostiques et pratiques*. Ed. Jean Darrouzès. Paris: Éditions du Cerf, 1957.

—. *Syméon le Nouveau Théologien: Catéchèses 1–5*. Ed. Basile Krivochéine. Paris: Éditions du Cerf, 1963.

—. *Catéchèses*. Vol. 3. Ed. Basile Krivochéine and Joseph Paramelle. Paris: Éditions du Cerf, 1964.

—. *Traités théologiques et éthiques*. 2 vols. Ed. Jean Darrouzès. Paris: Éditions du Cerf, 1966.

—. *Hymnen*. Ed. Athanasios Kambylis. Supplementa Byzantina 3. Berlin; New York: de Gruyter, 1976.

—. *Hymns of Divine Love by St. Symeon the New Theologian*. Trans. George Maloney. Denville, NJ: Dimension Books, 1976.

—. *The Discourses*. Trans. Carmino J. De Catanzaro. Crestwood, NY: Paulist Press, 1980.

—. *Symeon the New Theologian: The Practical and Theological Chapters and the Three Theological Discourses*. Trans. Paul McGuckin. Kalamazoo: Cistercian Publications, 1982.

—. *On the Mystical Life: The Ethical Discourses*, Vol. 1: *The Church and the Last Things*. Trans. Alexander Golitzin. Crestwood, NY: St. Vladimir's Seminary Press, 1995.

—. *On the Mystical Life: The Ethical Discourses*, Vol. 2: *On Virtue and Christian Life*. Trans. with introductions Alexander Golitzin. Crestwood, NY: St. Vladimir's Seminary Press, 1996.

—. *The Epistles of St. Symeon the New Theologian*. Trans. H.J.M. Turner. Oxford: Oxford University Press, 2009.

Symeon the Stoudite. *Discours ascétique*. Ed. Hilarion Alfeyev. Paris: Éditions du Cerf, 2001.

Theodore the Stoudite. Τοῦ ὁσίου πατρὸς ἡμῶν καὶ ὁμολογητοῦ Θεοδώρου ἡγουμένου τῶν Στουδίου μικρὰ κατήχησις. *Sancti patris nostri confessoris Theodori Studitis praepositi parva catechesis*. Ed. Emmanuel Auvray. 1891. Reprint, Thessaloniki, 1984.

Theoleptos of Philadelphia. *The Life and Letters of Theoleptos of Philadelphia*. Ed. Angela Constantinides Hero. Brookline, MA: Hellenic College Press, 1994.

—. *The Monastic Discourses: A Critical Edition, Translation and Study*. Trans. Robert E. Sinkewicz. Toronto: Pontifical Institute of Medieval Studies, 1992.

Theophanes the Confessor. *Theophanis chronographia*. Ed. Carl de Boor. Leipzig: BG Teubneri, 1883–1885.

—. *The Chronicle of Theophanes Confessor: Byzantine and Near Easter History AD 284–813*. Trans. with introduction and commentary by Cyril Mango and Roger Scott with the assistance of Geoffrey Greatrex. Oxford: Clarendon Press, 1997.

Thiermeyer, Abraham-Andreas. "Das Typikon-ktetorikon und sein literarhistorischer Kontext." *Orientalia Christiana Periodica* 58 (1992): 475–513.

Thomas, John Philip. *Private Religious Foundations in the Byzantine Empire*. Washington: Dumbarton Oaks Research Library and Collection, 1987.

Thomas, John and Angela Constantinides Hero, eds. *Byzantine Monastic Foundation Documents: A Complete Translation of the Surviving Founders' Typika and Testaments*. 5 vols. Washington: Dumbarton Oaks Research Library and Collection, 2000.

Thunberg, Lars. *Microcosm and Mediator: The Theological Anthropology of Maximus the Confessor*. 2nd ed. Chicago: Open Court, 1995.

Touraille, Jacques. "Introduction." In, *Philocaloe des Pères Neptiques*. Fasc. 2: *Pierre Damascène*, ed. Jacques Touraille. Bégrolles-en-maugés: Abbage de Bellefontaine, 1980.

Turner, H.J.M. *St. Symeon the New Theologian and Spiritual Fatherhood*. Leiden: E.J. Brill, 1990.

Vogüé, Adalbert de. "Monastic Poverty in the West." *Monastic Studies* 13 (1982): 99–112.

Vööbus, Arthur. *History of Asceticism in the Syrian Orient, A Contribution to the History of Culture in the Near East.* Vol. 2: *Early Monasticism in Mesopotamia and Syria.* Louvain: Corpus Scriptorum Christianorum Orientalium, 1960.

Ward, Benedicta, trans. *The Sayings of the Desert Fathers: The Alphabetical Collection.* Kalamazoo: Cistercian Publications, 1975.

Ware, Kallistos T. "The Sacrament of Baptism and the Ascetic Life in the Teaching of Mark the Monk." In *Studia Patristica.* Vol 10: *Papers presented to the Fifth International Conference on Patristic Studies held in Oxford 1967.* Part 1: *Editiones, Critica, Philologica, Biblica, Historica, Liturgica et Ascetica*, ed. F.L. Cross, 441–452. Texte und Untersuchungen 107. Berlin: Akademie-Verlag, 1970.

—. "The Spiritual Father in Orthodox Christianity." *Cross Currents* (1974): 296–313.

—. "Introduction." In *John Climacus: The Ladder of Divine Ascent*, by John Climacus, trans. Colm Luibheid and Norman Russell, 1–70. Crestwood, NY: Paulist Press, 1982.

—. "The Meaning of 'Pathos' in Abba Isaias and Theodoret of Cyrus." In *Studia Patristica*, ed. Elizabeth A. Livingstone, 20: 315–322. Leuven: Peeters Press, 1989.

Weyh, Willhelm. "Die Akrostichis in der byzantinischen Kanonesdichtung." *Byzantinische Zeitschrift* 17 (1908): 1–69.

Will, Cornelius, ed. *Acta et scripta quae de controversiis ecclesiae graecae et latinae saeculo undecimo composita extant.* 1861. Reprint, Frankfurt am Main: Minerva, 1963.

William of Tyre. *Chronicon.* 2 vols. Ed. R.B.C. Huygens. Turnhout: Brepols, 1986.

Worton, Michael, and Judith Still. "Introduction." In their *Intertextuality: Theories and Practice*, 1–45. Manchester: Manchester University Press, 1990.

Zeses, Theodoros N. "Ὁ πατριάρχης Νικόλαος IV Μουζάλων," Ἐπιστημονική Ἐπετηρίς τῆς Θεολογικῆς Σχολῆς τοῦ Πανεπιστημίου Θεσσαλονίκης 23 (1978): 309–329.

Index